BETTE, RITA, AND THE REST OF MY LIFE

BETTE, RITA, AND THE REST OF MY LIFE

GARY MERRILL

with a little help from his friends
John and Jean Cole

LANCE TAPLEY, PUBLISHER

Bette Davis's words on page 201 are from *Mother Goddam* by Whitney Stine and Bette Davis. New York, Hawthorn, 1974, p. 255-256.

Smedley Butler's words on page 215 are quoted in *The Plot to Seize the White House* by Jules Archer. New York, Hawthorn, 1973, p. 118.

Lao Tzu's words on pages 267-268 are from *The Way of Life according to Laotzu* by Witter Bynner. New York. English translation copyright 1944 by Witter Bynner; © renewed 1972 by Dorothy Chauvenet and Paul Horgan.

Design: Lisa Lyons.

Library of Congress Cataloging-in-Publication Data

Merrill, Gary.
  Bette, Rita, and the Rest of My Life.

  1. Merrill, Gary. 2. Actors–United States–Biography.
I. Title.
PN2287.M619A3 1988   791.43'028'0924 [B] 88-2151
ISBN 0-912769-13-0

Dedicated to all the children of the world . . .
including Gore Vidal

CONTENTS

1

MR. INKWELL

I hadn't always wanted to be an actor, but that was because for the first sixteen years of my life I didn't have the opportunity to act.

I was born in Hartford, Connecticut, on August 2, 1915, the oldest son of Benjamin Gary Merrill and Hazel May Andrews. I was named Gary Franklin because my father was playing games with Ben Franklin's name and his own. He was a Connecticut Yankee, and my mother was the daughter of Alice Mosher Andrews, from an old Maine family—so old that the originals were on board the Mayflower. Hell, they didn't just come over on the ship, they owned part of it.

I had a twin sister who died at birth. This information I wasn't given until I was almost twenty years old. In those days, no one talked about such things to children, and there were other things on my family's list of "not in front of the kids." I have wondered if, in the womb, I was responsible for the death of my twin, the first female I had contact with.

My father was a lovely, simple, gregarious man, at the time of my birth a clerk employed by the Royal Typewriter Company. Mother was bright, attractive but neurotic, an ex-schoolteacher from Westbrook, Maine. These two people were totally unsuited to each other. I can't imagine what prompted them to marry.

We weren't a wealthy family by any stretch, but we were comfortably well off. Later, Dad worked for the Aetna Life Insurance Company and, a true Yankee, was careful with his money. The Aetna offices were in downtown Hartford, but the company had a store for the convenience of its employees which my father ran. Singing with the Hartford Choral Club was one of his hobbies; he had a very fine bass voice. He also liked bowling and playing bridge. My mother, brother, and I spent quite a few evenings learning the game. I can see my father now: counting, making his bid, then waiting for me to answer. I answer, and there he is, recounting, trying to figure out where I'm getting my cards. I never had what I bid and screwed up a good deal.

My mother played the piano—probably not too well, which may have been the reason she was so adamant that I have lessons. Often after I had gone to bed I could hear her playing and singing. She was a teacher by training and knew how to push kids to do their work, but didn't understand them. She was the sort of person who pestered boys by always saying things like "wear your rubbers," referring, of course, to the ones worn on the feet.

It was painful to take piano lessons, and my parents would almost have to beat me before I'd practice. I wanted to be out playing ball or hockey, whatever the game of the season was, but there I sat, threatened with punishment if I didn't practice my chords.

"Hey Fats!" I'd hear, the voice coming through the door from a neighborhood boy as I practiced the piano. "Get your skates, the ice is holding." I can hardly believe I was called "Fats" when I was a boy, though I did weigh more than my cohorts. They were very skinny kids!

My first lucid memory is a minor trauma that occurred when I was about three. A little girl who lived on my street (Prospect Avenue, in Mark Twain's neighborhood) hit me over the head with my own little red wagon, which she was trying to take away from me. My mother decided the entire incident was my fault, and this injustice, along with the screaming and blood, impressed me greatly. I figure that started my problems with women.

The family moved around quite a bit. I remember a rambling brick house we lived in on Palisado Avenue in Windsor, a suburb of Hartford. It had large, shady porches and plenty of yard adjacent to the fields of tobacco. My father's parents lived on the first floor while my mother, father, and I lived in an upstairs apartment. The First World War had just ended, and Uncle Paul, my father's younger brother, had been released from the service unharmed. The family was planning a homecoming dinner. There had been plenty of talk around the house about the war, mustard gas, and the atrocities of the enemy. Uncle Paul's arrival was a real event in our lives. The house was filled with wonderful aromas all that day, and that evening the entire family assembled for the festive occasion.

Uncle Paul was greeted effusively. While we were eating, the conversation turned to a little black bag he was carrying, similar to the kind doctors carried in those days of house calls. The discussion was occasionally whispered and at one point I was sent out of the room. My imagination took over—I was positive there was nothing less than a severed German head in the bag, and that Uncle Paul had brought it home as a trophy. Many years passed before I found out that the bag contained nothing more exciting than French cognac.

When I was five, mother marched me to a one-room schoolhouse in Windsor which had six rows of desks, grades one through six. It was here that I began my formal schooling and became conscious of a girl (as a girl) for the first time. Her name was Josephine Smith, a sixth-grader, an "older woman," perhaps a portent of an involvement with an older woman later in my life.

My mother and her sister, Marion, had attended the Gorham Normal School in Maine. Teaching was one of the few careers open to women in those days. The sisters were opposites, and I'm not sure who was the better teacher, but I think it was my Aunt Marion, because she was much more of an extrovert. Mother may have been the more intellectual of the two, but Aunt Marion had an ebullience, a *joie de vivre* that my mother lacked.

From the time I was two years old, when summer came to Hartford mother would take me to Maine to visit Marion and my grandmother, who had a small cottage at Prout's Neck. My mother said it was necessary for little boys to have some healthy, fresh air to counteract the city's dust and bustle. Dad would join us for his two-week vacation, then return to Hartford. I was lucky enough to spend the whole summer at the cottage near the shore.

I always looked forward to our summers in this small community where Winslow Homer had lived and painted. It is a tiny promontory with a mile-long beach of magnificent white sand. At low tide this beach becomes a one-hundred-yard-wide football and baseball field, and at high tide it is a body-surfing paradise. I had the summers to myself: boat, beaches, fishing, swimming, playing with other kids; watching the lobstermen and *real Indians;* and that airy, open house, with its oil lamps, and the outhouse. I was living every kid's summer dream. On what we called the "back shore," we could dig enough clams in an hour to feed five or six people. Today, there are no clams and no one knows why. That cottage now belongs to my brother, but I have one on the next lane that Aunt Marion left me in her will because she wanted to be certain I would always have a place in Maine. I believe those summers were the reason I moved back to Maine in 1953. My conviction is that if a child is introduced to the coast of Maine in the summer, he'll be hooked for life.

The year I turned seven, mother did not take me back to Hartford. She left me to stay in Westbrook, just outside of Portland, with my grandmother and Aunt Marion. The three of us lived in a second- and third-story apartment, which was above another apartment and store which my grandmother rented out. She was a widow. My grandfather had died about the time I was born. Aunt Marion taught third grade in Westbrook's Forest Street School, and that fall she took me along to school with her. We walked, arriving before the other kids. I spent the time before classes writing love notes to a pretty girl named Mary Hallowell, who sat directly in front of me.

There was a feeling of excitement in the air—Aunt Marion was being courted. Her suitor came calling in a chauffeur-driven Lincoln town car, pretty impressive stuff to me. His name was George Caldwell and he had been visiting his cousin in Westbrook to counteract his loneliness since his wife's death. On one of his visits he met Aunt Marion. Before long, they started going out to dinner and the theater; it took them a year to get married. My aunt was younger than his daughter. He lived in Irvington in New York. I must say, he had quite a place there. As I remember, he bought it from an old actress who had built the house when her money was plentiful.

If you know Broadway, you know that Broadway is the longest street in New York. It runs from the Battery to Albany. Travel up Broadway to Irvington, and you may still see a brick house with six white pillars and two wings. On one side was the croquet court, and, behind that, a garden. George had his own gas pump, a chauffeur, a cook, and a maid—the whole deal. And each room had its own fireplace. I stayed with them one Christmas, and that's when I found out about Santa Claus. I had insisted on hanging my stocking in my own room and caught Uncle George coming in to fill it. And that's where I learned to live rich, when I was about eight or nine.

We'd often drive down Broadway to Times Square where I saw my first play, *A Connecticut Yankee in King Arthur's Court* with Billy Gaxton. I was ten years old. As we drove through the Bronx and Harlem, I noticed kids playing and peeing in the street, and I remember asking Aunt Marion, "Why do the poor have so many children? Why do the rich only have one or two?" It was a beginning, this questioning, of a social consciousness. I never got satisfactory answers to my questions. I have a friend, from the wealthy Main Line outside of Philadelphia, who got involved with poor blacks in that city when she was only ten or twelve. She doesn't remember how or why, but that early social awareness seems to carry through our lives.

That fall in Westbrook, at my grandmother's house, I found George to be a kind and generous man. I liked him, and I felt he liked me. During a passing conversation he asked me what I wanted for Christmas and, being a direct sort of kid, I told him my dream was to have a tricycle.

It was great being in Maine, and I never questioned my good luck at being able to stay on after school had started. But around Thanksgiving time I was sent home, and I discovered the reason for my prolonged summer visit: There was another kid in the house—a stranger. I had been left in Maine because my mother was becoming noticeably pregnant, and my parents didn't want me to know. I hadn't noticed a thing, but at Thanksgiving I met my brother Jerry, who had just been born.

No doubt this was quite a psychological blow. I started running away—not too far, just down the road to an elderly lady's house, and usually not until after supper when I had been left alone in the kitchen for a while. The lady always asked if my mother knew where I was, and I'd say "sure." We'd play cards or dominoes until mother started calling for me. When I got home, my father would be instructed to spank me and send me to bed. The spankings were not a very effective deterrent.

When Christmas rolled around, to my surprise and delight I found under the tree a grand present with my name on it. George Caldwell had sent me a specially made tricycle, one with pneumatic tires. All the others I had seen had hard rubber tires. It was truly a magnificent gift, but the tricycle had come unassembled and my father had to go to considerable pains, working until the small hours, to put the thing together. He had absolutely no mechanical talent, a trait I inherited, and the tricycle collapsed as soon as I sat on it. (Years later, a similar experience occurred with my son Michael. I thought I had bought a little motor car, but when I opened the package, there, in cellophane packets, were nuts, bolts, and parts. The only secret place to tackle the assembly was an unheated garage, and I swear it was twenty below zero while I assembled it, diligently following directions devised by the devil. Michael got about a hundred yards before the thing collapsed.)

In Connecticut that year, we moved to another upstairs apartment nearer the center of Windsor. Two more memories stand out from that time. One was that my mother wouldn't allow me to stay when my friend, who lived downstairs, was having his bath, presumably because I shouldn't be allowed to see naked boys (another indication of parental inhibition). The other was a visit from Aunt Marion and my new Uncle George. The two, just married, arrived in his big Lincoln driven by the chauffeur. The impression this made on the neighbors caused me to become aware for the first time of the concept of "status."

Then we moved again, and this time a whole house

was ours. It was next door to a family with five girls and a boy, and I had a problem trying to be comfortable with five girls around. I wasn't sure how to go about making friends, but there they were. I went to the fourth and fifth grades while we lived at that house, and I found my first my-friend-only friend, Willard Lovell. Willard's father had a pool table, a terrific attraction. I'd walk with Willard to his house after school, he'd make some mustard sandwiches, and we'd shoot pool.

My family was careful with money, what there was of it, and in an effort to teach me its value a paper route was arranged, a circuit I covered before school. My parents previously had tried to instruct me about money by giving me an allowance, but I always managed to spend it all the day I got it. They figured that if I had to work for the money, I might treat it with more respect. But I refused to take responsibility for collecting the weekly cash. If I got no answer at the door on collection day, I'd forget to write it down—so there went the profits. But before they admitted my incompetence and allowed me to give up on the paper route, I had somehow managed to save up three hundred pennies. I had my eye on a telescopic fishing rod which cost three dollars at the local hardware store. I carried my pennies to the store, counted them out, and returned home with my prize. My mother deemed this an extravagance and made me return it. As I counted the three hundred pennies again, I wondered what good it was to earn money if it wasn't mine to use as I wished.

Our parents make us what we are in odd ways. Like most kids, I tried to match up with the other kids in school. At the time, big belts and sweaters were what everyone was wearing. But when I asked my mother for the clothes in fashion, she'd say, "Why do you need them? You have a belt and a sweater." So now I wear what I please, and have become quite noted for it.

My father was concerned about my undisciplined nature. He tried to interest me in military academies, and had me join the Boy Scouts. The dues were twenty-five cents for each scout meeting, the same as the price for the movies. I tended to skip scout meetings and went to the movies, sitting as close to the screen as I could so I wouldn't miss any of the action. I got away with this for a number of weeks, but when Dad discovered that I was enjoying myself, "wasting time," I was forced to confront the scoutmaster and apologize for my misdemeanors.

I spent years doing all the usual boy things, sandlot baseball or shinny hockey on the pond—days of "Where did you go?" "Out." "What did you do?" "Nothing." I took excellent care of my spare time, and just had fun. I avoided organized sports, because I didn't like having someone say "No, not like that . . ." This allowed me to make my own mistakes, to learn on my own.

I had my first big-time crush when I was about twelve and in the eighth grade. Her name was Betty Dolliver. The school was having a bazaar and I knew she was going. I wanted her to notice me, so I exercised my mind trying to figure out something she might admire. I finally settled on my best shoes—surely she would notice those. But my best shoes were supposed to be saved for special occasions, and my mother wouldn't allow me to wear them. Her idea of special occasions and mine never quite jibed. So I put my everyday shoes on, placed my best pair at the back door, and after going out the front in the old shoes I went to the back to become glamorous for Miss Dolliver. I was too shy to ask her to walk with me to the bus, so I asked my friend Willard Lovell to walk with her. He obliged and got all her attention!

When I was about six, I had discovered a delightful pastime. One day while climbing a tree, I had accidentally massaged certain parts of my body against a limb, causing a tingling sensation that I liked and wanted to continue. I became an avid tree-climber until, when I was twelve, I found that masturbation did the job just as well. At about this time, when I was trying to look at the girls next door without their knowing it, I went to the attic in search of a more advantageous view. I came upon a series of Tarzan books. I became engrossed with the story of the ape man and would have spent hours reading, savoring the antics of Cheetah and of Tarzan's brushes with ferocious jungle creatures, but when mother discovered what I was doing, she took the books away. She was afraid of many things, though what Tarzan could have done to encourage bad habits I've never fathomed. It was the sort of incident that made her take to her bed, and at such times she liked to have me rub her neck. I felt this was all rather strange.

For a few of my teenage summers, I got a job as a caddy at the Prout's Neck Golf Club, and in this I was truly lucky. Some of my Windsor friends worked in the tobacco fields, gathering the leaves and hanging them in drying barns—the hottest job in the Connecticut River Valley. They made more money than I, but money has never meant a great deal to me. Caddies were paid by the hour, and if the players were fast, our fee came to as little as seventy-five cents, with maybe a ten-cent tip. But sometimes a really big sport would hand us a dollar. I wouldn't have traded places with my friends in Windsor for anything.

Up to the time I entered the eighth grade, my marks in school had been quite good, but then I began to falter and just squeaked through the eighth-grade graduation. I'm not sure what caused this change, apart from puberty and new interests, but mother thought a different school would be the answer. She chose Loomis, located in Windsor, one of the top New England prep schools. The school's policy allowed students who lived within a radius of ten to twenty miles to be day students at the nominal fee of a hundred dollars a year. Boarders paid around a thousand.

I had to take the required examination and passed everything except English. Instead of leaving for Prout's Neck that summer, I found myself with a tutor. My friend Willard was in the same boat and joined me for sessions at "The Island," so called because Loomis's buildings were usually awash during the spring flood, being situated near the convergence of the Farmington and Connecticut Rivers.

Our tutor, David Newton, was an English teacher at Loomis—a wonderful, informal man with a wry humor, who won me over almost immediately. He became my idol. My sloppiness of posture, my rebellions, and my smoking Lucky Strike cigarettes were results of my emulation, and I give him credit for it all. He was one hell of a guy, as teacher and friend, and long after Loomis had become history to me, we remained friends. My introduction to the theater was in part his doing. He gave me a lot of encouragement as well as an introduction to his brother, Theodore Newton, a movie actor. Teddy was the first actor I ever met, and he too became a lasting friend until he died of cancer in the early sixties. When Bette Davis and I married, we discovered that Teddy was a friend we had in common, and we saw him off and on during the Hollywood years.

As a result of Dave's tutoring, I passed the English exam and Loomis accepted me. It wasn't too long before I became aware that I belonged to a minority group—a "day boy." There were only a few of "us" opposed to the many of "them," the boarders. Because "they" spent twenty-four hours a day together, they were a more cohesive group. I was sure they were snobs because they knew we day boys were paying much less in tuition. But it's possible that they were envious of the day boys, some of whom had their own cars and were free to leave campus at the end of the day. Thinking back, my feelings of inferiority because I wasn't a boarder at Loomis seem ridiculous, but at the time I labored under the impression that everyone scoffed behind my back because I wasn't a wealthy man's son, as most of the boarders were. Through my Uncle George, who lived in Westchester County, New York, where many of the boarders lived, I was able to make believe I was one of the majority, at least during vacations when Uncle George gave me the use of his snappy car and chauffeur. But this flirtation with borrowed wealth, which to my mind gave me status, also left me in limbo. One day a boarder with whom I played football asked me out to lunch when his family came to visit, and I was forced to confess, "I can't. I'm a day boy."

"So what?" he countered. "Where does it say you can't eat lunch with us?" His acceptance of my condition lessened my skulking, and we became the best of friends. Years later, I was able to do him the favor of lending him five thousand dollars so he could save his family home.

I wasn't very interested in current affairs, but I recall voting for Norman Thomas, the socialist, twice, in straw polls. Something from the outside world was filtering through, but my lack of interest in studies had me staggering, and the weight of my poor grades forced me to repeat the freshman year. My long-suffering adviser, Mr. Newton, met with me to discuss my predicament.

"We prefer our students to have a balanced education," he told me. "You'll have to find something besides sports, Merrill."

"What should I do? I love sports best," was my reply.

"There are cultural activities we'd like you to try, like the Glee Club or the French Club, ceramics or the Dramatic Club," he continued. "Well-rounded, you certainly aren't— so try something new."

None of the things mentioned sounded particularly exciting, but the first thing Newton did was to take me out of football and get me into cross-country running because it took less of my time. This served chiefly to develop my lungs. Then I chose the Dramatic Club, not realizing what was ahead.

The head of the drama department was Monsieur René Cheruy, who was a former secretary to the sculptor Auguste Rodin. Monsieur Cheruy, a short man, a bit on the heavy side, was also my French teacher. He made himself memorable to me by marching me to the blackboard when I had made a mistake, holding onto my ear, and hissing, *petit cochon*. I wasn't altogether certain we could work together, but luckily his assistant was the Latin teacher, Larry Soule, and he took over most of the responsibilities for the Drama Club. Larry, whose father was a minister in Hartford, was an off-beat character who later was fired for spiking the punch at a school dance, or so I heard. On the weekend of the Senior Dance for the Class of 1932, a big day, the club was doing a play called *The Crimson Coconut,* a piece filled with characters called Mr. Ruler, Mr. Chalk, Mr. Blackboard. When Larry heard me audition he seemed stunned by my voice—even then, at sixteen, it was a deep baritone. "Is that your real voice?" he asked.

"Of course," I told him, and saw his eyes light up.

"You're Mr. Inkwell," he said.

Mr. Inkwell was the heavy, the villain, which is why the deep voice got me the part—the first of many times my voice got me the part. It is a gift of God and my father.

On opening night, Larry stood in the wings as we got ready to go on stage. "Make sure your flies are buttoned, boys," was his only instruction to his actors. It was a wild, physical comedy, a burlesque with seltzer bottles and bladders. I got out there and started horsing around, squirting seltzer at crotches, at faces, doing the gags and cracking jokes, and the audience loved it. They roared, yelled, clapped, laughed, and stood up and cheered.

Suddenly I realized that this was for me, this wonderful noise that rolled up in waves from the darkness beyond the footlights. It was Mr. Inkwell who was getting the biggest laughs, the loudest applause. When that sank in, my knees wobbled—I was overwhelmed. Nothing like it had ever happened to me before in my life. I was being appreciated. For the first time in my life I was getting the approval I so desperately wanted. I was being showered with more attention in that one hour than my parents had given me in sixteen years—my Yankee parents with their Yankee modesty and reserve, their Calvinism and repressed way of bringing up children, their unwillingness ever to let go of their emotions. It's that New England thing about never giving in, keeping such a stiff upper lip that you never cry, laugh, or tell people you love them and think they're wonderful. It wasn't the applause so much as the approval that I needed. I decided then and there to be an actor.

Between the Drama Club at Loomis, where I got my share of applause and became president, and the hockey team of which I was captain, my long-bruised psyche was partly restored. And there had been an ironic episode that helped sustain me. Some of my fellow students had names such as Steinway (of the pianos), Browning (machine guns), Loomis (insurance), and Rockefeller (Winthrop, who became governor of Arkansas). Just after the Crash of 1929, some of my classmates started bragging about how much stock market money their fathers had lost (all except Winthrop Rockefeller, who never got into the game). But I calmly announced that my father hadn't lost a dime—a statement that caused quite a stir. All the boys were impressed and my status soared. I saw no reason to tell them my family didn't have enough money to play the market!

My five years at Loomis were full of the usual fun with games and girls, and I usually went to Prout's Neck for the summer. The house at Prout's was just a few minutes from the ocean, and whenever I was away I dreamed about the place and plotted ways to get back. Some of my classmates from Loomis who were boarders summered at Prout's, and I became sensitive about the fact that I wasn't part of their sailing and tennis or golf sets because I was a caddy. A number of Portland and Westbrook people had small cottages at Prout's, like my grandmother's, but the majority of summer people had large homes, belonged to the yacht club and country club, and came from New York, Philadelphia, or Cleveland. So my status problems continued.

During my teens I tended to latch on to one girl, against my mother's advice to be friends with many. The girls I chose to be my particular friend did not always choose me, so I was jilted many times. Once, though, I did the jilting.

I had been carrying on a torrid affair with the daughter of an Episcopal minister. It was a wonderful summertime Prout's Necking romance. Our passion for each other was manifested by numbing our lips with kisses, and some petting, but we always stopped short of the ultimate goal. And we never took off a single item of clothing. As a result of these heated meetings, I often staggered home with damp pants. This incited me to plot ways to see her again as soon as possible, hoping the next encounter would end more satisfactorily.

I persuaded mother to invite this girl to Windsor for part of the Christmas vacation, after which we would continue to Bronxville, where Uncle George now lived and where the use of his town car would allow us an appropriate and available back seat. This plot backfired. That fall I met a beautiful redhead, a new girl in town named Janet Tilney, and I fell for her. In my new passion, the other was forgotten. But my summertime girlfriend arrived on the scene at Christmas, as planned, and I had no choice but to play the host. I took her out to dinner, but brought her home immediately afterward. I had a scheme up my sleeve. It was my chore to take my father's car to the heated garage he rented about a mile from the house, and that night I was eager to oblige. I told everyone I'd be right back. Instead, I went to Janet's house. When I came home several hours later, everyone had gone to bed except my grandmother, who was visiting us and who had waited up for me. She gave me a long look and said, "You ought to be kicked right in the ass." The use of this word by that dear lady jolted me so much that I was prompted to exhibit greater kindness to my houseguest before she returned to Maine. There was, of course, no trip to Bronxville.

A high spot in my sexual high jinks occurred one summer while visiting my friend Billy Braman. His older brother had a girl in his room one day, and Billy and I were downstairs, speculating on what was going on upstairs. When they emerged and found Billy and me sitting in the living room, the girl walked over and gave each of us a kiss. I had kissed girls before, but it was nothing like that kiss. Her tongue went deep into my mouth, almost to my throat, raising everything raisable on my body, including the hair on my neck. After that experience, I determined to find her on my own, though she was presumably involved, and a bit older than I.

I tracked her down and persuaded her to go out with me. When I got her in the back of a friend's Marmon touring car, I decided, "It's now or never." In my fevered anticipation of this meeting I had acquired a package of condoms—so determined was I to lose my virginity. With the subtlety of an ox, I began wrestling around, but she did a very good job of fending me off. Finally it all came to a halt and she sat up, saying, "Listen, you'll be pretty disappointed if, when you do it for the first time, you're in the back seat of a car going sixty miles an hour." What did I know? I believed her, and that was that.

Ah, but it was to come. A lovely lady had moved near us in Windsor, a married woman with a boy about four years old, and suddenly I found myself useful as a babysitter. It turned out to be easy money—he was a good kid, gentle to be with. Every time I went, I felt the woman's eyes on me, and soon I wasn't sure whether I was going over to do a job or so I could see her again. We found ourselves alone one evening, and from the way she touched me I knew we could get much closer. One thing led to another and before long I had a fantastic liaison going—my first experience with the real thing. I was like so many young studs; I didn't know anything about making love. I just banged away, never learning anything. Every surface was brought into play—the floor, the couch, bed, bushes. We did it anywhere, and as often as possible. I was pretty rabbitty. I had entered a man's world, but I hadn't learned the subtleties of love, which would come much later.

This idyll came to an abrupt halt after not quite a year of illicit fooling around. The brother of a Loomis buddy had a chicken farm which supplied nearby restaurants. I got a summer job there. One hot day, when I was down on my knees changing a tire on an old pickup truck, heaving against a lug-wrench to loosen the wheel nuts, a shadow fell across me. I glanced up and found myself staring at a pair of boots. Looking up a little further, I met a pair of eyes gazing at me with a mixture of rage and contempt. I recognized my fair lady's husband. Panic almost took over, but I just squatted there in front of him and swallowed a few times.

"I think you should stop fooling around with my wife," he said.

I thought that sounded like a good idea. He was more muscular than I was, and he had anger on his side. I'd be the loser in an argument.

The summer before, my father had discovered

CMTC (Citizens Military Training Camp). Because of Uncle Paul's stories about being a private in World War I, and my father's conviction that discipline would be good for me, my family decided that I should attend this camp. I had not yet turned eighteen, short of the age requirement, but apparently that didn't matter, because I found myself being dropped off at Fort Devens, outside of Fitchburg, Massachusetts, by my Aunt Marion and Uncle George, who were on their way to Maine.

I have never felt so alone in my life, a stranger among a thousand boys from South Boston, marching, making beds, having to accept military discipline. I was to spend parts of two summers at the camp. After the first week, I fell in with three brothers who were all boxers. They persuaded me to become one too, and set up a training program to teach me what they knew. I went along with the whole thing—though now I can't imagine I was all that enthusiastic.

This went on for about three weeks: fooling around, dancing up and down, jabbing, that sort of thing. One day they announced that the time had arrived for a match. I am not large-framed, and have never been bulky, but for some reason I was placed in the heavyweight division. As the matching-up and weighing-in began, I struck up a conversation with another fellow, who was a bit larger than I, and who had pretty well-defined muscles. He informed me that I was on the list as his opponent, and said, with very little humility, that he had been champion of his class for the past two years.

I couldn't explain to myself how I'd gotten into this, and felt some trepidation, but it was too late. I climbed into the ring, making sure my seconds had plenty of towels. The bell rang for the bout to begin. I started dancing toward my opponent as I had been taught, with my defenses up. I received a couple of blows, saw lots of stars, and yelled to my seconds to throw in the towels—all of them. My career in the ring was over.

2

COLLEGE
TO COMEDY

I n my last year at Loomis I managed to just get
by each term so that I could pass into the next.
One beautiful day in May I heard that two of my friends
were traveling to Brunswick, Maine, to take the entrance
examinations for Bowdoin College. The weather, the mention of Maine, and the fact that my friends were going to
stay at a fraternity house enthralled me to such a degree
that I raced to the headmaster and asked if I could go with
them. He said, "Well, since you're not going to graduate
from Loomis this year, what do you have to lose?"

With that less than enthusiastic encouragement, off
we all went to Bowdoin. We stayed at the Delta Kappa
Epsilon House, and the next day I took the exams along
with my friends. I must have been absorbing something at
Loomis, because, to everyone's astonishment I managed to
pass the exams—not exactly with flying colors, but at least I
passed.

So in the fall of 1933, I entered Bowdoin College
without having graduated from Loomis. To this day, the
only diploma in my possession is one from the eighth
grade, a fact that has never cost me any sleep. I became a

member of DKE and plunged into college life for the next few months. I hadn't really planned on a college career, and would have preferred to go straight to acting school, but my father, who hadn't attended college himself, wanted his son to be a college graduate.

The "rushing" season used up a couple of weeks. The freshmen found themselves pledged before they had made any significant new friendships. Even though I was pledged to DKE, and had friends there, I found my drinking buddies at the Beta house. We formed our own fraternity, the Club Stiff, which bore the scintillating motto: "You can't leave the Club Stiff until you leave the club stiff."

During one of our Club Stiff meetings, I was drinking beer, which was usually the mild 3.2 percent alcohol kind. But this time one of the guys had laced it with grain alcohol from the chem lab. I talked hockey with a visiting lecturer who was the poet laureate of Canada. On my way back to the DKE house I fell asleep in a snowpile, too blotto to find my way home. One of my nondrinking brother "Dekes," Harry Scholefield, got me back to a room, and may have saved my life.

(Harry later became the minister of the First Unitarian Church in San Francisco. It is more than likely that mine was one of the first souls he saved. I see him whenever he comes East, and we still phone and write between times—a lasting friendship of the best kind. Harry's church is the only church I've ever seen that was full every Sunday. From ten to eleven o'clock, he used to conduct an "adult forum" before the regular service, and he had the courage to let me use the pulpit to voice my antiwar and arms-control convictions.)

At Bowdoin, Dad arranged for me to have a free room in the football coach's house, in an effort to ease costs. The coach was Charlie Bowser, and I was a live-in babysitter. I got free meals at the fraternity house by waiting on tables, and took another job at the student union to earn spare change. I went out for football that first year and, to my surprise, Don Lancaster, the freshman football coach, selected me as captain. But he had no idea what my skills were; it was a random choice. As has always been the case, I had no follow-through. And so, by the end of the football season, not only was I no longer team captain, I was not even sitting on the bench—I was in the bleachers as a civilian.

Perhaps the outstanding event of my brief sojourn at Bowdoin was meeting Eaton Weatherbee Tarbell, who remains one of my oldest and best friends. Eaton's family came from Bangor, Maine, where he lives to this day, and they had some money. He had gone to Deerfield Academy, one of Loomis's rivals, and he had a car. But best of all, he had a double dormitory room on campus, and on the nights I didn't have to baby-sit, I stayed in his room, wore his clothes, and drove his car. As Eaton said, "I've acquired a roommate, and a well-dressed one at that." He went on to become a successful architect.

Soon, my college life began winding down. When I returned from the break in February, Dean Paul Nixon called me to his office. It wasn't an unusual occurrence. I think I spent more time in his office than any other freshman. But that day he said that my father had called to ask him if he was wasting his money by sending me to Bowdoin. He had replied that he couldn't answer, but would ask me. He sat there waiting for my answer, and all I could do was to tell the truth. "My father is wasting his money. I want to be an actor."

The dean leaned back in his chair, his demeanor calm but imposing, and said, "Well, Gary, I think you should go to New York and do your best. If it doesn't welcome you with open arms, come on back to Bowdoin." I always loved him for those words.

So much for college, I thought, and got myself ready to return home. On the road back, I took a little detour to Boston. Maine didn't have such a thing as a cocktail bar, something new on the horizon, so I thought I might as well make a quick visit to see what a cocktail bar was. The drinks had interesting names—Sidecar, Martini, Gin Fizz, Pink Lady, and Planter's Punch. I ordered one of each and drank them all within an hour, with no ill effects other than being happily drunk. Given only my brief training as a member of the Club Stiff, I concluded that my stomach was made of iron.

After a little research when I got home, I came upon a group of aspiring actors doing radio shows at WTIC in Hartford, the Guy Hedlund Players, and quickly became involved with them. The most illustrious graduates of the Hedlund Players were Ed Begley and Louis Nye. While we were "in training" we did everything from sound effects to leading parts, mostly for the experience. I think we got three dollars a week. I presume Mr. Hedlund made some money.

In my off-time, I played hockey with a bunch of amateurs who had organized a team. We played in Springfield and New Haven. This was my thing: I loved the radio job and the hockey. But Dad was after me about college again, wanting me to try Trinity in Hartford. He figured that if I could live at home I might get more studying done. Dad was a good salesman, and I finally agreed to give it a try. So in the fall of 1934 I entered Trinity, a freshman once again. All was not lost though; there was a chapter of Delta Kappa Epsilon at Trinity, and to sweeten the bitter pill of being a stranger, Ralph McEldowney, an old friend from the Citizens Military Training Camp, was on campus. What was more natural than to call home and say I was staying at the DKE House to study with an old friend?

Not much studying was done. Mac and I went off to

neighboring bars or, just as often, to girls' schools nearby, remembering old times and creating new memories. The denouement came one night when Dad lent me his car. I told him I was going to a local dance, but Mac and I took the car to Smith, a women's college, to pick up my girl of the moment and her roommate, who was a blind date for Mac. For some reason, we decided to head for Bowdoin College, a good two hundred and fifty miles away, instead of going to the dance. The girls told their housemother they were going bowling.

We drove along the wintry, early-December roads, having a gay old time, laughing and drinking, and in no time at all we were circling the city of Portland on Baxter Boulevard, twenty miles south of Brunswick. Suddenly, I hit a patch of ice. In my boozy inexperience, I twisted the wheel and slammed on the brakes and the car flipped over, landing on its roof, wheels spinning in the air. The glass was shattered, so we crawled through the broken windows. Miraculously, there was no evidence on our bodies that we'd had an accident except for a bruise on one girl's cheek. But there sat our transportation, upside-down by the side of the road. My heart was in my stomach.

I had spent a night in jail once, for driving without a license. It had been the same kind of thing. I'd said, "Let's go to Maine," and my friend had complied. We had gotten as far as Stafford Springs, Connecticut, when a cop stopped us. I had no license—no nothing—and wham, I was in the jug. My father came up the next day, a Sunday, with the other kid's father. My father said, "Well, the judge is out playing golf. I think you ought to stay in another day to think things over." He left me there. He'd paid the fine and I was released the next day, but it was an experience I was in no hurry to repeat.

But here I was, involved in an accident. Fortunately, I felt I was on "home territory." I called my uncle, Judge

Frank Pride, who lived in nearby Westbrook. He came to our rescue and drove us back to his house where he and my aunt put us up for the night. The next day, though there had been reporters, cameramen, and police at the scene, we were driven to the train station and shuffled off to our various destinations, all of us straining to come up with explanations for the night before. I assume the judge took care of the police, but I've always wondered how the situation would have been handled if the accident had been more serious. I didn't know one of the girls at all. Think of arriving at some stranger's house to say, "I have killed your daughter!" We used up all our nine lives that night.

I got home and said to Dad, "Here are the keys."

"Where's the car?"

"It disappeared. It's in Portland."

He was very gracious about the damage to his car, considering that his insurance policy didn't cover that sort of accident. He was a lovely man. Years later, when he lived in Florida, we got talking about winters in Maine, and that led to the time I flipped his car over. It had been years and years since he had mentioned it and, since I had never talked to him about it, I asked how much the repairs and the towing had cost. He said he couldn't remember exactly, but it was around a thousand dollars. I sat down and telephoned Tucker, the fellow who managed my money in Los Angeles, and said, "Write a check for a thousand dollars to Benjamin Gary Merrill and send it to him right away, in Fort Lauderdale." I put the phone down and turned around to see tears coming to my father's eyes. Soon I was crying too. I put my arms around him and said, "Well, I finally paid that off."

Northampton, Massachusetts, the home of Smith College, was conveniently close to Trinity. Students like myself, easily bored and not much interested in classes, could find diversion there. One day I went to see what

Northampton had to offer. There was a local beer bar that had a lot of private rooms, so I wandered in. I found some Smith girls sitting around, drinking applejack and studying, but they could not be budged from their books. I gave up and returned to Trinity, and settled down with a bottle of applejack and a book, in an attempt to emulate their studiousness. But, unlike the Smith girls, I ended up stark naked, trying to climb a telephone pole in two feet of snow.

With antics like that, is it any wonder that by the time midterm grades were posted I had earned five straight F's? At last Dad decided that I wasn't really college material. And my mother, surprisingly, became interested in helping me find a drama school. It was thanks to her energetic efforts that I could leave Trinity and go to New York. Aunt Marion's husband George had died, and she contributed some of her inheritance, which, along with the usual financial support from my parents, enabled me to attend drama school.

Shortly before I was to leave I had seen a notice in a Hartford paper that two scouts from Paramount Pictures would be in New York—Boris Kaplan and Oscar Serlin. I immediately wrote them a letter. I worked out a scene from *The Last Mile*, and Dave Newton, my old Loomis adviser, lent me some money to get to the city. At the time, Teddy Newton, his actor brother, was in New York appearing in a play called *Dead End*, and he let me stay with him while I did my thing for the Paramount scouts. As it turned out, I wasn't ready for Hollywood, but both Kaplan and Serlin encouraged me to keep acting.

I enrolled in the Hilda Spong School of Acting and Dramatic Arts on East Fifty-ninth Street, between Fifth and Madison. Hilda was an Australian actress of some note who hadn't managed to find work in New York. So she had started the school, hiring a playwright, a director, and a French fencing champion as staff. The playwright became

ill—probably from seeing his work murdered by students—
and Arnold Berke, from the drama department of Carnegie
Tech, took his place. When I first investigated the school, I
noticed that about twenty women and only five men were
enrolled, and it occurred to me that with so few men I'd
have a better chance of getting a good part in the plays. We
were constantly rehearsing for one play or another, without
actually performing for an audience, and we were exposed
to a lot of different art forms, techniques, and skills that
could be brought into use when the time came for us to be
on our own: diction, breathing, dancing, fencing, you name
it.

On the first day I was walking down the street with
one of the men students, chatting, getting acquainted, and
he asked where I was going to live. I didn't know, so I said,
"In some rooming house, I suppose."

"I have an apartment with two other roommates
and we have room for a fourth. If the others agree, and if
you agree, why don't you move in with us?" he asked.

Well, why not? It sounded great, although I couldn't
accept without first checking with my mother and Aunt
Marion. Not only were they taking an interest in my future
as an actor, but they also held the purse strings. My new
friend understood my reluctance to commit myself immediately and couldn't have been nicer.

"Bring your family around to the apartment tomorrow afternoon," he suggested. "They can look us over.
We'll have tea."

My mother and aunt had insisted on staying with
me in a downtown hotel until my housing problem was
solved, and when I told them about the offer, they thought it
was an ideal solution. The two ladies were delighted with
the invitation and got themselves decked out the next day—
hats, gloves, and all. We arrived at 145 East Fiftieth Street at
the appointed hour. I asked for Malcolm Atterbury's apart-

ment. "Yes sir," the doorman said, showing us to the elevator, and up we went—to a penthouse. The door was opened by a Filipino servant. Malcolm and his two room-mates came to greet us and ushered us to comfortable seats in a well-appointed living room. As we were served tea, Malcolm played the piano—and, I must say, we were swept away. The apartment had two large bedrooms and a living room, dining room, and kitchen, with a terrace running around three sides of the penthouse. Mother and Aunt Marion were entranced by Malcolm, who was a lean, attractive man, somewhat reminiscent of Leslie Howard. But when we got back to our hotel to discuss the pros and cons, we all came up with the same conclusion: too costly. There was no way I could afford to become a fourth in a place run on such a grand scale.

After classes the next day I told Malcolm the out-come of the family conference. "The other fellows have okayed you," he countered. "I can assure you it would be all right to move in. You can pay only what you can afford at first. Then when you get established, we'll talk about it again."

Of course I moved in, and that first year in New York I lived better than I ever did again until Bette Davis and I rented a triplex on Beekman Place while she was doing *Two's Company*, the revue that returned her to Broadway in 1952.

Malcolm was an Atterbury from the Main Line of Philadelphia. His stepfather had been president of the Pennsylvania Railroad and his mother's family was involved in the Merck pharmaceuticals company. Malcolm was prob-ably ten years older than I. Paul King, one of the room-mates, was five or six years older, and was studying for the opera. Warren Bergquist, the other roomy, was about the same age as Paul. Warren worked for the Waterman Steam-ship Line. With the exception of Malcolm, we were relatively poor boys.

Malcolm and I settled in as classmates at Hilda's, and, since he was not only attractive, but witty and charming, it wasn't long before he found a girl, Ellen Hardies. My girl was Betty Moran, the younger sister of Lois Moran, who had been a leading ingenue in musicals such as *Of Thee I Sing*. Lois had recently married Clarence Young, an older man, a Lafayette Escadrille pilot in World War I. He was with Pan Am at this time, and they lived in San Francisco. Betty and her mother, Gladys, lived at 277 Park Avenue, one of those houses with a big courtyard. Gladys Moran was a very interesting woman. Her husband had been an officer in the Army and had died during the war. She and Lois had lived in France while Betty was in school, because it was cheaper. Their circle of friends included F. Scott Fitzgerald. (It was said that he used Lois as the model for the girl in *Tender Is the Night*.) Gladys spent all day watching the stock market at a brokerage, and at night she plotted stock prices on graphs.

At the end of the first year at Hilda's, Malcolm went off to Cape May, New Jersey, where he'd spent many summers with his parents, and while he was there he leased a theater. He organized a stock company consisting of Betty, myself, and a few others, and we did one show a week—six nights and two matinees—rehearsing the next week's play during the day. More often than not, there were more of us on stage than in the audience, but we were doing plays— acting.

That August of 1936, Gladys wanted to take Betty to California, because Lois was about to have a baby. Since she was acquainted with one or two movie producers she had met through Lois, Gladys thought Betty should go as well, meet them, and get a job. Betty asked me to come along, with the idea that I, too, would meet these producers. It was too inviting an offer to pass up. I was sure I could get a job.

That's how green I was. I didn't know anything.

So away we went, leaving Malcolm in the lurch. I had just turned twenty-one, and should have known better. We traveled by train (a great way to see the country) and, though it was comfortable, it seemed to take forever to get to Los Angeles—about four days. No sooner had we gotten settled than Mrs. Moran arranged a meeting with her producer friends, and Betty and I did some scenes for them. I was under the impression it was as easy as that. You went out, did the scenes, and were offered a job. But I didn't labor under this illusion too long. We didn't get jobs. Then Mrs. Moran took Betty with her to be with Lois in San Francisco. I was left on my own in Hollywood, with instructions from Gladys to visit some studios and see what I could do.

It was hot in Hollywood and I was friendless, a little boy lost. For two days I kicked around, visited a bar or two, and went back to a room I had rented. Hollywood was not set afire by my presence, so I made a plane reservation, called San Francisco, and followed Betty and Mrs. Moran. It was late at night when I got in, and I'll never forget how warm and understanding Clarence Young was to me. He had been awakened from a sound sleep to go to the airport and meet me. I know that I would have been growling and out of sorts had it been me in his place. After ushering me into his kitchen, he handed me a beer and cheered me up. He was just fine.

The next morning Betty said, "My mother is madder than hell."

"Yeah?" I said, "Where is she? I'll talk to her."

"She's down at the market."

That meant a brokerage house. I found Gladys, and Betty was right. She said, "Well, I'm putting you on a train, you're going back to New York." So onto the train I went—and, boom, back to New York. I hadn't done what she told me to do and it had upset her. Later on we became friends, and I'd go to see her whenever I was in California. Once she even asked me to go to Newport Beach to talk to Betty, who was having marital problems—as though I had some answers!

On the street back in New York I ran into Bud Hurlburt, an old Loomis buddy, with another friend, Alan Gibson. None of us had anywhere to live, so we decided to get an apartment together. We went apartment hunting and came upon a one-room flat with a kitchenette and bath. Alan built a double bunk bed, and in this flat the three of us lived for about eight months while we tracked around the theater district looking for work. Finally, in October, I got a job. It was only for one week, and on the subway circuit— so-called because the theaters could be reached by subway. I rode to the Bronx, Coney Island, Brighton Beach, and around again. The play was a comedy about four Russian students, called *Squaring the Circle,* and my first job had me playing the male lead.

Milton Adams, a fellow student at the Hilda Spong School, had gone with me to the casting call in the office of Jules Leventhal, who operated the subway circuit. He was known as "Minimum Jules," no doubt because of his pay scale, but his word was his bond, and over the years he had given work to more actors than most of the more illustrious producers. The office was packed when we arrived and I was all for leaving, but Milton pushed me into the main office.

After I read for him, Jules asked if I belonged to Equity. "No," I answered, "but I'll join immediately."

"Good," he said. "You're hired."

I was hired, he said—but I didn't have the money for the union initiation fee and dues. You can't work without belonging to Actors Equity—the stage actors' union—and you can't join Equity until there is a job in the offing. There I was, the job in hand, ready to become a professional, a union actor. Fortunately, Dad came through with the money.

Beatrice DeNiergaarde played the female lead in *Squaring the Circle*, which she had played the year before in a short Broadway run, and was the most experienced of the cast of two young men and two young women. The director was a volatile Russian named Ostrov. Rehearsals lasted one week, and we opened the week before Thanksgiving at Brighton Beach. My father and mother came to see the play on Thanksgiving, and since Thursday was pay night at the theater, I received my enormous salary of twenty-five dollars right before their eyes. "How about that," I said to my father. "Twenty-five dollars for doing nothing."

That was my debut, and it gave me the courage necessary to continue making the rounds of producers' offices, where I was often greeted by pleasant secretaries. These overworked, badgered guardians of the producer's inner sanctum were the ones who kept us actors informed about when there might be some casting going on. But for an interminable two or three weeks there was nothing. One day, one of the secretaries told me about a casting call for dancers and extras for *The Eternal Road*. It was to be held on a Sunday at the Manhattan Center on Thirty-fourth Street, just off Eighth Avenue.

When the day rolled around, I was on the street pretty early, as I wanted to get a place in the casting line not too near the end. However, on the way to the subway at Fifty-ninth Street, I ran into another old Loomis buddy, Joe Mosenthal, whom I hadn't seen since school. What could I do? We had a couple of drinks at a nearby bar, talked over old times, catching up with what was going on in each other's life, and by the time I got to Manhattan Center for the casting, hundreds of people were already there, milling around. The line that led up the stairs to the casting office had two or three people on each step. I saw notices posted along the way and finally focused on one which read: PLEASE DO NOT USE THE ELEVATOR. The alcohol I had consumed had allowed me to reach a level of false courage and brashness. I took the elevator and got off almost in front of the casting desk. I pushed my way into the line about ten people back. The person behind the desk asked, "Can you dance?"

"Sure," I said. We'd had a few dance lessons at Spong's from a man who ran a dance company, so I gave his name.

"Report tomorrow to Brooks Brothers' costume department. You'll be measured for sandals and costumes. Do you know where that is?"

"Of course I know where that is," I shouted.

It appeared that I'd been hired as an extra, at fifteen dollars a week. My father was still supplementing my income, so I looked forward to being affluent for a while.

The Eternal Road was a play about the history of the Jews. Norman Bel Geddes was the set designer, Max Reinhardt directed. It had a cast of about three hundred, including Sam Jaffe, Sidney Lumet, and Dickie Van Patten. Samuel Goldenberg, one of the great cantors, threw lines to the actors so they wouldn't have to learn them. This was the norm in the Yiddish Theater; the actors didn't have to learn lines; prompters were always available. After a while the actor would remember his lines, but the effect was very dramatic. Meyer Weisgal, a devout Jew, produced the play along with Crosby Gaige.

Several rows of seats were ripped out of the orchestra section and this space served as a synagogue for a pogrom scene. From there to the stage and on up toward a "mountain," we extras were singing angels behind strategically placed screens. When we weren't singing, we had to crawl around on stage and be beaten. We all wore body makeup from head to toe because we were playing slaves exposed to the hot, hot sun of Egypt. Some nights, when I got home too tired or too drunk, I neglected showering and my white sheets turned to a lovely dusty pink. It upset my roommates at first, but they got used to it.

We dressed in the subbasement, and there were so many of us that we punched a time clock for our fifteen dollars a week. The next group up the pay scale were the dancers, who were probably making twenty-five dollars, and after that came the speaking roles, which paid thirty and forty dollars on up. The logistics of putting the play together were phenomenal. It was a hell of a *tour de force.* There were so many extras that it wasn't possible to keep track of everyone, and there were the usual games of people ducking scenes, sometimes not being missed. But occasionally there were so many angels or slaves missing that the stage manager was forced to beat the bushes to see where everyone was hiding. Usually they were in the subbasement, playing poker.

There were those who grumbled—I was one—about the low pay, the lack of decent dressing rooms, and one thing or another, and there was talk of a strike. Meyer Weisgal had a great deal of grace and apologized to everyone for the discomforts. A group of us had decided to go to his office and talk to him, but when I looked at him I realized how hard he was working.

"Shit, this man is exhausted," I said. "I think we're terrible to be here." I was taking his side, unexpectedly, and the others called me a fucking capitalist sympathizer, among a few other epithets, but I mollified them for a while.

Some of us had become friendly with a few of the women dancers. Through them we got to know some of the men dancers, one in particular. He lived in Greenwich Village with his wife, a schoolteacher. They had a charming apartment to which we gravitated on many occasions, and they welcomed us to their circle of friends. One afternoon when his wife was at school, Billy and I were alone sitting on the couch and talking. Usually when he talked, he gestured, as we all do, but on this occasion, after certain gestures, I found his hand resting on my knee or thigh and he was squeezing my arm in a friendly fashion. I didn't think much about it until he became pretty bold—and I suddenly realized he was making advances toward me.

I jumped up, shocked, and said, "Come on now, we're friends. Let's not louse it up." Fortunately, he immediately understood and backed off. I had heard of homosexual activity, of course, but this was my first experience. I suddenly understood how all those girls I had had in the rumble seats of various cars must have felt about my unwanted advances.

During the run of *The Eternal Road* I heard through the grapevine that auditions were being held for a road company of another play, *Brother Rat*, George Abbott's recent hit on Broadway. José Ferrer, Frank Albertson, and Eddie Albert were playing in it, but now they were recasting. Guy Palmerton, a friend of my father's involved in the theater, called me to say that he thought I'd be right for a part, and instructed me to get a crewcut. The play was set in a Virginia military academy and was about a group of cadets. He said that if I looked the part during the audition, it would help. So I got a crewcut and went off to the audition.

George Abbott had begun making a name for himself on Broadway. The famous critic George Jean Nathan described the "Abbott touch": "His is the theater of snappy curtain lines, wise-cracking dialogue . . . sentimental relief in the shape of tender young lovers, and various condiments, all staged as if the author had used a pepper shaker in lieu of an inkwell."

By the mid-1930's, Abbott was excelling in musicals. He went on to win six Tony Awards and the Pulitzer Prize with plays such as *Damn Yankees* and *The Pajama Game*. At one time he had three hits on Broadway simultaneously: *A Funny Thing Happened on the Way to the Forum, Never Too Late,* and *Take Her, She's Mine*. He counted directors Garson Kanin and Harold Prince as two of his protégés, and in his own career was director, producer, and even an actor. (At the age of one hundred years, he still is involved with Broadway productions.)

After my audition for *Brother Rat*, I was in a great frame of mind because he told me to report to his office on the twenty-second floor of a building on Forty-second Street later that day. I strolled around town spending the fine salary I was about to receive, then walked over. Several other actors were there, and then Mr. Abbott walked in.

"I called you here to say how good I thought you all were. You did an excellent job at the auditions, but I'm sorry, the company is formed. Perhaps later there'll be another company. Maybe then." And we were all excused.

My heart dropped twenty-two floors.

Well, what the hell, I thought to myself. At least I'd had a dream. So I returned to *The Eternal Road*, slaving along.

But two weeks later I got an unexpected call from Mr. Abbott's office: I was offered José Ferrer's role in the third road company of *Brother Rat*. A co-worker from *Road*, Burke O'Connell, was also cast. So we became big shots among the extras. Then *The Eternal Road* closed and I high-tailed it to Maine. With a job in the wings, I felt I'd earned a vacation, and I took Mary Perrine, one of the dancers, with me. No sex, just friends. I was not good with sex—partly because I was afraid. If I stumbled across it, fine. But I wasn't especially good at making passes or trying to talk someone into doing anything she wasn't willing to do without pressure—though I felt I was a bit better at it with a few drinks under my belt. A repressed character, I suppose.

Once, during a house party at Bowdoin, a chaperone had asked if she could read my palm. I gave her my hand, certain she would say something about my idiotic adventures. But when she began her routine she said, "I see a deeper side of you, a whole serious side that you don't show to your friends." This amazed me because until then she had only seen me drinking and horsing around. I had been trying to develop my sense of comedy, though at that point it was only released through alcohol. (Now I think it comes along quite well without drinks.)

Mary spent a week or so with me in Maine, and after she left I stayed on for a while, enjoying the sea's hypnotic rolling sounds, catching my breath. Then I got a call asking if I could join the New York company of *Brother Rat* until it was time to go on the road for the fall tour, and I said, "Fine!" The part I was given wasn't the one I expected, though. It had a couple of hectic entrances and exits, and, try as I might, I couldn't get it right. After a week my performance was just passable—and I learned later that Mr. Abbott was on the verge of firing me for my incompetence. But Edith Van Cleve, one of his assistants, suggested that I be kept on for the part originally offered me, and Mr. Abbott took her advice. Edith later became an agent at Music Corporation of America (MCA), and I've thanked her many times.

The cast and crew for the road company of *Brother Rat* included Eddie Bracken, Reese Alsop (who later left the stage to become a doctor), J. Richard Jones, Lyle Bettger, Hollis Mitchell, Fritz DeWilde (Brandon's father), and myself; as well as Jean McCoy, Clare Hazel, Mary Rolfe, Lorna Beaton, Eddie Rice, and Burke O'Connell. It was a wonderful comedy. Our touring group opened in Providence. In order to save a few dollars for entertainment, we stayed in a rooming house instead of a hotel, and then found a rambling apartment that housed five of us. Hollis

Mitchell, who played the lieutenant and was a bit older than the rest of us, asked if he could join us, and we said "Sure." When we got to the place, Mitch put his bags down and said, "I'm queer, but none of you interest me." So everyone knew where he stood.

We toured for nine months across the country, making seventy-five to a hundred dollars each week, depending upon the box office. In the late thirties, that was pretty damned good money, so much so that even I could save some of it, in spite of my indulgences. In Cleveland, Hollis Mitchell asked some of us if we'd like to go to a nightclub with him to see some "drag" acts. None of us knew what he meant, and he had to explain that it was a form of entertainment starring men who dressed and acted as women. We were all fresh from the country or from drama schools, not on to what was happening in the subcultures. By today's standards we would be considered really square—and we were square then, compared to the city boys. But we were curious and said we thought it was a great idea as long as we had Mitch as a chaperone.

The entertainment was really good. There was a magnificent dancer, a charming "songstress," and a thoroughly witty "comedienne." We clapped and laughed, and during intermission Mitch asked if we would like to meet the performers. We all thought that a capital idea and he went off to fetch them. While he was gone we debated whether we should rise when the performers got to the table, a reasonable point of debate, and the vote was that we should. As Mitch approached the table with the three glamorous entertainers, we arose as if on cue.

"Jeezus," the comedienne gasped, "the age of chivalry is not yet dead," and "she" raised her hands in mock surprise and pleasure.

That got a tremendous laugh from us all.

I remembered this occasion years later when Bette

Davis and I were doing *The World of Carl Sandburg,* and I took Bette to the famous Finocchio's in San Francisco. All the entertainers are men in drag. Bette refused to believe it until we went backstage. She'd never seen or heard of such entertainers—and she was about fifty years old then.

That evening in Cleveland, the singer seemed to take a shine to me, making me the object of a lot of his/her attention. It was all in fun. We were in such a good mood that nothing could spoil it.

About a week later I received a note. It said: "I will be arriving at your theater on such and such a date. We must meet again . . ." or words to that effect. It was signed by the singer in drag. Well, I was going crazy trying to figure some way to get out of that—how to disappear before any kind of meeting could take place. Each time I tried to talk it over with the guys, they just shrugged and walked away. Something had to be done. Finally, when I saw two of the guys talking to the girls in the cast, I went over, thinking that one of the girls could help me out. As I was describing my predicament, the group broke into gales of laughter. I was furious that they thought my panic was cause for amusement. It was then they told me that Lorna Beaton had written the note. I was relieved not to have to think up a phony excuse; I admired that group of entertainers in drag.

On New Year's Day, 1938, we were on tour in St. Louis. New Year's Eve had fallen on Friday that year, and, of course, we had two shows on Saturday, no matter what holiday it might be. A fraternity brother from Bowdoin days, Jack Goldman, lived in St. Louis, and when he discovered I was in town with the play, he invited me to his family home for an open house party on New Year's Day. I wanted to go and figured I could make it between the matinee and evening performance, so I accepted the invitation, saying I might bring along a friend or two. I invited Eddie Rice, the stage manager, and his girl, Lorna, who was working as an understudy, to go with me. A car was sent to pick us up at five-thirty so we might have more time at the party.

It was a wonderful party. We had driven up to a mansion all decked out for the holidays. My God, you could play Hamlet in the front hall. Jack Goldman's family had really put on a spread. Every time we turned around, there was another drink, but it seemed that no sooner had we arrived than Jack said, "Don't you have to leave? It's about seven-thirty-five." At that point, we were feeling no pain— in fact, we were in pretty sad shape—and the curtain was scheduled to go up at eight-thirty.

Fritz DeWilde, the assistant stage manager, threw Eddie Rice into the shower and then tucked him away. But I had to go on stage. I was in such a state that my words came out at a snail's pace instead of the staccato bursts that were called for. Unlike some English actors who mellow with a belt between acts, I couldn't drink and act—a good lesson to learn that early in my career. I still adhere to the rule today: not so much as a cocktail before dinner while working.

The train ride from St. Louis to Minneapolis, where we were due for our next performance, was almost a continuation of the New Year's party. At Chicago, while waiting to change trains, I bought an entire basket of fruit from a peddler and spent the time from Chicago to Minneapolis peddling it from car to car. I was loaded, and I always played the buffoon in that condition. My inhibitions were completely overcome. Someone hooked a couple of small wreaths to my ears, and I looked like a gypsy as I hustled up and down.

Since it was difficult to form any lasting relationships, moving as we did from town to town so frequently, most of the bachelors in the cast were girl-starved. Connie Nickerson joined the company and married Eddie Bracken, and they are still married. I've never forgotten that in the first act of the play, one of Eddie's lines was: "With a friggin' drug store on every corner in the United States, you go knock up a broad."

Lyle Bettger and Mary Rolfe had been going together since they were at the American Academy of Dramatic Arts in New York. I had taken a shot at Lorna Beaton—but she wanted Eddie Rice. I felt that my most persistent problem was not having a girl. When the tour ended, I made a quick trip to Maine, then within a few days I was back in the city to do the subway circuit. Here I met a new girl, a gorgeous girl, and I fell for her. Her name was Jewel Hart, and I did my best to make her notice me. The problem was that she was going with both Jack Warner, Jr., and Bobby Cohn— Warner Brothers *and* Columbia Pictures! Bobby's Uncle Jack ran Columbia in Hollywood; his father, the New York end. I managed to have a relationship with her in between, but Jewel eventually married Columbia Pictures.

This time around, I was rooming with Paul King, one of my earlier New York roommates. The year following the closing of the *Brother Rat* road show was pretty empty. I had saved enough money to tide me over, with a little extra for acting classes at Benno Schneider's, where I ran into some interesting people—Kay Loring, Joan Wetmore, Sara Burton, Burl Ives, Bob Sidney, and a few others.

Benno had us doing scenes from plays and occasionally I worked with Joan Wetmore, with whom I became entranced. She was a society divorcée and had a salon just off Park Avenue, where we often rehearsed. We'd have a few drinks, and then I'd wander home, wondering why I couldn't work up the nerve to make a pass. I guess the problem was that I was too properly brought up. Instead of talking "affairs," I talked "marriage." That's how it often was then. Sex and marriage went together. But even with all the freedom of operation today, I'm not sure I'd be any different. Eventually, however, the girls at Benno's understood that there would be no rehearsing with Gary on Tuesday, for that was his day with Jewel Hart. I'd been told by her that there would be no marriage, but sex was okay. I took the chance and finally learned something.

During the summer of 1940, John Most, Rex Williams, Don Richardson, and I landed a job with John Kenley at Deer Lake, Pennsylvania, doing summer stock. Every evening we did a show and rehearsed for the next week's play during the day. There were two other members of the company, Jim Gregory and Orpha Dickey, and we all lived at Mrs. Mootz's boarding house. We were training for our acting careers at Deer Lake, just as Muhammad Ali used the place some years later as a training camp for his boxing career.

About this time, I learned that my parents' marriage was coming unglued. There was talk of divorce. One day, Dad and I were driving somewhere in Windsor. He was being his usual gentle self, trying to get me to understand the dynamics, but I couldn't get it and suggested he just take a mistress and keep the marriage going. He said that he couldn't do that. So they got their divorce, and Dad later remarried—his new wife was a wonderful woman who understood him, and they got along beautifully. At first mother suggested that she get an apartment in New York to share with my brother and me, to maintain some sort of family unit, but I was smart enough to know that wouldn't work. So she moved to Maine with Jerry, who was fourteen; it was the best decision for everyone concerned. Jerry still lives in Portland.

After my summer stock stint at Deer Lake, I returned to New York. George Abbott was doing another play that fall called *See My Lawyer.* He was doing a lot of comedies at the time and was very successful on Broadway. He brought Milton Berle on the stage in his first legitimate acting role in *See My Lawyer.* (Berle had, of course, been a big star in vaudeville and on the radio.) Abbott hired Ezra Stone as the director. Millard Mitchell and I played the other lawyers; Mary Rolfe was also in the cast.

Milton was getting about two hundred dollars a week for his acting. But that wasn't enough, so he played at a big nightclub after the show, to bring in his accustomed thousands. He said he had to make a great deal of money to support himself and his mother, whom he treated like a queen. But she played the horses too often and sometimes lost big at the tracks. When Milton's mother died, he had so great a sense of loss that he began seeing a psychiatrist who, I assume, persuaded him it was all right to marry. In due course he married Ruth Cosgrove, a lovely lady from Portland, Maine.

I recall an evening when my mother and aunt came to New York to visit me. Milton was charming and insisted we be his guests at the International Casino after our evening performance. My mother and my aunt had a marvelous time and were grateful to this gracious entertainer. He is the sort of man who paid for an operation for one of his secretaries. The girl was a beautiful person, but had a horrible nose, and Milton's gift of an operation transformed her life.

That year, I roomed with J. Richard Jones, a fellow Benno Schneider classmate, who had appeared in several plays with me. It was the winter Pearl Harbor was bombed. We were both wondering what to do about joining the service. I didn't have long to wonder. In the spring of 1942 my draft number came up. I wrote my father, thinking that surely he would know someone at the Colt or Pratt and Whitney factories in Connecticut where I might get a job and thus be deferred. Dad replied, "You can't put a plug in a socket, so how could you work for those companies? You had better serve your time."

The army! For Chrissake! I was just getting started in the theater in New York and suddenly it appeared that I would be wearing a costume provided by Uncle Sam. That wasn't a particularly appealing idea. My enthusiasm was less than most patriots would want, but I finally realized that I would inevitably be drafted. I experienced a feeling of loss, of loneliness. I needed someone to share my feelings with.

I found her. While I had been absorbing the excitement of the sights and sounds of New York, taking in all the wonderful shows on my nights off, or visiting the restaurants and cafes that fabulous city is known for, I wandered about with small groups of actors, actresses, stage managers, and others involved with the theater. As we wandered, eventually a pretty young actress and I drifted together. Her name was Barbara Leeds, a bright young woman with ash-blonde hair, blue eyes, and an attractive figure. Although there was no startling recognition—"This is it!"—we were comfortable with each other. Gradually, we became "an item." She was lively and loved the theater— and her love of the theater was very attractive to me.

As we became acquainted, she told me she lived at home with her mother, her father having left when she was only about five years old. He had remarried after a short while, and I suppose this loss had unsettled Barbara's mother, who then began living vicariously through her daughter; she became dictatorial, and attempted to direct her every action. This only served to make Barbara, as an adult, increasingly uncomfortable and unhappy. By the time I met her she was determined to break away.

Barbara and I hadn't known each other long, less than six months, and we hadn't been going solely with one another for more than two months. But it was very easy for me to present her with a solution to her problems with her mother, and also to solve my problems of loneliness. "Why don't we get married?" I asked her. She wasn't exactly bowled over, but I pressed my suit over the next couple of days and finally persuaded her.

A Loomis friend, Jack Hardy, suggested I join a cavalry regiment on Park Avenue, one that was supposed to be going in as a unit, and with their own chef. I was surprised to learn that there was still such a thing as a cavalry unit, until I discovered that cavalry soldiers now rode in tanks instead of on horses. Jack Hardy joined, and I heard later that he had been killed on maneuvers.

I waited, and went in like everyone else when his number is called. That April the doors to the armory on Thirty-fourth Street clanged shut—and I was inside.

3

THIS IS THE ARMY?

C amp Upton was a two- or three-hour train ride out on Long Island at a place called Yaphank. After induction, it was one-two-three: shots, uniforms, lectures, housing, and so on. Most men were at Upton for only three or four days before they were assigned to a basic training camp, shipped off to places whose names were totally unfamiliar at first but became household words once the war engaged everyone. There was a building called the "Opry House" in which the actors who had been inducted performed sketches—and sometimes burlesque—danced, and told jokes. Another building was used both as a chapel and a movie house.

Through Mike Wardell, whose father had been in *See My Lawyer,* I was put on temporary assignment to Upton in "special services." Mike was trying to raise the caliber of activity at the Opry House. I knew there was not much a legitimate actor could do, but he grabbed me and anybody else who had been in the performing arts—dancers, comedians, anybody. Then the actor Ralph Nelson came along. I knew he'd been involved with the Lunts, the most success- ful acting team in American theatrical history, and with various big-time productions, so I asked Ralph if he'd been exposed to improvisation.

"Sure," he said.

"Improvisation is our only hope of staying at the Opry House," I told him. "Let's give it a try."

We worked out a few short routines, but for the most part we just walked on stage and asked the audience for ideas which we would then dramatize. Although there was a turnover of audiences every three or four days, the men had similar things on their minds, and they usually called out the same thing: "the Hook," they shouted, "the Needle." The Hook is what everyone called the multiple injections. Soon we got a routine going. Of course, the sketch ended with the doctor fainting instead of the soldier. Once in a while, when the GI's shouted out for something unusual, we'd *really* have to improvise, but we were very basic.

About two months after I got there, Ezra Stone arrived. Born Ezra Feinstone in New Bedford, Massachusetts, he had been doing "Henry Aldrich," a popular radio show. ("Hennnnree . . . Henry Aldrich!" "Coming, Mother . . .") Ezra contributed his salary from the show to an army fund and agreed to set up a legitimate theater, fully equipped and staffed, to tour each post in the area. This enabled us to take *Brother Rat* on a tour, and this time the cast included my wife Barbara. She had achieved acclaim in *The Children's Hour,* Lillian Hellman's play, a couple of years before, and had known Ezra at the American Academy. I had been a private, but was now promoted to corporal.

When we played at West Point, the officer in charge of the unit, Major Reybold, held a champagne supper for Barbara and me. We had been married (at the Little Church Around the Corner) shortly before. We could only be together when we were doing the show, and in between she continued to live with her mother.

Late in the spring of 1942, Ezra began to assemble actors, singers, musicians, stagehands, and box-office people for the production of a special show. Irving Berlin, who had written a musical about World War I called *Yip Yip Yaphank,* had been persuaded to do another about World War II. It was called *This Is the Army.* Ezra, the producer, pulled together an all-soldier, all-male cast. Wherever an available actor was stationed, Ezra located him and had him requisitioned. So Nelson Barclift (Cole Porter's friend), Burl Ives, and Josh Logan came to Camp Upton.

At about the same time, a boxing tournament was being staged. All of us misfits—actors, boxers, singers—were housed in a special area so we wouldn't upset the basic routine of the reception center. It was an incongruous group of fighters and artists. It was quite a sight to see uniformed men strolling hand in hand in the lovely Long Island sunsets. There must have been forty or fifty gays in the group, and they were in the habit of cruising the boxers every evening.

Then all those enlisted for the show were moved to New York. The married soldiers were given a per diem contract, so Barbara and I were able to find a little place of our own.

This Is the Army opened in New York on July 4, 1942. We drilled as soldiers by day and performed the show by night. For a soldier, it was an easy life. The major in charge was a reserve officer who in civilian life had been a detective in Brooklyn, and our captain from Upton had been a newspaperman on the *Brooklyn Eagle.* There was an assortment of lieutenants who had been agents or actors before the army found them, and I must say it was strange for an actor to find himself saluting his agent.

One of the most talented of the group, Jimmy McColl, had written several of the numbers and acted in several of the sketches. He made a ludicrous soldier—very intelligent, but quite incorrigible. When he was at his worst and the brass thought he should be disciplined, they made him stay backstage and put on his understudy. Instead of being upset, Jimmy considered it a night off and wandered around enjoying his leisure. Later, when we were making the motion picture of this revue at Warner Brothers, he was called in by his major.

"Corporal," the major said stiffly, "we have found that because of your uncooperative behavior, you will be demoted to private."

"My God, Major," he replied, wide-eyed, "This means I'll have to let one of the servants go."

There were three star ballerinas, all male sergeants, who had the star dressing room. On opening night flowers arrived to fill their room. The chorus line could have been called the "beef trust" because all involved were six feet or over, and burly—Tony Ross, an actor; Hank Henry, a burlesque comic; Burl Ives, the singer; and several others of similar build. The orchestra included musicians from a lot of the name bands of the time.

I had little to do at the opening of the show, but later I got to introduce Irving Berlin for his number. As I left the stage after the introduction, he would be standing in the wings waiting to come on while people clapped and cheered. He'd say, "You got a hell of a hand, boy," and clap me on the shoulder as he went on to do his number. Once when he and I were standing in the wings together we discussed how composers often steal from other composers. Berlin said he'd written so many songs he only stole from himself.

The show was well received in New York and we had a great time doing it. When it closed and we were ready to leave for a tour of the country, we were instructed to get into formation outside the theater with our regulation guns, gas masks, the whole thing, and march in soldierly fashion to

Penn Station for the train. But just as we formed the lines, it began to rain. In a rush, we were dismissed with instructions to reassemble at Penn Station, whereupon everyone broke ranks and scrambled for the nearest subway. You can imagine the surprise of the riders when they saw this odd group of fully equipped soldiers pouring into the cars.

Once we had reached Penn Station and were assembling in the vast waiting room, one soldier, Jerry O'Rourke, came sliding into place, and, while trying to be unobtrusive, dropped his gas mask. We all watched as a large puddle formed under the mask. He had stuffed a bottle of bourbon inside, though our orders specifically stated we weren't to have whiskey on the train.

We traveled by coach to Philadelphia, then on to Baltimore, and then Washington, D.C., where President Franklin D. Roosevelt came to the show. The Secret Service had milled around for days beforehand and were everywhere all through the performance Roosevelt attended. They had removed all the bolts from the guns, since they were regulation-issue weapons, and the meat cleaver used in one of the sketches was replaced by a huge turkey leg. As I sat in the orchestra pit and looked up at the president's box, I nevertheless thought how very simple a determined assassin's job would be, particularly if he didn't care about getting caught. After the presidential performance, we were given supper at the White House, and, with great flair, we were each introduced to President Roosevelt, who was a very impressive man. He seemed to exude what has sometimes been called "personality." When he died, I shed some tears—the only time I've ever done so for a president.

Then the sets were dismantled and we took to the road once more. Since we were still in the army, everyone had tasks to perform, such as loading trucks and helping with the wiring, lights, and scenery. And then we'd board another train headed for another opening night.

When the tour had almost wound down, Warner Brothers wanted to film the show, so our final destination was Hollywood. When the company got to Burbank, we found that a tent city had been set up for us just outside the studio. We were happy to settle down for a while and knew it would take a few months for the filming, so with our per diem contracts and wife allowances, Jimmy McColl and his wife Marjorie, Barbara, myself, and Henry Jones found a little house nearby. The house cost ninety dollars a month and consisted of two upstairs bedrooms, with two baths, and a downstairs apartment that Henry occupied. One night at a party a friend of Henry's said, "Henry, you'll always live downstairs." We borrowed a car and things worked out very well.

One day, up in San Francisco, Lois Moran and her husband Clarence Young held a small party for their friends Irving Berlin and Ezra Stone. Clarence had invited a friend, an admiral of the Pacific Fleet. One of the singers in the cast arrived escorted by a couple of sailors who were absolutely paralyzed when they were introduced to the admiral. He was a most gracious gentleman and did his best to put them at ease, but it was funny to watch. The rest of the cast were fairly nonchalant around brass because, night after night, generals and admirals would appear backstage.

As usual, many of us goofed off as much as we could, ducking the large ensemble numbers when our presence wouldn't be missed. The Warner Brothers studio was very active at the time, with projects such as *Saratoga Trunk* with Cooper and Bergman, a Bogart picture, and several others. We were all impressed to be in such company, some more than others. While playing cards one day, one of the fellows came back from a trip to the men's room in a state of high excitement. Apparently he had been using a urinal next to the one being used by Gary Cooper—and he couldn't wait to tell his friends back in Brooklyn.

When I returned to our house one day, I was met at the door by my wife and Jimmy McColl's wife. They were wringing their hands and knitting their brows. Jimmy had helped to get our captain into a sad state of intoxication and had then unceremoniously dumped him into the bathtub. It was a chore, believe me, but we managed to get him back to his quarters, with no help on his part. He slept through the entire incident.

When the end of the filming approached, rumors (the bread and butter of life in the army) were flying. During the theater run, one of Ezra's games had been to start a rumor a half hour before eight o'clock in the evening, just to see how long it would take to get back to him. The current one was that the show was going overseas, but the cast had to be cut and anyone who wasn't needed would have to fend for himself. But this rumor was the real thing. A captain came down from an air command in Sacramento, looking for actors and musicians for a show he wanted to do. So several of us—Jimmy McColl, Tony Ross, myself, and a few others—went on to Sacramento. Barbara returned to the East Coast to stay with her mother. There was talk of an Air Force show to be done in New York: *Winged Victory,* written by Moss Hart. So I wrote to Bernie Hart, Moss's brother, a stage manager I had gotten to know through mutual acquaintances—poker-playing actors and frequenters of Sardi's bar, where he liked to hang out. Bernie said that he couldn't do anything for me, but there were some women's parts and maybe Barbara could get a job. So she went to investigate.

When the filming finally had wound down, but before we had moved on to the Sacramento show, I was given a short furlough. Tony Ross—who later played the gentleman caller in *The Glass Menagerie*, with Laurette Taylor—traveled by train with me to New York. It was a hot summer, and the only air-conditioning on the train was the open window. Because Tony was over six feet tall, he took the aisle seat so he could stretch out his legs, and I got the open window, with cinders. Tony's only recreation during the trip was going to the diner on first call and then again on last call. I think our total stay in New York was about five days. The rest of the two-week furlough was spent on the train. I saw Barbara for a short while, and was greeted by her mother's complaint that she thought we were fools to get mixed up with the army in the first place, as though we had a choice.

I don't know what became of Tony after we went back to Sacramento, because I immediately got orders to return to New York City, as did some others in the group. Bernie Hart, Moss's brother, had arranged for Barbara to try for a part in *Winged Victory*. Barbara had waited until all the other women had done their auditions before going on. When it was her turn, she began by telling Moss, who was sitting in the audience for the tryouts, that she didn't care if she got the part or not, but that her husband *must* be in the play.

Upon my arrival at my tryout, I met Moss for the first time. He was an elegant man in his mid-forties whose dark curly hair receded slightly on either side of his forehead, leaving a widow's peak. His eyes were bright with intelligence and humor as he said, "Your wife played a hell of a third act." He apologized that the few remaining parts were so small but, as he put it, "It's not much, soldier, but you're back at Sardi's."

I fell for him, and my affection grew as I watched examples of his kindness displayed daily. I had heard that Moss had been a poor boy while growing up in Brooklyn. He had had a few early plays on Broadway which weren't very successful, but when he collaborated with George S. Kaufman, his career took off. When he had his first big success, he went to Brooklyn, loaded his mother, father, and brother in a cab, and moved them to an apartment in Manhattan, complete with new furnishings. He had taken nothing from the Brooklyn apartment, leaving everything behind but his family.

Winged Victory's story line traced the life of six air cadets through the war. I was already too old for one of the leading roles, and the other parts involved short scenes as the cadets' careers progressed. Lee J. Cobb played a doctor, I played a captain in charge of their first solo flights, and Alan Baxter, Ray Middleton, Peter Lind Hayes, Red Buttons, and Mario Lanza all had small parts. The plot of *Winged Victory* was similar to that of *This Is the Army*, but *Winged Victory*, a play with music, not a revue, called for actors and singers and no dancers. David Rose came in from California to conduct the orchestra. *Winged Victory*, like *This Is the Army*, allowed performers who were military personnel to be used in the jobs for which they were best fitted. Though there was some fuss from people whose sons were overseas being shot at, we had our orders to carry out, did our jobs as best we could, and felt extremely fortunate.

Moss indeed was a marvelous man. As servicemen, we could have been kept around the theater all day waiting to rehearse our small scenes. But Moss scheduled rehearsals so that we'd appear at a certain time, rehearse, then leave. This free time annoyed the brass, but Moss held the reins. On the day before the opening, we were to be marched to Riverside Drive for calisthenics on a very cold day, as part of the army drill. But when Moss heard of it, he hit the roof and stopped the order. Exposing his performers to colds and flu would have jeopardized the entire show.

Our officers, in the main, weren't particularly knowledgeable about show business, but the stage manager, Jerry White, had formerly been employed by George Abbott for his musicals, and was experienced in running big shows. He had been inducted into the army, entering as a master sergeant, a title that seemed appropriate given his dictatorial ways. He had been accustomed to dealing with young actors and actresses, but handling three hundred men required a different approach. He was slow to catch on, and we had our ways of showing disgust at his orders. One day an announcement flowed through all floors and dressing rooms on the intercom: "All hair will be cut GI!" Being in uniform is tough enough for actors—who are confirmed individualists—and the only way to express oneself in uniform is tonsorial. I got tired of listening to all the flack about hair, so I got the shortest crewcut I could—so short, in fact, that when the stage lights hit my head, I might as well have been bald. What hair remained was barely visible.

My main scene took place in a large hangar. About forty cadets were ready to complete their solo flights; there had been a crash and the men were assembling to hear what had happened. I was their captain, and, on a dimly lit set, they awaited my arrival with the news. I entered, took off my hat, and announced that the entire crew had been killed. A brief dialogue followed, after which I dismissed them, and we gradually wandered off. That was the entire scene.

The day I'd gotten my crewcut, I had deliberately concealed it until the evening performance. When my hat came off I looked absurdly bald, and every man started to break up, trying to hold the laughs. They turned upstage, and I assume that their heaving chests made the audience think they were overcome with grief. Alas, my joke backfired: I found I had the very difficult job of delivering tragic news while trying hard to keep a straight face.

As I returned to the dressing room, I was startled to hear my name over the loudspeaker. "Sergeant Merrill, report to the stage manager's desk." I complied and was duly chewed out. But what could be done? My haircut was GI—just a bit exaggerated. None of us was as disciplined as we would have been as civilian actors. In general, actors are extremely self-disciplined, but in the army, in response to the constant nagging, we tended to relax.

Surprisingly, there seemed to be no rules about drinking, and there were always some who were bitten while on stage. Word would travel through the company and we'd wait in anticipation for the inevitable goof. Usually we weren't disappointed, and some of them were particularly funny.

One night when the show was on the road in San Francisco, we tried to keep one of our friends, Ray Middleton, from going on. He insisted he could play his role—no problem. The scene was a Christmas celebration of the shore police and our boy, playing the colonel, had a touching speech about Christmas. We watched as he stumbled onto the platform, but he made it and launched into his speech. It was a perfect delivery, slow and deliberate. He was given a tremendous hand as he made his exit. It was the only time he'd ever been given a hand after his scene, and he was too drunk to hear it. It was his best performance.

As we toured from place to place, we spent our time on the train playing poker. On the trip from New York to L.A., which took four days, there were eight of us who played every waking hour. I was broke before breakfast one day but managed to borrow some money in the diner from another player, and, by the time we arrived in L.A., I was a hundred and fifty dollars ahead. Men and women weren't allowed to mingle on the train, so Barbara rode in the ladies' car, where she, too, played poker, and sometimes we'd both be broke. But at other times, if one of us had lost, the other had been lucky. The only time I've gambled in my life was when there was nothing to lose. Our pay was so small that the only place to go was up. But some players had money from other sources than their pay. They were the targets.

We were on our way to California again because

Winged Victory, too, was to become a motion picture. Moss Hart had promised that we'd each play his own part in the picture. There was a great flurry of dental appointments prior to leaving New York. Dental plates were made, and teeth were capped with permanent or temporary crowns. During the trip some of the temporary caps were lost; and there was much comparing of plates and prices. One of the more serious actors had a major amount of dental work done. Later on, in his big scene out on the desert, the entire production was brought to a halt as the cameraman tried to find the cause of a very bright reflection. The source was the sun bouncing off his beautiful new teeth. The make-up man was summoned to dirty up the lovely choppers, much to the chagrin of their owner. When he discovered later that this episode was a put-up job to embarrass him, he went berserk, screaming that we had wasted money and had held up production, all for a lousy joke. But escapades such as these helped us keep our sanity.

Early one morning, as a friend and I were returning from an all-night shooting—still dressed for our film roles, he as a colonel and I as a captain, we walked by the parade grounds. A squad of recruits was being drilled. When they all saluted us, we were sorely tempted to dismiss them. But the thought of going to the guardhouse for impersonating officers was a compelling deterrent.

When the filming of *Winged Victory* was over, we actors were again allowed to fend for ourselves for a time. Through some friends I found a job with a radio unit in New York that did weekly broadcasts on the four major networks (NBC, CBS, ABC, and WOR) of radio dramas about the army. Millard Lampell, then involved with Pete Seeger in a group of singers, the Weavers, had written a radio play about returning veterans. Marty Ritt, myself, and a few others were cast, and I stayed with the series for about six weeks.

Barbara and I were having a trial separation at the time—though we were separated more than we were together throughout the marriage. She was cooling her heels in Maine. A fine actress, Mercedes McCambridge, was also with the series, and when she and I discovered each other, we had a fast-paced romance that lasted as long as the show.

Mercedes was divorced and had a little boy. Some men get to know girls by first patting their dogs. I always notice the kids first. So I got to know the little boy, then his mother. With her dark-brown eyes and sultry voice, she was an attractive woman, with a self-assuredness that projected a "go-to-hell" attitude. It usually resulted in her being cast as the woman in charge—a woman lawyer, the behind-the-scenes power, a woman capable of directing the affairs of a single husband or an entire army with ease. She was pretty well put together, too, and her direct, authoritative manner completely disarmed me. A sexual explosion occurred.

When the war ended, Mercedes and I were on Fifth Avenue and helped celebrate the victorious conclusion. But I was still married, and when the radio series was over, I packed my barracks bag and headed for Maine to try to patch things up with Barbara, a move that was quite unsettling for Mercedes. Her last words were: "Well, you're some kind of son of a bitch." Barbara, too, had something to bitch about, for sure, but somehow I managed to straighten things out for a while.

A short time later, when Barbara and I were back in New York, a friend at an advertising agency helped me get auditions for radio shows. I wound up doing "The World's Most Honored Flights," playing the role of Captain Eddie Rickenbacker in the dramatization. This was a biographical series, with the real Eddie Rickenbacker as the host and narrator. Some said our voices were so alike that it was difficult to distinguish between the two of us. Up to this point, Barbara and I had worked out an existence on army pay, but now we felt as though we were living in luxury. To open the mailbox and find a check for ninety or a hundred dollars was like finding the pot at the end of the rainbow. This pleasant period lasted for about six months.

I was released from the army just after Thanksgiving in 1945; I had achieved the rank of sergeant. We had a small apartment in New York. For us, there was the feeling that anything could happen, and I began to look for productions.

4

ACTION, PLEASE

M y release from the Army was just that, a great release: freedom to be on my own, to choose—or not—from whatever jobs might be available. Being in New York was a fine prospect, too. That's where the action was for stage work and broadcasting jobs. Radio work, which I continued with vigor at this time, particularly in soap operas, was a special extension of my freedom: I could dress as I pleased—forget about wardrobes, fittings, and makeup—just be the voice.

I had always sought the casual—shorts and sandals in the summer, for example. In those days you were allowed to wear shorts to Sardi's, though a shirt and tie and jacket were required. Now you can't wear shorts but can go in without a tie and jacket. After the war, there was a drift toward more casual fashions, but in the company of theater patrons or on visits to fine restaurants, a good suit and tie were still required. Women were also expected to be at their formal best in many situations. This remained the status quo until the Kennedy assassination. As the sadness changed our psyche, styles began to change dramatically; this change was the result, too, of the revolution of the young against our involvement in Vietnam. But I hadn't needed that war to prompt my sartorial rebellions, which began to be noted in the press. Eventually, *Esquire* would do a full-page photo of me wearing a kilt on the New York streets. Much later, I would wear skirts on hot summer days. My unusual garb would draw a lot of comments, and get a fair amount of publicity, which as an actor I was never averse to.

In 1945 Barbara contracted to portray actress Ruth Gordon as a girl in an autobiographical play, *Years Ago*. Ruth Gordon was director Garson Kanin's wife, a sprightly, dark-haired dynamo whom Barbara had met only recently, though she had known Garson before the war at the American Academy. I knew him only slightly.

Gar was currently directing Bob Sherwood's *The Rugged Path*. He had given Rex Williams a part in it to hold him until a new play on the horizon, *Born Yesterday*, written by Kanin for Jean Arthur, went into rehearsal. But during *The Rugged Path* Gar told Rex he no longer thought he was right for *Born Yesterday*. Meanwhile, Rex told me he was quitting *The Rugged Path*, and maybe I could replace him. I went to see the play and found the part to be a small one, which I could have done—but it didn't mean much. When I went backstage to see Gar, I told him I could do the part in *Path* but it would be just for the money; it wouldn't do anything for my career. Gar's response was that Spencer Tracy had the final say, so we went along to his dressing room. Tracy was pleasant enough. (Soon after, he gave his notice, saying the theater was for idiots and children, and he went back to California.) A few days after the meeting, Rex told me that Gar thought I was pretty mercenary. Well, what could I say? The part wasn't great and I'd been honest about it. But I wouldn't get the part.

In due course, *The Rugged Path* closed and *Born Yesterday* went into rehearsal. I stopped by one day, interested in whether there might be anything for me, and Gar and Ruth announced that they had a divine cast. I said "Fine," and that was that.

Several weeks later, *Born Yesterday* opened in New Haven and received great reviews. Then it moved on to Boston. One evening, just before Barbara and I left home for a party, I called my phone service to check the messages. The operator said, "A Mr. Kooner . . . Carmen . . . Kanin was trying to reach you from Boston." I couldn't imagine what was up, but decided to go to the party. I could call from there.

Montgomery Clift and Karl and Mona Malden were at the party—everyone was happy, in good form. After greeting them, I made my excuse. "I got a call from a Mr. Kooner . . . Carmen . . . Kanin and I think I ought to see what he wants." This prompted everyone to draw his own conclusion, but the general consensus was that there must be some sort of trouble with the show. They hung around the phone to hear the news, and the babbling subsided when I said, "Garson Kanin, please." Gar came on the line.

"Could you come up to Boston to see the show?"

"Well, Gar, I read the reviews. I thought everything was just great."

"We've had a few problems," he said. "I'd appreciate it if you could come on up." He was giving nothing away.

Everyone clustered around, encouraging me to act blasé. "Don't get excited . . . don't act interested," I heard them hissing.

"I do have a radio commitment right now," I told him. "But I might be able to get to Boston on Saturday evening."

I hung up. As far as we could figure it, someone was going to get the axe, so we ran over the possibilities. Everyone thought I had Gar over a barrel, and we sat around talking about how to screw directors and producers, and such enlightening subjects, for quite some time.

That Saturday I flew to Boston. In this business, when the word is out that an actor is going to be replaced, it's like a general casting call. Vultures hover around the dying man; agents and actors run all over the place. John Forsythe, David Wayne, and I were there, along with assorted agents. Someone tapped me on the shoulder and took me over to be introduced to George Kaufman. I later discovered that Kaufman and Moss Hart were Max Gordon's partners, and that Max Gordon was the producer of *Born Yesterday*.

Then we all sat down for the show. As the play progressed, it wasn't difficult to see the problem: The actor who had the part of the reporter was dreadful. In the long second act scene he played with Jean Arthur (who had the role of Billy Dawn), she virtually had to drag him across the stage. I remarked, "I wouldn't play the part like that!" Kaufman said, "If we wanted it played like that, we wouldn't be replacing him."

When the show was over, I found myself being bustled into a cab with Johnny Forsythe. The man who hustled us also got in. Johnny and I were chatting about the play as the cab pulled out, not sure where we were headed, but when it stopped, we found ourselves in front of the Ritz Carlton Hotel. Our fellow rider, whom I mistakenly took to be Johnny's agent, told him to wait in the lobby, but to me he said, "Come along." I followed him as we wove through the small lobby to the ornate doors of the elevator. He wasn't a talkative sort, this fellow, but as we rode up two floors he did mention we were on our way to Gar's and Ruth's suite.

A short way down the corridor, he knocked on a door that was opened by Gar. "Hello, Max," he said to my companion. So our mysterious hustler was no less than Max Gordon, the producer. Ruth was in the room. I don't recall being offered a drink, but Gar launched into a speech about me for Max's benefit. "What a magnificent actor . . ." Ruth said, "When I saw you standing at the door with Max, I thought Max had brought a reporter up here at this time of night!"

With all this shit flying, I began to roll up my pants. Gar continued to list my sterling qualities—although he barely knew me. Then Max turned to him and said, "Where was this guy in the first place?"

There was a bit more small talk, after which Gar excused himself, gesturing for Max and me to follow him. Apparently, money wasn't to be discussed before the lady, so we went into a bedroom and stood by a bureau. "What do you think about doing the part?" he asked.

"It's a great play," I replied, making a stab at appearing interested but not bowled over. "It has to be a hit—probably. I think five hundred dollars a week would be fine."

Obviously I had said the wrong thing.

"You've been in the army four years. Before, you worked for George Abbott for a hundred a week," Max countered, trying to bring my price down.

"That's immaterial," I said. "I want five hundred dollars."

I had my jobs on radio, I wasn't starving, and five hundred dollars seemed pretty reasonable indeed.

"We better go see Jean Arthur," Gar said, implying that she had the deciding vote. So Gar and I took the elevator up to her suite. I had loved her in the show that night, and had been entranced by her films, so I felt like a kid meeting Santa Claus. When we were let into her suite she was sitting in front of a cheery fire, looking adorable. Gar introduced me, repeating some of the flattery that had flowed earlier that evening. I could have sworn she said, "Well, at least he's got balls."

She claimed later that she had said, "Well, at least

he's a man." Either way, it was music to my masculine ears. Gar went on about the issue of my salary, then, after chatting a few more minutes, preceded me to the door. As I said to her, "It was a real pleasure to meet you," she mouthed to me silently: "Get what you want, get what you want."

Gar must have caught her, because as the door closed he said, "You know, Jean doesn't control the show."

We said goodnight, and I thought we had left it that Max would call me in the morning to let me know their decision.

I called Barbara as soon as I got back to my room to tell her that I was in Boston with her friends—and that I was in a den of thieves. Though I'd said five hundred dollars, they were insisting on three hundred dollars. The original actor had been paid three hundred dollars and they couldn't replace him for less, according to a rule of Equity, but if it hadn't been for that, I'm sure their offer would have been one hundred dollars or a hundred and fifty dollars. I believed that Paul Douglas, the other male lead, was being paid five hundred dollars.

In the shower the next morning I was thinking, "I've got to do this play. It's a hit. I've been away a long while and this is my chance." But at the same time, I really resented their being so cheap. I had just finished shaving when the phone rang, and Max Gordon was on the other end, shouting at me, "Where the hell are you?"

"Right here. You were supposed to call me."

"So, okay, but here's what I want you to do. Come on over to the theater and watch the direction. Learn the first two acts. The third act is being rewritten, so wait on that."

The upshot was that I accepted the three-hundred-dollar salary and went to the theater. I watched closely for a few days and rehearsed the first two acts. Then I got another call to see if I felt ready to go on stage.

"Yeah," I said. "Except, what about the third act? I haven't done anything on that." Max replied: "That new third act hasn't been completed. You go on with the old one. There isn't much dialogue."

"Well, hell, I haven't even bothered with it," I said. "I'll need another day or two on that." They agreed.

On the assigned day I got to the theater and went to the dressing room to start making up. But there on the table was the original actor's makeup. His clothes and things were still around. The stage manager was behind me, so I turned and said "What's this?"

"Oh, God," he said. "He hasn't been told yet he isn't going on tonight."

"Get me out of here!" I said as I left the room, really steamed. "What do they want me to do, tell him myself that he's fired? Christ!" They gave me a room way upstairs to use that night.

I got through the play that night, but it was the only one, as it turned out, I got to play with Jean. The next night she was exhausted and couldn't continue. My opinion of Gar had begun to decline a bit. I felt he had handled the replacement of my predecessor with great insensitivity. My opinion of him continued to sink when I talked to Jean about her exhaustion. Though Gar had actually written the play for her, he and Ruth had not given her the care she needed. She had been away from the theater for years. (I have found that the most talented actors are often the most insecure.) It seemed that they had promised her a replacement before New Haven for the part I took over, as well as a new third act. Here we were in Boston, and neither had showed up.

Jean is a tiny woman, blond-haired, whose voice has a breathless, hesitant, and slightly husky quality that never failed to delight her fans. At that time, she wasn't exactly timid, but she wasn't strong, either, which prompted some of my protective instincts to come to her defense—though I couldn't do much but rail against her adversaries.

At the end of the week, we moved on to Philadelphia. We were supposed to rehearse the new third act for a week before the opening there, but, as we read through the script, Jean said that she couldn't bring herself to say many of the lines—they were repugnant to her. I played the rest of the week with an understudy, which gave me a lot of rehearsal time.

Next the actors were told that Jean was withdrawing from the play. "A replacement will be found." I walked the streets that night with another actor and swore that, if I could afford it, I'd leave too.

Born Yesterday is the story of a former junk man who had parlayed junk and scrap iron into millions during World War II, had retained a drunken former Supreme Court justice to wheel and deal and buy him a United States senator to help with all the underhanded deals. The entire action takes place in a five-hundred-dollar-a-day suite of a Washington hotel where the junk man is ensconced with his mistress, a former chorus girl. The man's older brother is his valet and general flunky. The chorus girl has an innate intelligence, and her intellectual curiosity is stimulated by a reporter, working for the *New Republic,* who has come to the suite to interview the Big Man. The reporter is intrigued by the girl, physically as well as mentally—and, as he becomes more entranced by her, he begins to help to educate her. Eventually Billy Dawn, the former chorus girl, uses what she has learned from the reporter and the lawyer to bring down the junk man. In the end she goes off with the reporter.

Jean had acted like a chorus girl in the first act, then became more "herself" from the second act on. Jean had a quality that I'd seen only once before—the ability to make an audience laugh and cry with the same line. Laurette Taylor, the greatest American actress I've ever seen, also had this quality.

When the curtain went up on the second act, Jean was sitting on the divan surrounded by books, newspapers, and magazines, and was dressed as a miniature George Washington. Her blond hair was done up to look like Washington's wig, and she was wearing knee pants and buckled shoes. She looked adorable.

A day or so after Jean left, Judy Holliday was brought in as her replacement. She was comparatively unknown; she had done only one or two plays and some nightclub work with Betty Comden and Adolph Green, who have since written innumerable hit musicals. Judy was a big girl, a contrast to Jean Arthur. In her own way, she was as talented as Jean. Hers was a much tougher, harder quality. She had a genius I.Q. She really knew her business. We rehearsed for a few days and opened on Saturday evening. Judy wasn't even given the Sunday off before the Monday show. Her life was rehearsing, studying, and Benzedrines.

Paul Douglas had been a sports announcer before accepting the part of the successful junk man in *Born Yesterday*. He seemed to think that with Jean gone he could take over the show, although the play really belonged to Billy Dawn. He must have figured that with an unknown coming into the part, he had it made. But on opening night, he didn't know what hit him. He'd never been up against such a tough pro in his life: He looked bewildered, a sparrow caught in a badminton game.

When the notices came out he was on the verge of quitting. A new star had been discovered; Garson Kanin had uncovered a major talent. Judy could get a laugh with her squeaky voice and her blank expression more easily than anyone I knew. She was very good. Paul didn't quit, but I don't think he ever quite recovered. The play was a smash. People laughed, cheered, clapped, and for me it was almost as good as the approval I had received with Mr. Ink-well.

Standard Equity contracts run from September to June and can then be renewed at the actor's and producer's discretion. In those days, when a show became a Broadway success the producer would ask the performer to sign a contract for the run of the play. Casts weren't shifted to new players as they are today, and some actors would perform the same role for two or three years. As I remember, Howard Lindsay and his wife, Dorothy Stickney, were in *Life with Father* for five years. I was asked to sign a run-of-the-play contract for *Born Yesterday*, with a raise of fifty dollars. I said no. I wanted to be free.

After a few months with *Born Yesterday* in New York I began looking around for a new play. I should have gone straight to Hollywood from *Born Yesterday*, but I was agented by the William Morris office and, as Garson Kanin and Judy Holliday were with Morris, too, I got no action because they didn't want to interrupt the play—didn't want to take any of the machinery out. Some time later I learned from Josh Logan that there was an unwritten law among producers that they wouldn't raid actors from each other's plays. I had sacrificed my fifty dollars for nothing. Today, actors such as George C. Scott leave plays after a few months, with no untoward results at the box office. Since producers realize that sometimes an actor loses interest in the part after performing over a period of time, they will easily sign on someone else—no recriminations.

Another, parallel lesson I learned about that time had to do with going to California. One of the top Hollywood agents, Charlie Feldman, came backstage one afternoon to inquire if I might be interested in going out to make a few screen tests. I told him I couldn't because I was with the Morris agency. Because Gar was also involved with the movies, an agent would not consider me available until Gar said I was. The bigger the client, the more protection and service he has. Had I not been with Morris, I might have begun a career in motion pictures earlier.

During the day I performed on radio doing the early version of the soap operas "Young Dr. Malone," "The Second Mrs. Burton," and "The Right to Happiness"—and appeared in *Born Yesterday* in the evening, on Broadway. Ah, radio! You just had to be sober enough to read—and not too much time was taken up, either. We spent one hour in rehearsal for a fifteen-minute show. Except for "Superman," which I played occasionally. That took even less time.

We had opened the play in early 1946, and when the contracts expired on June first, the games began. I don't know what Judy was paid when she first joined the cast, or what she settled for ultimately, but I'm sure there was a considerable difference between our salaries simply because she was tough. I dressed in a room above hers and could hear her arguing with Max—or Gar—night after night. Later on, she recounted some of it to me. After one of the shows Gar and Ruth came backstage to take Judy out for supper. They had come up through the front of the theater instead of going to the stage door because their car was waiting for them. Judy related that as she got settled in the car, Gar started in: "What do you want all that money for?" Judy reached across him for the fur lap robe, saying, "So I can have one of these, too, Gar."

After *Born Yesterday* had opened on Broadway, my wife went into rehearsals with Ruth's play *Years Ago*, also directed by Gar. There was a good deal of trouble getting it off the ground, and ultimately Barbara left the play. It finally opened in New York starring Frederic March and Florence Eldridge.

About the time *Born Yesterday* had opened in Philadelphia, I found out that Moss Hart had been instrumental in my getting the part. When he came backstage to congratulate me, I thanked him not only for his approval but for helping me get the part, and without letting anyone know. He told me he had advised getting me in the first place.

My regard for Moss grew steadily, but for Gar and Ruth it diminished. I observed their callousness on another occasion. They had cajoled an old friend to come out of retirement to play Ruth's mother in *Years Ago*, but after the opening realized they had made a mistake. Instead of talking with her and apologizing personally for their mistake, they sent her a wire saying she was fired. Hit and run! Not pleasant.

I played the part of the reporter in *Born Yesterday* for a year and a half. It gets boring, doing the same lines over and over again. Ray Middleton was playing opposite Ethel Merman in *Annie Get Your Gun*, down on Forty-second Street. He was a trooper; he lasted for the entire Broadway run. I walked into his dressing room one day and told him I had quit. "I can't get it up anymore," I said.

"It's your job to get it up!" he responded.

"Well, when *you* get it up, you get a lot more than I do for doing it. I'm quitting."

I suppose it was part of my soon-to-be-famous "no follow-through" syndrome, but I later learned that most of the good English actors seldom played a show longer than six months. The great Lunts would open for six months in New York, then do six months on the road the following year. They believed they owed it to the people outside of New York.

I went to Maine to enjoy the beautiful summer, returning to New York to do the radio bits and to keep one eye open for any new plays. Instead I found a three-week job in a Twentieth Century Fox film called *Slattery's Hurricane*, starring Richard Widmark. It was going to be filmed in Florida and the cast included Linda Darnell and Veronica Lake—added enticements.

This was my first film as a civilian. It had been arranged by an agent, Frances Robinson, and was a free-lance job. Working through a California agent, Paul Wilkins, she had managed to get me a small part as Widmark's commanding officer. Wilkins had a friend in the Fox casting department, Bill Mayo, who had seen my performance in *Born Yesterday*. Bill figured that if he could show the powers at Fox a sample of me in uniform he could get me into a bigger film, *Twelve O'Clock High,* and make a good client of me for his friend Wilkins.

Slattery's Hurricane ran into filming difficulties in Florida. It was about airplanes, and we were using a small airfield with a small tower, and small private planes continued using the field. The cameraman, Charlie Clark, couldn't get things right. The light was wrong, there were clouds, rain—it was always one thing or another.

"Shit, Jeeezus! This is ridiculous. We've got to go back to California," he said, and just stopped filming.

Johnny Johnstone, the assistant director and production manager, was a guy with real integrity and a lot of personal courage. He called the studio. "We've had it. We've got to come back to California to reconstruct this thing. We can't make it right here."

I went up to him. "Johnny, I live in New York. Since this is going to go through Christmas, and it seems to me it's going to take a while to reconstruct things in California, how about if I go to New York till you're ready?"

He said, "Hell, yes. You go on back to New York and we'll call you when we need you."

Most fellows in his position would have been so frightened of studio brass that they would have refused to take responsibility for allowing an actor to do this, and would have said, "No, no. You've got to go on to the next location and wait." But Johnny Johnstone had guts and took the responsibility of giving me my freedom until everything was set up. It worked in my favor and three weeks of work turned into eight weeks, some of it spent on my own, back in New York.

Except for Widmark's performance, *Slattery* wasn't much as a movie, but I ended up with a seven-year contract at Twentieth Century Fox, starting at seven hundred fifty dollars a week, escalating two hundred fifty dollars a week each year the option was picked up. But the best part was meeting Richard Widmark, who became a good friend.

Dick is a serious, hardworking actor, as well as a serious person. I call him the Melancholy Dane since he is both dour and of Danish descent. It became my mission to make him laugh, and I succeeded. Our temperaments are opposite, and my zaniness has amused him often enough.

He had started out as a teacher in Chicago, then became a radio actor. When he worked on the stage in New York, he was known for his comic characterizations, but when he went to Hollywood in the forties, he made it big as a thoroughly evil man in *Kiss of Death*—with the famous scene in which he pushed a crippled woman in a wheelchair down a flight of stairs and laughed in sheer malevolence. That evil moment transformed Widmark's reputation from a good comedian to a dramatic star.

He is the gentlest of men, married to a bright, attractive, creative woman. Jean was always tolerant of my unconventional ways, and when I dropped by at odd hours, saying, "Hey, anybody home?" and helping myself to a drink, she was always warm and welcoming.

Later, Dick and I did another movie together, *The Frogmen*, which also was shot on location, this time in the Virgin Islands. The agent, Jennings Lang, arrived at our hotel with the beautiful Joan Bennett. It never occurred to Dick that they were having an affair because Joan was married to a big Hollywood producer, Walter Wanger. He assumed that the agent was seeing to it that his client was properly treated. As history has recorded it, Wanger later shot Lang as close to his private parts as his aim would allow. But when Dick saw Lang and Bennett together, his observation was: "Gee, they [agents] don't give me that kind of treatment."

In *The Frogmen* I was a naval captain whose ship had suffered a torpedo hit from a Japanese sub, and it was Widmark's task to defuse it, heroically saving us all. During the shooting Widmark kept telling me, "Stop squinting, Gary."

"I can't help it," I told him. "The sun is in my eyes."

"It can't be—this scene is at night!" I kept forgetting it was meant to be a night scene, and the camera lens would make it appear to be so; it was up to the actor to take care of the squinting. Widmark always remembered the importance of such details.

I loved the story Dick told about his father. He had grown up in a small town, and whenever a Widmark picture was showing at the local theater, his father would ask the manager, "Say, how's my boy doing?"

When *Slattery's Hurricane* was through in California, I headed back to New York. The plane was grounded in St. Louis because of storms and fog, but, instead of being stranded, I went to see my old friend Jack Goldman. While I was there, I was surprised to receive a phone call. From some recesses of his mind, Ezra Stone had remembered the New Year's party I had attended in St. Louis while touring with *Brother Rat*, and managed to track me down at Jack's. He called to ask if I would replace an actor in a show currently playing in Boston, *At War with the Army*. I told him about my option with Fox Studio, but he said, "That's O.K., I'll take my chances. Just help get the show to New York." I agreed.

For the next couple of weeks I split time between my soap operas in New York and *At War with the Army* in Boston. The day before the play was scheduled to open in New York, my option was picked up by the studio. I gave my two weeks' notice on opening day and played out the two weeks—in my experience, a terrific way to open in New York. There was no need to worry about the critics or their reviews—though, in this case they were favorable. So back to California I went. The call from the studio was for the picture *Twelve O'Clock High* with Gregory Peck and Dean Jagger.

I played a squadron commander in the Eighth Air Force who was always circling his group to help any lame duck return to the base, thereby endangering the entire squadron. I was relieved of my command because I showed too much compassion and was replaced by a stern disciplinarian (Peck) who turns the squadron into a tight, super-efficient unit. In the end, the new commander suffers a breakdown. Years later, the film was used at the Harvard business school as an object lesson in creating an efficient organization, the message being that the needs of the company are more important than the welfare of an individual—aberrant thinking on Harvard's part. Millard Mitchell, my old friend from *See My Lawyer,* was also in the cast. He was a beautiful character actor, and he went on to do a lot of other films.

The script was written by Sy Bartlett and Beirne Lay, Jr., two fellows who really knew their material. It was about the Eighth Air Force, and they had been in it. Henry King, the director, had two passions—flying planes and directing movies, so the script was perfect for him, too.

We lived at Fort Walton, Florida, and every morning the cast was flown ninety miles north to a deserted field with a couple of runways and empty buildings. It was part of Elgin Field, one of the largest bases in the country. All the air force flyers there knew the script. Elgin Field was pretty much deserted and had been made to look as though we were in England. It was hot as hell in our heavy uniforms and the only shade was under the wing of the chartered plane that delivered our lunch.

When the time came to do the crash landing of the B-17, the air force advisers told Paul Mantz, the greatest of stunt flyers, that it wasn't going to be easy. Henry King added that there was only one take and one plane. "B-17's aren't easy to come by," he said, then added, "There will be a couple of tents at the end of the runway and it would be great if the wings of the plane would catch the tents and pull them down."

Paul Mantz took that big four-engined Flying Fortress up by himself, with very little gas in the tanks. He flew around the field once or twice, then called down on the radio, "This is it!"

So, in he comes with the B-17, and Bing, Bingo! The two tents go down, each one pulled along on a wing tip. He sets the plane down on its belly, and there's all this noise and dust . . . It's perfect!

The air force hotshots were looking at each other, "Wow, this guy really is a hot pilot," one of them said. "I don't know if we could have done it."

Paul climbed out of the plane and asked, "Anybody got a Coke?" He was magnificent.

After *Twelve O'Clock High*, I was sent to New York. Producer-director Otto Preminger was doing the film *Where the Sidewalk Ends*, and I was cast as a gangster. Preminger was a stickler for realism and wanted me to have a dapper suit. I brought in a few things I had selected from my wardrobe to show him, but each time he'd mumble, "Ummph, not the right cut," or "that lapel isn't right," or something else. "All right, so we'll have taste. Let's go to Saks," I said, and finally I got the right suit. But I couldn't get into being a gangster. I wanted to talk to Otto about it, but he was such a presence I wasn't thrilled about consulting him. In desperation, I worked up the courage to go to his hotel. I found him sitting in the tub, shaving.

"Otto, I've never played a gangster," I told him. "I'm having trouble getting into the part."

Otto interrupted his shaving only long enough to say, "Don't tell me. Tell your psychiatrist."

I didn't have a psychiatrist, but I gave the part a shot. My performance was all right, nothing great, but passable.

In those days I did everything that came my way. I was loaned to MGM, and did a picture, *The Girl in White*, with Arthur Kennedy and June Allyson about the first woman doctor. It was set around the turn of the century. This was my first experience since the war in a studio, as opposed to on-location filmmaking, and the MGM lot seemed huge. There was an enormous concrete sound-stage, more like a vast prison complex than a setting for making films. The facilities were pretty antiquated. They didn't even have bathrooms. Some architect without a bladder must have designed them! Can you imagine one of those multimillion-dollar productions stalled because a cameraman can't find a place to take a leak? This was also true of the Warner Brothers lot, where Bette Davis was known to disappear for an hour and no one knew where she went for relief.

I got another job, because of my voice, narrating a little film about a boy who lived in a ghetto, and I also did a film with Dorothy McGuire. I was really into the swing of Hollywood.

When I left New York, Barbara stayed behind at first. My brief affair with Mercedes McCambridge and a few other differences of opinion had put into discord what harmony there was. Things weren't really right, but we thought we'd try to rebuild our marriage. I rented a small apartment in a wonderful modern house off Laurel Canyon. Barbara came out. We lived there for a year. Then we found a lovely gray wooden house at the beach. We tried to be smart about money, but neither of us had much fiscal sense. As soon as I had a job under my belt I'd start to spend more than was prudent; this time, I started with a big yellow Oldsmobile convertible. For the premiere of *Twelve O'Clock High*, which opened to tremendous acclaim, I thought that Barbara must have a little mink stole. Meanwhile, our marriage drifted a little closer to the rocks.

The studio was gearing up for their big new project, *All About Eve*, directed by Joe Mankiewicz. My role was to play a Broadway director. Before this, because of the shows in which I had appeared during my army career, the studio had slotted me into war movies, as lieutenants, commanders, and the like—roles in which I felt comfortable as a good, not really heroic, but honest guy, a man who says what he believes and is a few cuts above average intelligence. These movies were not as challenging as Broadway, though *now* I could walk the streets and be recognized—mothers showed me their babies, fathers shook my hand. With the *All About Eve* role coming my way, I felt good. I felt I might have a fair opportunity ahead to work with many talented actors and actresses. I looked forward to learning and stimulation.

5

THE QUEEN

O n Sundays a large film studio is nearly deserted. The empty sets for westerns, New York streets, or Arabic marketplaces are rather eerie. One Sunday in 1950 I had been called to the studio for a makeup test with Miss Bette Davis who, at the last minute, had been called in to replace the ailing Claudette Colbert in *All About Eve*.

In the thirties, while I was slapping two blocks of wood together to generate sound effects for the Guy Hedlund Players, a film was made in Hollywood that would move the young Bette Davis the first long step on her way to becoming an American superstar. A contract actress with Warner Brothers, Bette Davis had been in Hollywood three years when she launched a persistent campaign, which she won, to play Mildred Rogers opposite Leslie Howard in a movie based on Somerset Maugham's novel *Of Human Bondage*.

The combination of bitchy Davis (who had worked for months to perfect her Cockney accent before she got the part) and Leslie Howard's graceful acting earned the movie raves from every serious critic. *Life* said Davis had given "probably the best performance ever recorded on the screen by an American actress." She was nominated for an Academy Award for "Best Actress," an honor she would win the following year for her role in *Dangerous* with Franchot Tone. From that point on, she performed in numerous films, always the star, always working very hard on her part. As I was to find later, she was an absolute perfectionist. Over the years, with her tremendous drive, talent, and star billing, she made her points of view acceptable to those she worked with, producer and actor alike, and often she was right. She had been cast almost by accident in *All About Eve,* and was given the role of Margo Channing, a fading Broadway actress whose role in a play is usurped by an ambitious and unscrupulous young woman whose star is on the rise. If Claudette Colbert hadn't hurt her back, how different my life might have been.

I had been chosen for my part mainly through the efforts of Joe Mankiewicz. Darryl Zanuck, the Fox production chief, hadn't been convinced I was the best choice because, as he said, I had "only played around airplanes." What's more, Mr. Z. had a hair fetish: He didn't like too much of it. I had a hairy chest and a messy head of hair. (In a later movie, in one scene that showed my shirt opened to the second button, Zanuck had the makeup man clip off all the hair on my chest!) But Joe got his way, thank God, and landed me the role in this important picture.

On that Sunday I went to the test stage, and there, being turned this way and that on a stool, as though she had just been picked up from a counter at a jewelry store, was the Queen, Bette Davis. I was appalled. The makeup people should have been pampering her, remarking on her abilities and skills, but instead they were twirling her around, rather callously examining her facial lines. I guessed they were trying to see if our age difference would be too noticeable. Bette is seven years my senior. But that question had never been raised with Miss Colbert, who is older than Bette by a few years. I thought, "My God, what are they doing? This isn't right." But the professional attitude Davis adopted throughout the ordeal was impressive.

The entire cast was scheduled to leave shortly for San Francisco, where we would begin several weeks of shooting in an actual theater instead of on a set. Hugh Marlowe and I had worked together before and were old friends, and I had been tested already with Anne Baxter, but the rest of the cast were new to me. They all proved terrific to work with: George Sanders, a droll, witty fellow; Gregory Ratoff; Celeste Holm, a funny lady; Thelma Ritter, a character actress with great common sense; and a young actress new to the films, Marilyn Monroe.

The testing and makeup session that Sunday wasn't long, and the story line and cast, as I thought about them, filled me with a general sense of elation and good feeling about the picture. When I returned to Barbara and the beach house at Malibu, I spent some time regaling her and our guests with my story of meeting The Star, Miss Davis.

There is truth in the idea that an actor's personality is created in the parts he or she plays. My role was that of Bill Samson, who was in love with Margo Channing, and as the film progressed, I became infatuated with Bette. At first, I noticed her three-year-old daughter, who was often on location, and since I love kids—all kinds, all ages—I played games with her, trying to make friends. As B.D. (her name is Barbara Davis, but Bette always called her B.D.) became more comfortable with me, so did her mother, and as I earned more of their trust, Bette opened up and began confiding in me about some of her problems. She was separated from her third husband and in the process of getting a divorce. I noticed a fellow lurking around while she was filming or in her dressing room, and I asked about him. He was her bodyguard. Her husband, she said, had been abusive, a wife-beater, so she wasn't taking any chances in case he came after her unexpectedly.

The age difference between us may have caused the directors of *Eve* some qualms, but it meant nothing to me. Bette had a few character lines around those incredible eyes, but she was a dynamic, attractive woman who knew what she was doing. As I had noticed with Mercedes McCambridge, here was a magnetic woman, with a compelling aura of femininity, but who might also be willing to confront dragons. I was irresistibly drawn to her. My first feeling of compassion for this misunderstood, talented woman was quickly replaced by a robust attraction. Before long we were walking about holding hands, going to the movies, and doing other things together. From simple compassion, my feelings shifted to an almost uncontrollable lust. I walked around with an erection for three days.

Sometime during the next few weeks, Bette hosted a party for the cast at a famous San Francisco restaurant. Marilyn Monroe was seated next to Hugh Marlowe. The party went on quite late but Marilyn excused herself early because she had to work the next morning. We all knew that the scene Marilyn had to work on the next morning was really Bette's scene, and that Marilyn had only a few lines. After she left, we all wondered what was going to happen to the dumb blonde. (My judgment, as far as predicting success goes, is invariably bad. When I was in England years later, I was asked about the Beatles and I said, "They won't make it in my country because we're into folk music.")

The next day Bette and Marilyn played their scene. I recall that Marilyn had four or five lines. Bette had more, but she was an experienced actress and accomplished the scene with little bother. It had to be done in ten takes, however—Marilyn kept forgetting her lines. Obviously, this problem did not injure her career.

At the end of filming in San Francisco, I got permission from the studio to drive back to Bette's home for the weekend, along with Bette's sister, Bobby, and B.D., with the bodyguard in tow. Our affair was becoming more serious.

Shortly afterward, Barbara and I were asked to attend a dinner party at which I had a drink or two beyond the far side of prudence. In my alcohol haze, while talking to the other guests about Davis, I stated that I'd marry Bette if she'd have me—not exactly the sort of thing to say in front of one's own wife. When we returned to the beach house, the dishes began to fly.

Barbara and I had been playing "make believe" with our feelings. Our marriage wasn't made in heaven, but came about because I needed someone to hold onto, and we happened to fall in together. Barbara was sexually independent all along, but I was too dumb to notice. However, when I began to follow the dictates of *my* appetites, trouble followed. Amongst the ruins of the china, we decided to get a divorce.

At the very beginning of our acquaintance, Bette and I discovered that we had both spent our childhood summers in Maine—I at Prout's Neck, she at Ocean Park, a summer community quite close by. Because of her early introduction to the coast of Maine, we found that our love for it was similar—a happy discovery, common ground. As Barbara vacated the house at the beach, my relationship with Bette deepened.

One Monday, after Bette, B.D., and B.D.'s nurse had spent the weekend at my house, the phone rang. Hedda Hopper, the gossip columnist, was at the other end of the line, and opened the conversation: "I know Bette spent the weekend with you . . ." She continued to prattle on about what a great person Bette was, what she had gone through already, and ended with: "If you treat her badly, you'll be in for a great deal of trouble."

Hedda had spies everywhere and let me know in no uncertain terms that she was *powerful,* and that dire things would happen to me if I didn't behave. After a fairly one-sided conversation, I hung up and Bette, who was still there, said, "I thought you were talking to an old friend." I figured it was better to have Hedda with me than against me. Somehow I managed to tame her, and eventually we became friends.

Damned if I didn't get another call straight off—this time from Louella Parsons, Hedda's archrival. We had the same general conversation. The news was out: Bette and I were gossip column "items." Gossip was Hedda's and Louella's livelihood, and, though sometimes they could be quite vicious, I felt they ought to be able to earn a living, though not at my expense. I was extremely agreeable to them, which resulted in a fairly good press—although both wrote in their columns that I was basically a slob who lived with unmade beds and dirty dishes in the sink. When Bette and I adopted a poodle—a small, neat pet that B.D. might enjoy—they focused on the fact that poodles need clippings, combing, and proper care. I responded by saying I planned to let the poodle become a bum—and they loved it. Such is the substance of gossip columns.

My mother followed my career with keen interest, clipping everything she read that included my name. She had seen the gossip columns, and I got a call. She was upset. I at first had no idea what was wrong, but, as she talked, I understood. She pictured Bette as a typical Hollywood siren, with a long cigarette holder, luring her poor little boy to his destruction. I reassured her by saying, "But Mother, she loves lobster."

Finally Bette's divorce came through, and I asked her to marry me. Her response was to tell me that she couldn't have any more children. I said that was okay—we'd adopt some. She had a girl, so we would get a boy, and it would work out fine. She agreed to marry me. This was in 1950. I was thirty-five and she was forty-two.

Bette rented a house in Gloucester, Massachusetts, and sent her sister Bobby and B.D. on ahead. Our plans were to drive across the country for a honeymoon in Maine. But first we had to stop in El Paso and cross to Juarez, Mexico, where I was divorced in the morning and remarried that afternoon—without even a coffee break. It was a lark: The two of us piled into Bette's black Cadillac convertible—I had unloaded my yellow Olds—and took off across the country. For five long days I drove that damned car. It felt more like horsing a truck around, and added nothing to our equanimity. There wasn't the contemporary convenience of having one of the motel chains available in every town. It was a rough trip all around. Each time we checked into a place, something was wrong with it, and out we'd go. I'd be tired, saying, "What the hell, it's a bed." But no, it had to be better. Before the trip was over, my normally easygoing attitude was wearing thin and I began to wonder.

We were happy to arrive in Gloucester, and stayed for a few days to see Bobby and B.D., and to reassure them that we were still in one piece. We then left for Westport Island, Maine, where we had rented a camp on an ocean point. It was quaint, all right, including the oil lamps and an outhouse. We chartered a boat to sail to a grocery store for food and five-gallon jugs of water—which I lugged up a ladder in order to get them into the camp. Bobby and B.D. joined us for a few days, at my invitation, and we all had a good time. Luckily, they enjoyed the great outdoors as much as I did.

After the honeymoon, we rented a house adjoining the Black Point Inn on Prout's Neck, so Bette could meet the in-laws—Mother, Aunt Marion, and my brother Jerry and his wife. There was a slight apprehension on Bette's part, which disappeared quickly after the meeting. And Mother and Aunt Marion were surprised to discover that they liked Bette. They had pictured what the magazines and gossip columns dredge up to work on the readers' imaginations: glamor, sin, nonsense. The two ladies knew that Bette had had three husbands prior to this marriage and were ready to do battle. Instead, they found a New Englander much like themselves.

Like many others, they were a little in awe of her, too, though they appreciated her practicality and down-to-earth qualities, and were proud of her Puritan work ethic and energy—all the qualities Yankees most admire. However, these very qualities, combined with her compulsive perfectionism, also intimidated people. Her perfectionism helped give Bette the reputation of being a bitch to work with, and all these personality traits, as well as her intelligence, made for trouble with the second-rate directors and actors of which Hollywood has had more than its share.

When I found myself being badly directed, I let some suggestions go in one ear and out the other. I'd do what I felt was right, the director be damned. No discussion. More often than not he would say, "Fine. That's just what I wanted," not really knowing what it was he wanted until he saw it. Bette, on the other hand, would have at them—tell them they were idiots. She seemed to feel confrontation was necessary to protect her reputation on the film. She was the star, and, as such, the picture was a reflection of her abilities. She would be blamed for any failure because, at that time, the star carried the picture. Today, the director's character comes through more clearly, and he or she is equally responsible. A director can't just sit by and let the star carry the picture, as Bette often was called on to do. She worked hard for her successes.

I'm not sure how they found us, but we got a call from Claude Rains and his wife Frances, who were on their way farther down east to visit their daughter Jennifer at a summer camp. They said they would stop by for dinner on their way home to Pennsylvania. I arranged for them to stay at the inn. This would be my first meeting with Rains, a friend of Bette's, and she advised me to get some Irish whiskey for his visit.

Bette arranged to have a few people come in after dinner, among them my friends Ernest and Betty Angell. Ernest, a New York lawyer who summered at Prout's Neck, was quite active with the American Civil Liberties Union. Bette had not met them before. When the Rains's arrived, Claude was using a cane. He'd sprained his ankle at Jennifer's camp and was ready for a drink. I asked how he'd like his whiskey and he said, "Just give me a glass and put the bottle beside it."

As we were having drinks and hors d'oeuvres, I watched the whiskey go down in the bottle as it went down Claude. After dinner, when the other guests had arrived, I heard a loud exclamation from Claude above the general chatter, "That's a lot of bullshit!" Since the Prout's Neck people were pretty straight, this cleared the house quickly, except for the Angells, who were tolerant people. Claude and Frances spent one night at the hotel and left the next morning. Several days later Bette received a card from Claude saying, "Frances tells me I used the word 'bullshit.' I know that 'shit' is a household word, but 'bullshit'—my apologies."

Soon after we had moved into the house, Bette rearranged things to suit herself while Eaton Tarbell, my old Bowdoin buddy, and I went off to play golf. I guess we were late coming back because Bette had begun to barbecue a chicken—which I guess I should have been there to do. As I walked in I said the house looked a little like *Good Housekeeping*. For some reason, the chicken came flying at me.

I made my peace before I left for Germany to make *Decision Before Dawn*, one more military movie in the post-war film marathon. In this role I wore a colonel's uniform. Richard Basehart had the leading role, and Oscar Werner and Hildegarde Neff co-starred. The film's basic point was that Germans are human, too. I rarely did violent scenes in it, but Basehart was shot at, dodged heavy bombardment, and twice had to throw himself into icy rivers to swim for his life.

While I was gone, Bette returned to the West Coast to find a place for us, since my Malibu house was too small. She found one also in Malibu, right on the beach; it had belonged to Richard Barthelmess, one of the first stars she had worked with. It was a great place, a compensation for transplants from the East Coast, though the waves of the Pacific are different. Their constant rolling and booming doesn't match the icy clarity of the waves I grew up with. When I returned from Europe, I wasn't home very long before I was summoned to the Virgin Islands to do *The Frogmen* with Dana Andrews and Dick Widmark.

For some of the filming of *Frogmen*, the cast and crew left the Virgin Islands to rendezvous at the submarine base in Key West. During the war, the navy had taken over a hotel built by Henry Flagler. He had envisioned Key West as the main stopping-off place for businessmen or performers en route to Cuba and South America, after his railroad had linked the Keys to the mainland. It was here that I got a call from Bette.

"You're the proud father of a beautiful baby girl," she announced.

What? This couldn't be right—we had planned for a boy next. Bette had been thirty-eight when she had B.D., and then had felt she was past the age for bearing children. During her rise to stardom, she'd had a few abortions so as not to interrupt her career, and medical advice was that her baby should be delivered by cesarean section. An osteopathic surgeon from Laguna Beach was her doctor, and he

Gary and his mother, Hazel May Andrews Merrill, 1918.
"I imagine the book was a prop the photographer put in front of us. I was three years old."

Above: Benjamin Gary
Merrill, Gary's father.
*"He was four years younger than
my mother, and probably was in
his forties when this was taken."*

Above right: Gary's aunt,
Marion Haley Andrews
Caldwell.

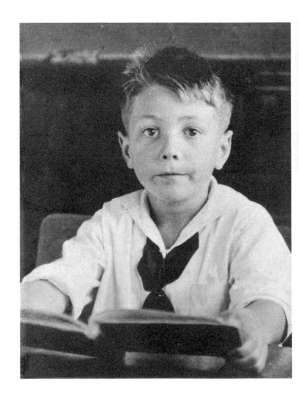

Gary at seven years old at
Forest Street School,
Westbrook, Maine.
*"The picture was taken in school,
so they put a book in front of me.
The stern expression is probably
because I was in school."*

Right: Gary at seventeen, 1932. *"This was taken in Windsor, Connecticut. I already wanted to be an actor. I've always been a slob. I got dressed up here to show off the outfit."*

Below: *"This was a New York photo studio shot taken when I was starting in the theater. I wanted to get an agent."*

Below: Partial cast list from *The Eternal Road,* 1937. *"We were extras, getting paid fifteen dollars a week. A lot of people went on to future success: Sam Jaffe; Sidney Lumet, the great movie director; Dick Van Dyck, who played the kid Moses took up to sacrifice on the mountain."*

SERVANTS, SLAVES, SOLDIERS, ISRAELITES, REAPERS, ARCHERS, BRIDE'S MAIDS, PRIESTS, ETC.

Misses Bernbaum, Bliss, Boone, Castle, Coates, Cooper, Cubitt, Curtiss, Druce, Heller, Hellman, Kubert, Lester, Lyons, Paduit, Petcheski, Quimby, Reilly, Dewey, Romaine, Saunders, Seranne, Woodfin. Messrs. Adams, Alsop, Arndt, Bowden, Brock, Brooke, Budd, Burns, Beech, Chain, Clarke, Berwick, Dassori, Davis, Fuente, Dickens, Donahue, Ferguson, Firestone, H. Fisher, J. C. Fisher, Foote, Frank, Gardner, Gompers, B. Gordon, D. Gordon, S. Gordon, Graves, Gray, Grimshaw, Haas, Halpern, Hare, Heure, Hinkley, Holmes, Jovanovitsch, Johnson, Kossoff, Leffler, Loeb, Lynch, Mahra, Martin, Merrill, Michael, Morgan, Murray, Nason, Nelson, O'Connell, Prince, Putnam, Rand, Reppetti, Richards, Rowland, Samuylow, Schein, Seymour, Shannon, Sheehy, Shem, Sherry, Shipman, Simons, Slocum, Stange, Stevens, Sullivan, Tandberg, Thomas, Thompson, Thor, Waxman, Zwrit.

See My Lawyer, 1939.
"*Milton Berle (center) was a lovely guy. He made two hundred dollars a week as an actor in the theater, and thousands in nightclubs. He was already famous. Millard Mitchell (left) later played with me in* Twelve O'Clock High."

This Is the Army, 1943 (Gary seated, in officer's uniform).
"*I was a narrator, and got to introduce Irving Berlin.*"

Barbara Leeds, Gary's first wife.
"This was a picture taken before I knew her. I don't know how I ended up with it. When you split up, things go every which way."

Gary and Barbara at Prouts Neck, 1947.
"Barbara liked Maine all right, although she wasn't a Maine type of person."

"BORN YESTERDAY"

*The tough gentleman (Paul Douglas) is protecting Judy Holliday,
so to speak, but Gary Merrill wants to marry her, the minute she learns
how to read. Garson Kanin's comedy is at the Lyceum.*

In a clinch with Judy Holliday.
Born Yesterday, 1946.
"Judy was a bright lady. A tough
broad: hard-working, knew her
business. Whatever she did was good.
I wouldn't group her with Bette Davis,
though . . . Judy was sane."

At War with the Army, 1948. Below: with William Mendrek and Maxine Stuart.

Gary with Claudia Morgan in a radio show, 1948.
"Claudia was the niece of Frank Morgan, the Great Oz in The Wizard of Oz. *I liked radio because it was nice and easy. All you had to do was be sober enough to read. No clothes, no makeup, no nothing."*

RIGHT TO HAPPINESS

In Germany for *Decision Before Dawn*, 1951, with Oskar Werner (third from left)
"We were having a poker game while they set up the lights."

Twelve O'Clock High, with Gregory Peck, 1949.
"This was the film Bette Davis saw me in and thought I was a good actor. Greg was a nice guy. I never got to know him, though. He's not knowable - he's off by himself."

Above: Bette and Gary, *All About Eve*, 1950.
Below: with Anne Baxter, *All About Eve*.

Bette and Gary, newly married,
1950.

Bette's 43rd birthday, on the set
of *Another Man's Poison*, 1951.

Above:
Another Man's Poison.
"I'm probably leaning like that because I couldn't hold myself up!"

ette and B.D. greeting ary at an airport.

At home in Malibu with Margot and B.D., 1951.

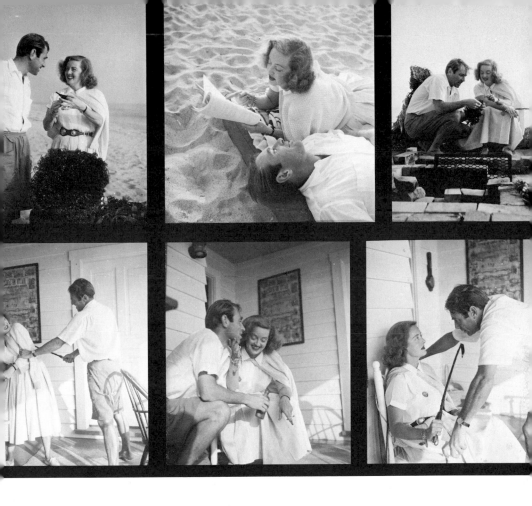

"Phil Stern, the photographer, was down to the Malibu house. We were getting ready to do Another Man's Poison, *but here we were just fiddling around, getting some action in for the pictures... Actually, I don't know what the hell we were doing in some of these.*"

he prefers tee shirts to tails
but he's no slouch as an actor

GARY MERRILL

REBEL
IN
WONDERLAND

Even in the studio, Gary likes slippers

It's a cozy thing about the heavenly stars. If you know where to look for them, you can always spot them. Ditto for a huge dipperful of Hollywood stars.

But not Gary Merrill. He's a star who swings an original orbit. It takes a lot of looking to track his flickers down.

Ask Bette Davis if Gary fits into the celestial jigsaw puzzle. She'll laugh and say, "Heavens, no!"

All of which means that Gary says what he wants to say, goes where he wants to go, does what he wants to do and wears what he wants to wear—and just let ANYONE object.

Bette doesn't. She wants Gary to be Gary. She married him because he IS Gary. And to be Gary in Hollywood takes courage.

Remember the night Gary was escorted from a swank party at the Mocambo Night Club for heckling? Three hundred of Hollywood's blue-book set remember. Seems that Gary thought the party was a private affair and then he learned that it was tossed for a political bigwig. He had come to have fun and he let it be known. After his exit, Esther Williams found him outside signing autographs for clamorous fans.

Some say it's Gary who persuaded Bette to leave Hollywood to do that musical revue. He could have nixed the idea when he heard about it one Manhattan day. But he saw that Betty got the script. And Bette didn't mull over it. Her okeh came one-two-three.

Gary is a rangy five foot, ten inch, 170 pound he-man whom some call handsome and some call charming despite a slooped-in face and a straightforward push of personality. In other words, he's handsome and charming because he DOESN'T fit the conventional mould.

Nor does his marriage to Bette—described by her as the only real marriage she's had. Their union contains none of the usual trappings about dressing and going out to dinner or speaking to the governess about the three kids. It's a free, rough-and-tumble, tender life together —full of children and work and bounding love and mutual respect. Because Gary is Gary and Bette is Bette and they want to keep each other that way.

From Gary's New England childhood to his success in Broadway's Born Yesterday, he's managed to resemble a beachcomber at every relaxing opportunity. This state of sartorial seediness is maintained in Hollywood, and does Gary care if he doesn't rate Esquire? And does Bette care? Here's how much.

They bought a toy poodle for the children only after Gary said the fancy

46

SHORT NOTICE

THE handwriting's on the wall: shorts have come to town. Gary Merrill, a man's man, leads the van in the shorts parade from resort centers to your favorite urban spot, come summer. Don't say we didn't warn you: shake a leg and get yours.

PHOTOGRAPH BY ZINN ARTHUR

Opposite page: *Screen Fan* , 1953.

Above: *Esquire*, 1953.
'They were defending my wearing skirts (a kilt) by saying I was 'a man's man.' "

15

"Witch Way," Cape
Elizabeth, 1954.
*"That was a great spot —
three or four acres, and the
ocean was your front
yard."*

Gary and Dexter "Wig" Hunnean.
*"We played hockey out in the backyard at Witch Way. In this picture we were just playing
a little hangover hockey ."*

delivered B.D. just beautifully—with the world looking over his shoulder, so to speak. Many people were concerned about the welfare of the reigning movie queen and her child. After we married, Bette agreed that I could adopt B.D., with her father's approval, but B.D.'s father thought he ought to be paid fifty thousand dollars for the privilege. We settled for five thousand dollars and had gone ahead with the adoption. Our plan had then been to adopt a boy next, then a girl, then a boy. So my response to her announcement was "Wrong fucking sex!"

Apparently, when we'd been in Maine during the previous summer, she had talked to a cousin of hers, a doctor, about adoption—but I was told nothing of this. Bette hadn't consulted me but went ahead on her own, and her high-handed way of doing it irritated me.

However, when the filming of *Frogmen* was over, and I returned to the Malibu house, it was all right. When I saw the baby, I melted. She was a little blonde doll, and we settled on the name Margot.

Not long after my return to the Malibu house, Bette received a script in the mail from an English producer, Daniel Angel. Neither of us thought it was particularly good. Then Daniel Angel appeared on our doorstep. He walked with canes because he had been afflicted with polio; this made him seem "Rooseveltian," which quite affected us. He was completely charming, and in order to persuade Bette to do the film, he said that Emlyn Williams had already agreed to play in it and Douglas Fairbanks, Jr., would be involved in the production. Bette had visited England but had never worked there, so if she agreed it would be quite a feather in Angel's cap. He offered her nearly the whole world, plus a part for me if the Fox Studio would loan me or rent me.

When an actor is under contract to a studio, he is guaranteed forty weeks of pay per year. Often, a studio with no assignment on the agenda would loan a contractee out. The word "rent" is a more apt description, because the agreement allowed the loaner to make a profit on the deal. For example, the "rent" paid to the studio might be twice the actor's salary, and the studio would pocket the difference. It was standard practice and no one complained—and, in this case, it worked beautifully. Angel agreed to pay all our household expenses while in England, with a proviso that a certain amount of meat would be flown over from America for us. England was still in the grip of strict rationing. Since Bette didn't like flying, we could travel to England by boat.

The film was *Another Man's Poison,* an implausible story about a mystery writer who murders her husband, an escaped convict, and makes a stab at murdering another escapee, but then dies by accidental poisoning. Bette was going to involve herself in some script revision, with Emlyn Williams's help; as for me, I would have gone to England without the script. Bette was able to order up the director, Irving Rapper from Warner Brothers, a real run-of-the-mill talent. He had directed Bette in several films which had turned out all right, so she took him on again.

At this point, our family consisted of Dell, a wonderful woman who had been with Bette for a long time as cook, washer, ironer, and general factotum; B.D.; her nanny; and Margot, our three-month-old, complete with her own nurse. We were a small troop and took up a good deal of space—just about the entire top deck of the *Queen Elizabeth* (the old *Queen*). This seemed fitting, because Bette's imperious manners were probably like the first Queen Elizabeth's. (In fact, Bette made a movie about her, *The Virgin Queen,* in 1955.) It was a February crossing and the seas sometimes became quite rough, which caused Dell to remark, "This boat kind of takes you over and then brings you back." It so happened we did return on the same ship because we were unable to book reservations on the *Queen Mary*.

We had spent some time with Dick and Jean Widmark before our departure, and Dick had warned us about the English press. "They're rough on Americans arriving at Southampton," he had said. But Bette was quite sure she could handle them, and I had no doubt that she could—a premature assumption, as it turned out.

When we arrived at Southampton, Bette was ready. She threw open our suite to the reporters, offered them booze and hors d'oeuvres, was overly generous with her time, and was very pleasant. The next morning when she saw the papers she was furious. All the reporters sang the same song—about rich American actresses with hundreds of pieces of luggage, fur coats, and a mention or two about the kids and "Mr. Davis." Bette's anger was directed at herself for not heeding Dick's warning, and, probably, because there was no way to soften the sting of the reporters' words.

As if to compensate ourselves for some of the hurt inflicted by the press, we found a charming old inn not far from Walton-on-Thames, where we enjoyed the incredibly picturesque countryside. Moreover, it meant that Bette and I had a lovely drive along the river en route to the studio each morning. We had anticipated with pleasure many things in England, and one of them was meeting and working with Emlyn Williams. Some years earlier, Bette had played the lead in the picture *The Corn Is Green* (directed by Rapper), about a dedicated teacher in a Welsh mining community who helped a brilliant young man get out of the mines. It was the story of Williams's own life—he was the young man—and he had written the play on which the film was based. During our filming of *Another Man's Poison*, Emlyn brought his former teacher to meet Bette.

Many of my writer friends have said that when a script is bad, it can't be fixed. Better to tear it apart, preserving the basic premise if it happens to be solid, and start over. The basic premise of *Another Man's Poison* was pretty crummy to begin with. But Bette believed that with Emlyn's help the script could be improved. So the two of them went to work, altering this and that. When this happened, I generally found a place to lie down, being my usual lazy self, to wait for the action to begin. The fact that I wasn't doing anything bugged the hell out of Bette.

One of the scenes called for Emlyn to drive a jeep, but, as far he was concerned, there was no way to accomplish this because he had never driven anything in his life and wasn't about to learn. The problem was solved by attaching ropes to the jeep, and about ten men pulled it along as the scene was shot. There was another problem: Emlyn couldn't drive—but I couldn't ride a horse. There aren't many stunt riders in England, but a jockey was located to do my riding for me. However, in several scenes I had to be filmed while seated on the horse . . . which refused to cooperate. The director asked the jockey what was wrong with the horse and the jockey said, "The horse thinks he has a monkey on his back."

The sidelights of our stay in England were the highlights. One in particular was dinner at the Lord Chancellor's apartment at the Houses of Parliament. Some years before, Bette had fled to England to fight a contract at Warners that she felt was unfair. She had chosen a lawyer to represent her named Sir William Jowett. When she arrived in England this time, Jowett was Lord Chancellor. He was a beautiful C. Aubrey Smith colonel type who was convinced that the Labor Party—his party—would be out in the next election. He wondered if he would be able to land a job in Hollywood. I said, "Sure, I'll be your agent."

One evening we were invited to John Gielgud's house for dinner, but arrived late because we had been working. As we drove up, I saw Ralph Richardson just leaving, and scrambled to get out of the car. He'd been a favorite of mine for years and I wanted to meet him. Bette nettled me with, "Why didn't you bring your autograph book?"

Later, upstairs, I met Alec Guinness, who was acting in a modern *Hamlet* and was sporting a mustache for the part. I went downstairs to tell Bette that the Guinness brewer was upstairs and that I wanted to introduce her. It was a while before she realized she was talking to the fine actor, not the brewer—a small satisfaction for me for her remark about the autograph book.

Good plays are always being staged somewhere in England, but one evening we ended up seeing a play of no particular note. We had taken some American friends along, Justin Gray, an architect, and his wife. When we left the theater afterward, we discovered a throng of people crowding around, waiting for Bette. We were jostled and elbowed before finally making it to the car. Justin remarked, "Wow, this is like traveling with the Queen!"

"Didn't you know that you were?" I said to Bette, laughing. From then on, it was my favorite name for her.

The climax of the trip was the afternoon we spent with the Oliviers. Laurence Olivier was married to Vivien Leigh, and at the time they were appearing in a double playbill, *Two Cleopatras*—Shaw and Shakespeare—which we attended. Laurence Olivier was magnificent, as usual, though I had the feeling he was holding back a little, perhaps because of his wife. He is considerate and honest, and it bothered me to see him struggling—it was somewhat like watching a thoroughbred being held back to throw a race.

After the play we went backstage to see them. They had recently bought an old monastery, and they invited us to visit them there on Sunday. Of course we accepted. The shooting of our film finished on Saturday, after which a party ensued, a frequent occurrence when a film is in the can. It turned out we hadn't been the only ones who had been partying.

We drove up through the beautiful grounds the next day, noticing someone playing tennis off to the side. We walked to the door and rang the bell. There was a slight delay but the butler finally appeared. "Very sorry," he said, "no one's down. Please follow me." We trailed after him to the drawing room where he ushered us in and pointed out the bar. "They'll be down shortly," he said, and left us.

We fixed ourselves a drink and were just getting comfortable when Larry bounded in, apologetically explaining that they'd been up until all hours. He fixed himself a little eye-opener and asked if we'd like a tour of the "great pile," and of course we said we'd love it—who could resist a tour with such an extraordinary guide?

The abbey was an ancient and lovely building. We ambled around looking at this, commenting on that, all the while being thoroughly entertained. The abbey was surrounded by paths and gardens and outbuildings, and as we passed an outbuilding that looked like a storage shed, Larry said, "Those were originally pig sties. It will eventually be a projection room."

We approached the side of the house where we had seen the tennis court and, as we did, the players came toward us. Larry introduced them as his stepdaughter and her father—Vivien's first husband and their daughter. I muttered to Bette how much more civilized the English were than Americans. In the United States I'd never seen a man entertain his wife's first husband.

Following the introductions, we returned to the bar to mix another drink, and saw a man descending the stairs. He "hallo'ed" in our direction and visited the bar before he joined us. It was Nöel Coward, who had stayed on after last night's party. Soon after, Vivien made her entrance, greeted us, and also headed for the bar. As she poured herself some seltzer, Peter Finch appeared and followed suit. Apparently we weren't the only ones looking for an oasis—everyone's night before had obviously been long.

Lunch was announced. As we were gathering to go in, a car drove up and Bobby Helpmann hopped out. He came in and also made a beeline for the bar. Helpmann explained that he was on his way to rehearsal at Stratford but needed a pit stop. (Robert Helpmann was a famous ballet dancer and actor, as well as a choreographer.) At this point, with all the remarkable talent surrounding me, I rather regretted not having an autograph book—never mind Bette!

The lunch was perfect—light but filling. We all pushed back our chairs and trooped out to the lawn. Bette and I watched while the rest played a pickup game of bowls, a version of lawn bowling. Helpmann clowned around and did a wild imitation of Dame Edith Evans bowling—as he imagined it. Suddenly a swarm of bees flew by, and we all rushed after them, Larry intent on getting some home-grown honey.

As I sat on the patio to rest, I was joined first by Nöel Coward and then Miss Leigh, who was wearing a large hat and carrying a basket of flowers. Coward explained, "She's doing her gardening bit."

She smiled and announced that tea was going to be served.

"Tea?" said I. "Not a drink?"

Coward said, "Surely, old chap. They're not religious about their tea." He then joined me at the bar.

It was an incredible afternoon, and my conversation with Nöel Coward was a high spot. I found him to be a warm man, though many people think of him as having been the brittle, witty character he so often portrayed in films. They forget his more poignant writings. He related some of his war experiences, when he had entertained the troops practically at the front line. During that time the government had had him shadowed by Scotland Yard. When I expressed my amazement, he explained: "They had the idea I'd demoralize their young soldiers." He had served his country in his way, and tried to ignore the interference of stuffy bureaucrats. To me he seemed a remarkable man.

We'd been asked by the Oliviers to come for the day and had dressed for a romp in the country, but the romp extended to dinner—and that was black tie. We hadn't brought a proper change of clothes, and when I mentioned this to Peter Finch, he admitted that he hadn't either. So, although it was a rather formal dinner, some were dressed and some undressed, so to speak, but no one seemed to mind.

That Sunday was our last day in England, and it was one hell of a day. During our few weeks there, I had met "royalty"—the cream of the English theater. The advantages of being married to the Queen of Hollywood were obvious. I had hobnobbed with the Lord Chancellor, Laurence Olivier, John Gielgud, Alec Guinness, Vivien Leigh, Robert Helpmann, Nöel Coward, Emlyn Williams—people whose accomplishments make an average American feel giddy, especially one who enjoys English actors and English theater.

We also had seen some American theater royalty. At the Palladium, Judy Garland had been performing to a standing-room-only crowd. Danny Kaye was in our box, saying how great Judy was, and carrying on.

"Quiet," I said. "We came to see Judy."

Bette and our whole entourage left England to return to Malibu. I was to start *Phone Call from a Stranger,* a movie in which a group of people is locked together on an airplane trip across the country, and the plane is repeatedly forced down because of severe thunderstorms. The cast included Keenan Wynn, Shelley Winters, and Michael Rennie, and I played a lawyer. As the storms continued, each of us had a story to tell and an intimacy developed. The plane crashed and there was one survivor—me. I dutifully went about visiting the next of kin, the last of which was Bette Davis, playing a small third-act part, a three-day bit that had been scheduled to go to some other actress. Bette had talked the producers into letting her do it, for which she was paid a handsome thirty-five thousand dollars, as opposed to fifteen hundred dollars called for in the budget. The producers got back more than that in publicity alone—the "star playing a bit part."

Some years later I was on a flight to California when I was caught in a real storm with ferocious lightning and thunder, and the plane was buffeted this way and that. Farley Granger was on board also and *Phone Call from a Stranger* kept flashing through his mind. He was sure everyone on the plane was going to be killed but me, and moaned, "How did they ever allow that picture to be made?"

As the family settled back into our Malibu beach house, Bette decided to throw a clambake. We weren't particularly social, as many others in Hollywood were—in fact, we were usually the opposite. We enjoyed our privacy and casual style of living, so this clambake was an exception. Some of the top echelon of Hollywood arrived: MCA chief Jules Stein, producer Lou Wasserman, Hedda Hopper, the Widmarks, and Ray Middleton, to name a few. Extra rest rooms on the beach had to be built. One was painted pink, one blue, and guests were encouraged to leave graffiti on the walls. I often wondered what happened to those "outhouses," because, shortly afterward, Bette found a terrific, old, wooden California-style house at the corner of Camino Palmero and Franklin Avenue in Hollywood, just above Sunset and Hollywood Boulevards, and we relocated. Lillith James and her husband, Dan, who together had written the musical comedy *Bloomer Girl*, lived next door.

This was in the early fifties and the gloom of McCarthy's witch-hunts had hit Hollywood. Good, decent people became fodder for the ego of a ridiculous demagogue. It seemed that wherever I went political issues were the subject of discussion. People vigorously took sides. Before 1945, I had ignored what was happening in the world, and had largely gone along relying on the good fortune life had dealt me. But when the atomic bombs were dropped on Hiroshima and Nagasaki at the end of the war, I decided I had neglected my political education too long. I read everything I could get my hands on, digested it, and came up with ideas that I felt needed attention.

When Winston Churchill introduced the concept of the Cold War to Americans at Fulton, Missouri, along with his now-famous comment on Russia's "Iron Curtain," I was on the picket line that surrounded the Waldorf Astoria to protest his arrival in New York. When President Truman fell in with this new ideology, I became active in support of his former vice president, Henry Wallace, during his campaign for the presidency in 1948. I joined the protest against the atomic bomb because it became the symbol of America's intimidation of the entire world. For what other reason was the stockpiling of new and larger weapons, such as the hydrogen bomb, becoming so important to the military? War had become far too horrible even to contemplate.

When the House Committee on Un-American Activities began digging out "radicals" in the movie industry, I was prepared to speak up for what I believed. I began looking for ways to establish my new political position: I gave money, lent my name, and spoke to various public demonstrations of protest to the committee's activities. In 1950, the House Un-American Activities Committee had sent ten movie actors and directors to jail for refusing to discuss their political positions at committee hearings. During the subsequent years, the blacklisting of actors, writers, directors, and others was rampant in both the movie and television businesses. Through it all, though I associated with more than a few of these unfortunate victims and gave my name to several organizations listed as subversive by the U.S. attorney general, I was never named as a radical nor called before any committee to testify, nor did I lose any jobs because of my associations.

I found myself resenting this apparent immunity, as though it were an assault on my integrity. What right had the blacklisters to ignore me? I put it down to the old Merrill luck.

Then, at the height of the McCarthy witch-hunting years, I received a call from the FBI. They wanted to pay me a visit. It was when I was in New York doing the David Susskind series, "Justice." I thought, "Well, finally! Here it comes." When I told Bette, she was immediately frightened.

"You can't go to jail now. You've got a wife and children!"

I did not look forward to this visit and was shaken when the two federal agents arrived at our door. After showing them in, and asking them to sit down, I sat there staring at them, determined to be silent and uncompromising, all the things I'd admired in others. There would be no information from me, even if it meant being blacklisted or going to jail.

"Mr. Merrill," one of them began, his voice free of any emotion, "we're here to check out an applicant for a federal appointment, who . . . ah . . . might present security problems. We'd like to know, in your opinion, if this man is a homosexual."

What horseshit! I said I had no inkling of his sexual preferences—and that was as close as I ever got to the political hot seat. As for Bette, we later learned that the FBI had her categorized as a "hyperthyroid type with a heart of gold."

My neighbor, Dan James, had been blacklisted, for

which I felt a deep regret. It was through him that I met Dalton Trumbo, one of the successful screenwriters who had been charged with contempt of Congress and sentenced to a year in federal prison. Dalton was an intellectual and had spent much time protesting the de-emphasis of Latin in the public school system. Along with his other sterling qualities, he loved martinis as well as I did. When we first met and sat down with our martinis to talk, I heard Bette ask Mrs. Trumbo about our conversation. She answered: "Wait till they stop flying and come back down."

In the fall of 1951, mother and Aunt Marion came to California for a visit. That same year my father and Pauline, my stepmother, also visited us. In an attempt to help out, I hired Pauline to handle my fan mail—and it turned out to be a blessing. She compiled a massive scrapbook, from which many of the pictures in this book have been selected. Had it not been for her assiduous collecting, few would have survived—they would have gone the way of my money.

When Bette had adopted Margot in January of 1951, the legalities had been handled by a wonderful Maine lawyer named Jake Berman, and we weren't required to go through state examinations. With our next adoption, we applied through the proper agencies for interviews, and though we might have been considered a little older than many prospective parents, we were found acceptable. In February of 1952, a little boy was born who came to us right from the hospital. We named him Michael. We had wanted to start from scratch rather than with a two- or three-year-old. Our luck with our staff held, and we were able to find an excellent German nurse, a tiger in her vigilance of Mike—solid as a German alp.

Michael's background was good on both sides, probably better than either Bette's or mine. Compared to me, he has turned out pretty square—but that's not a difficult accomplishment. Once, when he was being interviewed, he was asked about his father. Trying to come up with a description, he was stumped for a while and the interviewer asked, "Is he eccentric?"

"Yeah," Michael said, "that's the word. He's eccentric."

So here, at last, we had our boy, Michael.

6

THE BEST YEARS

In the late spring of 1952, while we were ensconced on Camino Palmero in Hollywood, Ralph Alswang, an old army friend, called me from New York. He was larger than life, a madcap architect, set designer, and erstwhile producer. Some of his friends, who were also my acquaintances, were planning a revue, *Two's Company*. Vernon Duke was to do the music, Ogden Nash the words, and Nat Hiken, who had been a writer for Fred Allen and who had evolved the successful TV series "Sergeant Bilko" for Phil Silvers, was to work on the sketches. He had lined up Jerome Robbins for choreography and the ballerina Nora Kaye, who was later married to the talented and successful movie director Herb Ross. Ralph wanted to know if Bette might be interested in doing the revue and taking it to New York. She would have to do some singing and dancing. I told Ralph I'd ask her about it.

Bette had often mentioned returning to the theater in New York, where she had begun her career. But she hadn't been on the stage since arriving in California in the early thirties. We talked it over at length and decided it might be fun for her. There wouldn't be the critical pressure that is always present when doing a dramatic role, and the singing and dancing seemed an appealing change of pace.

Light comedies and musicals appeal to performers who have only been involved with serious roles. I suppose it's the "grass is always greener" syndrome, or a need to test themselves and prove their versatility. Usually, however, the more successful crossovers are the dancers and singers who move on to serious acting—people such as Gene Kelly, Fred Astaire, Shirley MacLaine, and Mary Tyler Moore. But, then, Rex Harrison and Richard Burton were terrific in musicals. When I called Ralph back I told him Bette was definitely interested.

Two weeks later, Ralph arrived with producers Jimmy Russo and Mike Ellis in tow. They brought sketches, songs, and the overall idea of the revue, as well as suggestions for the casting director. Bette set the pace: After considering the time needed for voice training, dance routines, and a general shaping-up—something like training a boxer for a championship bout—we all realized she should be given a lot of time to become comfortable with her part, since the play was a considerable risk for her. Rehearsals were put off until fall to allow for everything to settle in.

Bette spent the next few months in training, and in September we loaded the family onto a plane bound for New York. The boys (as we called Russo and Ellis) had found us a triplex on Beekman Place, a wonderful and spacious apartment—and we certainly needed the space. Michael was about seven months old, Margot twenty months, and B.D. was five years old. Because Bette was working, we had more help than usual. Bette's sister, Bobby, came with us, bless her heart—always reliable in emergencies. In times of stress, Bette had a tendency to take out her frustrations on whomever she ran into first. Frequently this was Bobby, who, by her presence, enabled the children to be once removed from Bette's short circuits. For some reason,

Bette treated children as miniature adults, so they weren't exempt from her blistering tirades. With her nervousness and apprehension about being back in New York, and about doing a show in a medium that was new to her, the tirades were heightened. As a perfectionist, she concentrated on her work, and the fact that everyone else wasn't as single-minded drove her to distraction; she made bystanders feel guilty as hell for not working as hard as she. She'd let you have it—words flying like balled fists, right between the eyes.

Shortly after our arrival in New York, I was sitting on the terrace of our Beekman Place apartment, twenty-odd floors above the street, engrossed in the *Times*. I thought I heard the whisper of my name in the air (an eerie sensation), but I ignored it and continued to read. Seconds later, I heard it again and thought, "This can't be happening. I must be going crazy." But I heard it again, this time in a more normal tone of voice. I looked around and saw, in a nearby hotel window, Mary Harding's face. She was a friend whom I hadn't seen for several years. I shouted our apartment number to her.

"Come on over. Meet Bette and the kids."

It was a joy to see her and, as I answered the door, I asked, "What in the world are you doing here?"

"I'm at the tag end of my divorce," she replied. "I consider him an ex-husband. I'm on my way to Italy to get away from him. He's a brute."I was shocked that anyone could mistreat this charming, tiny woman.

She met Bette, but Bette's tension upset her. Mary was sailing the next day, and I accompanied her to the boat. As she was boarding, she took my hand. "Poor Gary, you are in for trouble with your wife. So are the children. Be careful."

With that, she kissed my cheek and was gone. I attributed her apprehension to Bette's involvement with the play, and almost forgot it.

(As it turned out, Mary Harding never returned to the States to live. She loved Rome and wrote a book, *Dear Friends and Darling Romans,* which brought her briefly to New York and the Jack Paar show on a promotional visit, after which she returned immediately to Rome.)

Bette invited everyone concerned with *Two's Company* for cocktails. The official purpose of the party was to become acquainted, and things went beautifully, everyone warm and friendly. As they filed out, each person had a gracious word to say. When everyone but Ralph Alswang had left, Bette announced that she knew from meeting him that she would be unable to work with Jerome Robbins. Mistakenly, she was certain his attention would be on the ballet numbers and he would forget about her. Ralph and I assured her that Robbins was the very best choreographer to be found, and somehow managed to calm her. A case of jitters, we thought, though now we felt tremors of our own.

A performer carries an enormous amount of baggage on stage, and insecurities need to be addressed constantly. (During this time, I was reminded of Jean Arthur's problems in *Born Yesterday.*) Returning to the stage after the security of studio work can be especially traumatic. Reassurances are necessary. This is what Ralph and I tried to do for Bette, with some success, and she managed to ride out the storm. Jerome Robbins stayed on, and Jules Dassin, who is now married to Melina Mercouri, was brought in to stage the sketches. One way or another, the show got to Detroit for its premier.

The theater was packed. I was standing at the back when the overture began and the curtain went up. Within seconds there was Bette, alone on the stage for her opening song. She had only appeared on stage, but people were applauding her.

The applause went on for what seemed like five

minutes; the orchestra vamped; finally, Bette began. I realized that something was wrong. She was fumbling her words—very unlike her. Then she dropped to the stage as though she'd been poleaxed. There was a gasp from the audience as she lay there, and, as a stagehand walked on to drag her off, I hurried to the wings. I thought she had had a heart attack and had died. The curtain dropped.

When I finally got backstage and saw her, I began breathing again. I could see she hadn't died. I mumbled something inane, then said, "Don't worry, she'll go on."

Someone gave her smelling salts to help her revive and she looked up, rose to her feet, and walked back onto the stage. As the curtain rose once more, she said to the audience, "Well, you can't say I didn't fall for you." And she went on with the show.

She had never been ill in her life and I couldn't imagine what was wrong except sheer fright, though nothing like this had happened before. The play went as smoothly as an opening night on the road usually does, and at the end of the performance the audience gave her another ovation. Bette told me in the dressing room afterward that she had played the entire show by rote, hadn't been aware of any audience reactions, not even the ovation at the end. The next night she was back on stage.

Within a couple of days she began to lose her voice, forcing the cancellation of two or three performances. Doctors were flown in from New York. Josh Logan came for a look at the play, to see if he could help firm it up. As for Bette, he felt that she should just get on the stage. I think he felt she was simply overanxious.

When the show reached Boston, Jimmy and Mike, our neophyte producers, decided to call in John Murray Anderson, an old-time musical director, to take a look at the play. His pronouncement was that the production was more amateurish than a Princeton Triangle show. He proceeded to tighten things up, to make it a more professional vehicle.

During the entire time on the road, doctors were in and out to see Bette. Finally the show opened in New York. The reviews were bad, but the box office couldn't be stopped. I think the show could have run for as long as Bette stayed with it.

During the New York run of *Two's Company*, I was called back to California to do a picture, *Night Without Sleep*, with Linda Darnell. It would take about six weeks. It was in January that Bette phoned to say that she had an impacted wisdom tooth which had been the cause of her illness, poisoning her system. She assumed that this was why she had blacked out on stage. She arranged to go into the hospital for its removal on a Sunday so that she wouldn't have to miss a show. Stanley Behrman, a fine oral surgeon, did the operation. When the tooth was removed, Dr. Behrman ran some biopsies which showed osteomyelitis, an infection of the bone, and informed Bette that it was necessary to perform a fairly serious operation on her jaw. That did it—the show had to close.

Bette's problems occurred around the time Walter Winchell, the New York gossip columnist and broadcaster, was raising money for his pet philanthropic effort, the Damon Runyon Cancer Fund. The night of Winchell's weekly broadcast—I believe it was a Sunday night—the phone rang. It was Stanley Behrman and he was pretty upset. "Did you hear the Winchell show tonight?"

"No. What's going on?"

"I was afraid you might have been listening and just wanted you to know that what he said isn't true."

"Jesus, Stanley, what did the guy say?"

"Now, Gary, don't get mad yet, but if I heard him right, Winchell said that Bette's operation was for cancer. He must have gotten wind of the surgery I've done and just assumed . . . at least he implied that she had cancer."

"My God," I said, beginning to get riled, "that man will do anything to get money for his project. Telling stories to get people to contribute to his fund."

Stanley went on to say he'd been called by the head of surgery at his hospital, who had given him a hard time. He told him that it had been the first thing he had looked for, but there was no evidence of cancer. Stanley was more concerned about our welfare than his being called on the carpet. He wanted to reassure us.

Again the phone rang and this time it was Bette's mother. On and on and on she ranted. I got madder and madder and told her I'd take care of it.

It was now my turn to use the phone. I called Dorothy Schiff, owner of the *New York Post,* who had had trouble with Winchell in the past. "What the hell can we do?" I asked her. She set about giving me some pointers. I then called Winchell and screamed at him for spreading lies about Bette's illness to his listeners, and warned him that if he harmed her career, I'd sue.

"I'll print a retraction and mention on the air that I had misinformation," he said. "As far as suing goes, you'll have to stand in line."

He had accomplished his ends. Few people see retractions, and although we were able to reassure our close friends, the whole world believed Bette was stricken with cancer. I subsequently heard that Winchell's cancer appeal had been very successful. I assume something good may have come from a lie just this once.

While Bette was recuperating at Beekman Place, she heard that Anna Magnani, the great Italian actress, was in New York for the first time and had expressed an interest in meeting her. Bette couldn't have been more excited at the prospect. The meeting between these two dynamos was tremendous, a real scene as they communicated in fractured French and Italian with a bit of English thrown in.

They admired each other's work; and the passion that Magnani displayed on the screen was magnified in person. A friend said that if Con Edison, the power company, could have plugged into that meeting, it could have lit the city for a couple of days.

The instructions to Bette were that she would need complete rest for the summer, to the extent that she shouldn't even be responsible for running a house. Our Beekman Place triplex was fine, but our lease expired in May. So we decided that a summer in Maine—or maybe longer—would be just the thing. But where? At that time in Maine, there were few hotels open before mid-June at the earliest, and it was only April.

As I idly thumbed through a magazine, probably *Down East*, I came across a familiar place on Casco Bay, near the town of Yarmouth, called the Homewood Inn. I noticed that it planned to be open in May, so I called immediately. A Mr. Webster came on the line. We established a sort of rapport. He'd gone to Williams, a Bowdoin rival, a starting point. He said he might have something that would suit us for a while. So we went to investigate. We found a tiny cottage on the shore of Casco Bay; from it, I could throw a fishing line out the window to catch supper. The place could hold all of us, if rather too snugly. It would do nicely until we found a house somewhere. We were thinking increasingly about living in Maine.

We discussed terms. I wound up giving Mr. Webster a check for five thousand dollars, just about our last money in the world, and told him we'd take the place until the end of October or so, which would give us enough time to locate a house. As far as I was concerned, it was a bargain, about one thousand dollars a month for three adults and three children, including board, for we took our meals in the main dining room.

We settled into the Homewood Inn in short order.

When we began house hunting, occasionally we would arrive late to the dining room for the evening meal and find that Mr. W. had sold our table. On those occasions, anyone who had come for dinner hoping for a peek at the Queen got both a peek and a performance. Bette would go through a routine that caused me to conclude that Mrs. W. had deliberately arranged it in order to build up trade. Word of mouth is the best way to sell tickets.

The Websters were fairly new to the trade, perhaps a bit overeager for success. Bette was sitting in the lounge near the registration desk one rainy morning, writing cards, when she overheard one of those notorious, white-haired, pearl-chokered, elderly Boston ladies say to Mr. Webster as she was checking out, "Mr. Webster, I want you to know that never have I been charged so much for so little."

It's possible he was trying to make up for what he felt he was losing on my family and me. I suspect that when he discovered my wife was Bette Davis, he hated himself for not charging twice the price. Movie stars are supposed to be loaded, right? Like everyone else, some are, some aren't; some handle money well, some don't. We belonged to the latter category. Bette and I had in common the skill of mishandling money.

In due course my Aunt Marion discovered an historic place for us, the oldest house in the nearby town of Windham. It was fairly remote, very quaint, and could be rented for seventy-five dollars a month. We settled for it, in case we'd be unable to locate a larger one near the ocean. The Windham house was quite small but adequate, so we had the furniture shipped out from California.

Very few pieces were placed inside the house, just enough to get by, and the rest was carried into an old barn, a rickety structure, but a shelter nevertheless. Bette arranged the furniture and played house, having to be reminded to rest when her nesting instincts ran away with her.

It was almost certain the company which insured our furniture would have shuddered had they seen the barn, but that bothered us not at all. I had learned about insurance companies, having lived in Hartford. They are basically odds-makers. At this time, Bette and I were involved with Lloyds of London, the biggest odds-makers in the world.

The year before we had come East, we were going over what finances we had and discussed dropping Bette's disability policy with Lloyds. It was a large policy with very large premiums, which were predicated on her salary at Warner Brothers at the peak of her career. The policy was to compensate her in case she was completely incapacitated. Fortunately, we continued the policy, and, seven months later, here she was, incapacitated for the first time in her life. We were receiving a good sum each month, our only income, but the Lloyds people were becoming disagreeable. Here was Bette, up and around, having a nice summer. Why didn't she get off her ass and go to work? Was she trying to best them out of money?

When Stanley Behrman performed the jaw surgery, he worked from the inside, so that no scars would be visible on the outside, and they weren't, although the nerves around the mouth had been badly damaged. It was an unreal sensation for Bette now to have no feeling around the lips and mouth, a sensation distinctly disconcerting for one so voluble. Stanley and the other doctors had clearly stipulated that for a time she shouldn't run a household, much less work on the stage. But the Boston Lloyds reps, with their suspicious nature, had her appear monthly at the Boston office, where they'd stick pins into her face to prove she wasn't fooling.

Finally, a letter was sent to her saying the company wanted to settle the case for a lump sum, but the lump turned out to be half the amount we were owed in total monthly payments. We were dumbfounded, and, of course, angry. I called a lawyer friend in New York, Charlie Ballon, who went over the situation. He suggested we settle. I screamed and said all lawyers were alike, and other uncomplimentary things, but he explained that by the time we got through fighting the case we'd spend all the money we might get in legal costs. We settled. The money saw us through until we both started working again that fall.

All that summer of 1953 we drove and drove, still looking for a house on the coast. We found one in Boothbay Harbor that we loved, but it wouldn't hold all of us. We weren't pressed because we could get by with the house in Windham if we had to. We spent many pleasant hours driving along roads, public and private, looking everywhere. One day we drove down a private dirt road and came upon a fine large house beside the ocean. It was remarkable.

"There it is!" I shouted. "That's it. A dream of a house! Why in hell are these kinds of places never for sale?"

The house was obviously inhabited, so we backed the car quietly out the drive, turned around, and left. I comforted Bette with, "Don't worry, we'll find one just like it."

About a week later, our real estate man called to say he had something we might like. Bette and I drove to his office. He said, "Follow me," as he jumped into his car, leading the way.

We followed along. Eventually he turned left on a dirt road in Cape Elizabeth. My heart started thumping. A minute later, there we were, at the house we'd loved when we had first seen it just a few days before. Magic! We offered the owner a rent for the winter, to be applied to the purchase price if we decided the place was right for us. We had spent many summers in Maine, but no winters as yet. We had learned to take one look before we leaped—but we needn't have worried. We found winters to be more exciting than the summers. The Atlantic Ocean is magnificent even in raging blizzards. It is a presence with a life of its own. It is as beautiful—but in a vastly different way—as on those summer days when the sea lies tranquil in the fog.

The house was on four or five acres, with the ocean for a front yard. Heaven! Bette named it "Witch Way," explaining, "A witch lives in it, and we don't know which way we're going."

So there we were in Maine, a couple of rolling stones who had finally rolled home. Here we could relax, and Bette could be as unglamorous as she pleased—wearing slacks and other Maine-style casual clothes. Our children would be brought up in Maine instead of Los Angeles. Neither of us wanted the children to be raised "Hollywood style," which meant offering material objects in place of love and attention. B.D. was of school age and was enrolled in Waynflete, a private coeducational school in Portland just a few miles away. Since several of the neighbors' children also attended the school, a car pool was arranged.

Bette was as pleased with the house as I and felt she could manage, but help with the children was most important. We found Elsa Stokes, who had raised two boys in Virginia until they had left home for school, after which she returned to Maine and semiretirement. The children called her "Coksie." I've had my share of luck in life, but Coksie was one of the high spots, and though she no doubt took a psychological beating during the years she spent with us, she gave Michael much of the mothering of which he was deprived.

Some adults cling to small cuddly babies. Not Bette, she didn't have much patience with them. She preferred the four-year-and-up age group, though she was convinced that as soon as children could speak they should be dealt with on an adult level. As Bette and I had more and more difficulties, she was apt to take out her frustrations and disappointments on Michael. In retaliation, I used B.D as a target for my discontent. In my defense, I must say that B.D. needed a great deal more disciplining than she had received. Though she was a hardheaded, stubborn little girl who was prone to come up with stories not based on fact, Bette rarely found fault with her, saying she had an active imagination. Coksie said she couldn't understand girls. Fortunately for Michael and me, she did understand men and boys, which offered security for Michael when I was away from home.

Our staff grew gradually when we found a woman to do some of the cooking and another to do the laundry and help out in a general way. Until then, Bette, who was a very competent housekeeper and cook, did the domestic chores—and liked doing it. She was thoroughly a nest builder. This got us through the first winter. But the next fall, having gone through a hurricane with a frightened cook, Bette said she needed a man in the house. We came up with the seemingly brilliant solution of trying to find couples and, adding up their days off, we figured we'd have the house to ourselves one full week out of four. We enjoyed our home but we didn't want to do all the work, nor could we, since one of us had to be away earning money. We would do turns. One of us would be home with the children. My first job after we started living in Maine was a TV series for David Susskind, "Justice." I flew to New York every Wednesday for rehearsal, and we did the show on Thursday evening. I returned to Maine by midnight of the same day. I discovered this was my ideal—two days' work and five off. This approach is one reason my career has been sporadic. (But the time off is what counts for me. When, in my sixties, I started doing a lot of commercials, it became four weeks of work and forty-eight off. Very bad for ambition, but not a bad deal.)

For the next year or two we ran, as I called it, "a transient hotel for help." Three or four couples came and went, and they were always gone when we needed them most. Once, when we'd been invited for a cruise along the coast, one couple had just been relieved of their duties, and so we were unable to go. The boat came by our cove for its crew to wave good-bye. We turned from the beautiful sailing vessel to go into the house to prepare dinner, and, as we walked across the lawn, we were both tearful from disappointment and frustration.

I think my favorite transients were a black couple who lasted about a month. The man was a lay minister who enjoyed being called "Reverend." I delighted in saying, "Rev, would you mix me a martini, please?"

The pattern was that Bette would hire but I'd have to fire. The discontent in the couples was, oddly, constant and very palpable. One would always claim he or she was doing most of the work; often the arguments at the back of the house, where the help lived, were more intense than those at the front. Probably some came to the house to be around Bette for a few days. Finally, I suggested we find a single man and a single woman for the jobs.

I went to the Portland railroad station to see my old friend Eddie Cummings, whom I called the unofficial mayor of Portland. Eddie was a grand man who'd been head porter at the station for years, hustling to put his kids through college. He knew practically everyone in the small city. Many of the summer visitors arrived in the state on the old State of Maine Express, from Philadelphia and New York or Boston, and either were dropped off at Portland or continued on down east to Bar Harbor. Eddie had helped me before, and this time I told him that we needed a man who could drive and take care of the house.

A couple of weeks later I saw a car come up the driveway. It was Eddie Cummings and beside him in the passenger seat was a smiling black man named LeRoy Thomas. LeRoy had been a dining-car waiter. He had seen the demise of railroad dining cars looming and was looking for another kind of job. He said he knew how to serve, he knew how to drive, and wanted to try out for the job. He preferred being called "Thomas," he said. Finally, we had luck! He was jolly, loved kids, loved gardening, and became a wonderful butler. We were in heaven with all the fresh vegetables he produced from a plot of ground he restored to a lush garden.

Domestically, we were almost there. With the addition of Ogletha, a lovely young black woman who cooked like a dream and enjoyed experimenting with new dishes, we finally got the household running smoothly, and with people we loved and respected. No more argumentive married couples to contend with. In that category, Bette and I filled the bill.

We bought the house. With the change of name on the deed, it followed that we would begin implementing our ideas for the place. One of the first things we did was to add a pond. I had noticed a swampy area behind the house that looked promising and sought advice from the state geologist. It proved possible to bulldoze the depression into a basin to collect water from a natural spring as well as rainfall. Most homes in the countryside benefit from a pond as a form of fire protection, but my design had other dimensions: I envisioned a trout pond in summer and a hockey rink in winter.

An area by the barn/garage was fenced in. Now that we were country folk, we wanted to have a few animals. We started with a couple of sheep, which, when sheared, eventually provided sweaters for all of us. Then came the baby goat. B.D. had been sick at Eastertime, and I bought it to cheer her up. When I brought it home I let it run down the hall to her room. She was delighted. Being a novice about such things, I didn't realize it was a male and that males become odoriferous. That goat was something else! Bette and I often walked our few acres, stretching our legs and enjoying our new role as landowners . . . and one warm summer day, as we walked by the fenced area, she turned to me and said, "Gary, I thought I told you to take a shower!" I had been playing golf and *had* taken a shower.

"Bette, that's not me, it's the goat. He's in heat. Jesus, I hope I never smelled like that!"

The children named the sheep but weren't particularly attached to them, which surprised me somewhat, but it was just as well. They never became upset when the time came for lamb chops or mutton stew. They would say, calmly, "I wonder if we're eating Mark or Luke."

Eventually, B.D. was given a horse that she had asked for. She learned to ride as well as to care for the animal. The next addition to the menagerie was a burro. We had seen an advertisement and ordered one, giving no thought to how it might be delivered. We assumed that those details would be taken care of. Imagine our surprise when we received a phone call from the train station: Our burro had arrived at the depot, and would we mind coming to pick it up?

Every self-respecting farm has a pickup truck. We had a black Cadillac convertible. I put the top down, rounded up the kids, and off we went to pick up the burro. At the train depot, we hauled and pushed and got the burro into the backseat. The kids piled in, and with me driving, we rode through the city of Portland with the burro. He was a very good passenger and sat there with his ears flying in the breeze, giving us no trouble at all.

But we found that he was one mean burro. When he was in the fenced area with the other animals he ran after the sheep, bit the goat, and kicked at the horse. This earned him a separate fenced area, but he didn't stay around long—we found a farmer to take him off our hands.

During our animal acquisition period, the interior of

125

the house was being altered. Eaton Tarbell, my Bowdoin buddy and architect friend from Bangor, had drawn up a remarkable set of plans for opening it up. An old screened porch was glassed in to extend the living room. The windows framed the ocean, creating living paintings of the sea. Walls were removed, bookcases replaced, and the porch which opened off our bedroom was enclosed with screens so we could sleep there on warm summer nights. The effect was like being on a boat without the movement. The sound and smell of the sea were truly amazing.

(It always astonishes me to find sophisticated people who cling to the idea of primitive simplicity when they think of Maine. Bette and I attended a party in New York and ran into Doris and Jules Stein. Jules was the founder of MCA. Doris asked how we liked living in Maine, and then, in all seriousness, asked, "Do you have central heating?" It took awhile, but I responded, "We were lucky enough to find one of the only houses around that has it.")

A year or so after we had moved into the house, a few leaks developed which made it necessary to replace the roof. Bette was working in California at the time, so I discussed the problem with the roofer. He'd given me a price for asphalt shingles as well as for the wooden ones we both preferred. I called Bette to explain that the roofer had said the asphalt would last a lifetime, but the wooden shingles would probably last only twenty years. Bette laughed and said, "Put on the wooden shingles. As far as I'm concerned, twenty years *is* a lifetime."

That was a typical remark when she was in top form. Bette is a very bright lady. Thus, her short circuits were incandescent. It was almost a compulsion with her to create scenes. I remember a party where she had created an unusually acidic scene that caught everyone, including me, by surprise. The hostess said to me, "What did I say? What did I do?" I honestly didn't know. The next day Bette felt remorse and sent an apology, by way of flowers and a note.

The years at "Witch Way," regardless of such difficulties, were the years I loved most. My love of the elements—especially stirred by the winter seas glimpsed through the windows of the living room, the tremendous waves battering themselves against the rocks—reinforced for me the rightness of our decision to move back to Maine. The Pacific at Malibu served its purpose by helping me forget that I was in sterile Los Angeles, which was basically a desert. If the water were turned off for a month, Los Angeles would blow away. Most of the greenery there has been transplanted. The constant sun, the lack of seasonal variety, always made me hunger for New England's changing seasons.

But there was a shadow over these years. When Margot had been just a tiny thing, she had cried a lot and wasn't easily mollified. I'd said, "All kids are different—don't worry, she'll grow out of it," and we just went along. But she didn't grow out of it. She had amazing stamina, refused to take naps, and seemed never to sleep. I couldn't imagine where such a small child could find the energy to just go on and on. Our pediatrician suggested she be taken to New York to have some tests done. After a number of tests, the conclusion was that she was brain damaged and would be a retarded child, though the doctors were unable to determine how far she might progress. I discovered later that her mother had been an alcoholic, which may well have been a contributing factor to her condition, but we hadn't known anything of this when we adopted her.

The doctors suggested a home for her, the Lochland School in upstate New York, but I resisted, thinking we could manage by ourselves. A little vest was made for her, which could be attached to the bed, to keep her in, and when she finally understood that she was secure, unable to climb out of bed, she began to nap. We got along with that for a while, but, placed as she was between two very bright children, her deficiencies were magnified. She wasn't able to keep up with them, and her frustration resulted in temper tantrums that were difficult to control. She was quite strong—though never strong enough to hurl furniture about, as B.D. suggested in her book, *My Mother's Keeper.* But she did manage to knock things over.

When she was about three the doctors again suggested we look into the Lochland School in Geneva, New York, which was run by Florence Stewart.

We were by then devastated by Margot's misfortune. We also realized that if anything happened to us (flying back and forth across the country as we did), there would be no one to care for her. It should never be B.D.'s or Michael's problem to cope with, but ours, and we decided to visit the school.

The setting was lovely, a big old Victorian house on a sloping lawn near a lake—but, God, it was depressing. Miss Stewart had about twenty kids there, one or two of them with Down's Syndrome, and all of them quite handicapped in some way. Our Margot was a beautiful child, a doll, with no outward signs of anything amiss. We didn't know what to do. We talked with Miss Stewart and she said, "Let me take your number. I'll call you."

Weeks went by with no word, but finally we got a letter from Miss Stewart in which she said, "I don't take anyone until I visit their home. I would like to spend a few days with you."

The visit was arranged and Miss Stewart came to stay with us. We had long talks that convinced me she was a caring person who could take Margot in and give her what we weren't trained to do. After she left, we heard nothing for a while. Bette became upset and said, "What the hell is going on?" Finally Miss Stewart got in touch to say that she would take Margot. We agreed it was the best thing.

"I can't drive her to the home," Bette said. "It's an eight-hour drive from Portland."

That's when I first met Hal Katz, the one-eyed pilot. Hal was a wonder. Everyone had told him it was impossible for him to get a pilot's license with his handicap, but he learned how to adjust so that when he took his examination no one was able to detect that he had sight in only one eye.

(He was an amazing man with great spirit, a person who never complained even when cancer of the bone made it painful for him to walk. When he died, he left me, along with five other friends, a small bequest, with this explanation: "I give, devise, and bequeath equally to the following named dear friends, if they survive me, all of whom are persons inclined to do nice things for other people . . ." He was one of the good people.)

I chartered Hal to take us to Geneva. Bette dressed Margot in an exquisite little dress, and we flew to the small airstrip near the home. As I looked at her, after saying goodbye, she looked so pretty, so normal—but, of course, she was not. Leaving Margot at her new home was extremely difficult. Miss Stewart said, "Remember, it's tougher on you than it is on Margot. We'll do what we can. She'll be fine."

That was in 1954, and Margot has been living there since then.

In the winter there was hockey on the pond. There were enough players around to enable us to have wonderful games. Those of us in the neighborhood came up with a title, "The Icemanship Society of Cape Elizabeth." I called Blaine Davis, a sports reporter at the *Portland Press Herald*, to let him know we wanted to organize some competition. He was a real hockey buff, but in those days there was not much hockey being played around Portland. There were few rinks and no televised games; hockey had fallen on hard times.

The following Sunday, I read in Davis's column, "The Icemanship Society of Cape Elizabeth challenges Falmouth Foreside and other outlying communities to a hockey match." Falmouth Foreside, a community to the north of Portland, was the "Gold Coast" of Portland. On Cape Elizabeth at the time, there were mostly farmers and lobstermen, though it, too, was becoming a well-to-do bedroom community.

This original challenge in Davis's column was followed by another, which claimed that we trained on cracked ice. This got a lot of attention. Henry Payson called to say that a group from Falmouth would arrive the following Sunday to test our skills. Bette decided to get into the act on behalf of her pet charity, the Children's Theatre of Portland, so the hockey match became a charity event. Balloons were filled with helium, chestnuts were roasted in the outdoor fireplace, and a cocktail bar was set up where Bette could collect donations.

The Falmouth group arrived. Hank Payson had assembled everyone he could find who had ever skated—brokers, doctors, lawyers, and even some retirees, a group ranging in age from seventeen to fifty. I was around thirty-eight or thirty-nine then, and our team ranged in age from me on down. I recall that our Icemanship Society won the hard-fought game.

At one point, when I was off the ice, Bette ran up to me.

"The guests are drinking all the booze."

"So what?" I asked, "Aren't they contributing?"

"Yes, but there won't be enough left for the home team."

I sent for more. That was the kind of game it was.

At the end of the day, the men from Falmouth wanted to join our team. Hank Payson is an ebullient, gregarious man. We joined forces and formed a better team, which Blaine Davis named "Merrill's Marauders." All the players had businesses or worked in Portland: Bob Jurgenson had a fish business; Hank Payson had an insurance company; Bobby Porteous had Portland's major department store, Porteous, Mitchell & Braun; Sonny Morrill worked in his family baked-beans business, Burnham & Morrill; Robinson Cooke (the goalie) had an insurance business; Parker Poole had the Shurtleff salt business; and John Robinson had the C. H. Robinson Paper Company. Most of these were old family concerns, but there were those of us who were just workers. I was the only gypsy.

By no stretch of the imagination could we have been described as hockey professionals, but most had played in school. We were challenged by teams from all over the state, and, since Maine's population has a large proportion of French Canadians, well known for their skills on the ice, we were defeated a few times. No matter, the games were beyond imagination—full of fun, sometimes expert skating, and always bruised shins and elbows. We wore no helmets, no padding, just an extra layer of clothing to provide warmth.

Eaton Weatherbee Tarbell brought a team down from Bangor, a hundred and fifty miles northeast of Cape Elizabeth. They arrived in a Greyhound-type bus and provided us with one of the biggest games on the pond at Zeb's Cove. In those days, the elite of the business world still formed clubs. Good restaurants were all but nonexistent in Maine, except for those that served shore dinners, and these were open only during the summer season. Eaton was a member of the Tarratine Club of Bangor, and that day he supposedly brought the club "members" to play hockey with us. The snow began to fall as the game got under way. Within seconds of the face-off, Bangor scored the first point, and, within a short period, scored again. Our team was at a loss—we were playing fairly well, we thought, but

Bangor scored again and again. We were no match.

I buttonholed Eaton. "For Chrissake, Eaton, some of those Tarratine Club members must have joined the club as they entered the bus. I'll bet they retire from the club when they get off again at Bangor."

Eaton may have sprinkled a few Tarratine Club members into the mix, but I swear that the rest were ringers, most likely from the farm team of the Montreal Canadiens. He didn't deny a thing. We lost badly, but it was a great game.

Our team stayed together until we began playing indoors on the Bowdoin College hockey rink. After hearing those pucks booming into the boards, we realized it wasn't shinny hockey in the fields anymore. We gradually dropped out.

During one of the last games at Bowdoin one of the players asked me to speak to Cookie, the goalie, because he was having a drink or two. I found Cookie and asked, "What goes?"

He said, "You don't think I'm going in there sober do you?" That response took care of further complaints. I think we won that game.

Many of the hockey team members belonged to Portland's staid Cumberland Club, and, in order to stay in touch as well as to enjoy the good food, I thought I might as well join. I found a sponsor. He prepared me for the interview, when I would be asked questions about associations, clubs I belonged to, and that sort of thing. "I'm not much of a joiner," I told him, "but I do belong to several unions."

My sponsor cautioned, "We don't mention that."

Possibly I was the only member of a union to belong to the Cumberland Club, and the same might be true at the Portland Country Club, which I also joined. The country club provided Bette and me with many diversions, and I returned the favor. Its members were a conservative group, with codes for just about everything. One late summer's day, after I had just returned from Los Angeles, a board member informed me that my club privileges were being revoked. I was stunned, and of course asked him why.

"You took a shower in the ladies' locker room!"

Weeks before, there had been a Fourth of July golf tournament and these businessmen had shed their inhibitions and reverted to adolescent madness. They set off firecrackers on the green, and the tournament became a lark instead of a competition.

In the shower room a cherry bomb was set off, blasting ear drums and creating pandemonium. (Those conservative types are a bit scary when they let loose.) I stepped out of the men's locker room with a towel around my waist and asked if there was anyone in the ladies' locker room. No, no ladies were around. So I had used the ladies' shower. I found their locker room to be well decorated, with wicker chairs, scented soaps, and so on, and it was considerably neater and more stylish than the men's.

After my explanation, instead of my being kicked out, renovations were begun in the men's locker room.

At the club, my outfits were always on the casual side, but on one occasion I arrived for my golf date in a skirt, which I like to wear on warm days, and I had bare feet. This sent a flurry of comments wafting through the club chambers. I wasn't wearing colorful trousers and stout golf shoes. Though my golf game is fairly respectable, the skirt and my bare feet got the attention. I received a letter of censure from the club's board. Now, I must wear shoes.

Beginning with the hockey team, Bette and I were able to meet the local worthies. We made many fine friends, among them Prout's Neck's most conservative patriarch, Shaw Sprague. I had come home to Witch Way after one of my jobs, and Bette greeted me with the news that she had met Shaw Sprague at a cocktail party. She had told him that

I'd spent many of my summers on Prout's Neck, but he couldn't recall having met me.

Bette had told him, "Of course you don't remember him. He was your caddy."

I remembered Shaw—a great, rugged, athletic, bonny guy—and, despite our very different political and social outlooks, we hit it off. He lived on several thousand acres. His house was brick and glass, with a saltwater pool that was refreshed when storms broke waves into it. Offshore rode his eighty-five-foot yacht, the *Lion's Whelp*, and in the fields was a beautiful herd of cows, which produced the rich Devonshire cream that graced his table. Shaw lived exactly as I would if I had his money. His house was on the southeastern coast of the Cape, ours on the northeastern. I told Shaw, "You're the king of Cape Elizabeth, and I'm the crown prince!"

Along with several other couples, Shaw and his wife, Jenny, were guests at Witch Way one Thanksgiving, and Shaw suggested the group get together for New Year's Eve at his house, an idea we all agreed to.

A few days later I called Jenny and told her to discourage Shaw from trying to provide musicians. I wanted to provide the music as a late Christmas gift. I asked her to convince Shaw that records would do just as well, but reassured her that I'd get the musicians.

But I found that musicians are booked for New Year's Eve well before Thanksgiving. There was no one available for my party. I was doing "Justice," commuting to New York every week, and since MCA was my agent, I turned to the greatest talent agency in the world. Eleanor Kilgallen, Dorothy's sister, was my personal representative. Once, when no one knew where I was—I was sailing the New England coast—she found me by using citizen's band radio. I trusted her abilities, and now laid my dilemma at her door.

Two weeks before Christmas she called: "A terrific musician has been touring abroad, in Europe. He's just returned and wants to do something over the holidays in the way of a job. He plays the trumpet. His name is Jonah Jones, and he's good. How about it?"

"Damned right." I hadn't heard of Jonah Jones, but if Eleanor said he was all right, he was. Jonah went to work locating a few of his musician friends to fill in, and I had my combo. It was going to be a great New Year's Eve!

We had a tradition of interesting starts to the year. I recalled the first year we moved to Maine. Bette and I had settled into Witch Way, but we knew very few people in the area. We looked at each other and asked, "What shall we do for New Year's Eve?"

Then we'd thought of a couple of friends in Quebec, Mark and Lucille Donohue, whom we'd met on the *Queen Elizabeth* on our trip to England, and we called to see if they could join us. They couldn't, but immediately asked, "What is to stop you from coming up here?"

The weather held for us on the trip to Murray Bay, and our visit was the best tonic imaginable. On the way back, we ran into a blizzard and were forced to spend a cold, snowy night at the Jackman Hotel, just across the Maine border. As we sat in the lounge waiting for a bite to eat, in walked a Maine woodsman, tall and lean, wearing an old sheepskin coat. He ambled to a nearby table.

"What you doin' out on a night like this, Joe?" the woman behind the desk asked. As the two of them talked, we learned that the fellow was Emile Beaudoin of Bingham, a French Canadian whom the locals called "Joe Bean." He was on his way to Quebec, in the driving blizzard, to borrow money from a relative to buy a piece of woodland. The woman kidded him about his thick accent, so I spoke up, inviting him to our table. "Come on over. My wife speaks some French," I told him, and he came over to sit with us.

He told us about the land he wanted to buy—some timber lots he wanted to work during the winter along Wyman Lake. It was one of the prettiest places around, he told us—and I immediately pictured having a hunting lodge on a remote lake. I offered to lend him the money for the land and gave him a check for fifteen hundred dollars. He said he'd show us the land the next morning, and I could take back the check if I wished.

By the following morning the storm had subsided and we followed his Jeep along a narrow, snow-banked highway. When he finally stopped, we saw that Wyman Lake was on the right and on the left were the snow-laden trees on a steep embankment, and up and up and up over the hillside, as far as I could see, were more trees. I walked to where he was standing near his Jeep and he turned his back on the lake, pointing up the small mountain, describing the woodlots he wanted with the sweep of his arm up, up toward the top. It wasn't at all what I had imagined—a rustic lodge nestled in pine woods, with the lake a short distance away. You'd have to be a mountain goat to get to a place level enough to build on.

I looked back at Bette, who was sitting in the car. She was laughing her head off, knowing it wasn't at all what I had had in mind. But I said that I'd go through with the deal anyway, and I've owned it jointly—now with one of Emile Beaudoin's sons—ever since. A day or so later, the Bangor paper headlined: "Hollywood Couple Buys Land in Moscow, Maine." Eaton Tarbell called us at Witch Way and asked, "Who got loaded in Jackman the other night?"

Now, as another New Year's Eve approached, I was looking forward to my surprise for Shaw Sprague. I heard that Jean Arthur was in New York. Bette and Jean hadn't met, so I asked Bette if we might invite Jean to Witch Way over New Year's. Jean was a reticent lady, but she surprised me by agreeing. She would become my *piéce de résistance* for

Shaw's New Year's surprise.

I had to work in New York up to the last minute and had to take the last plane to Maine. I asked Jonah and his group to meet me at LaGuardia. Jean and I arrived together and greeted Jonah. He pulled me aside and asked, "Who's the chick? The vocalist?"

The next morning Jenny Sprague and I planned Jonah's appearance at the party to the last detail while Bette talked to her about seating arrangements. As a thoughtful hostess, she selected a witty, intelligent friend who was one of the leading neurosurgeons in Portland as a suitable dinner companion for Jean—a notable and amiable conversationalist who would make her feel comfortable.

Alas, when finally the dinner took place, the good doctor decided this was his night to howl and celebrated with too many before-dinner libations. He didn't even finish his soup before he dropped into it.

With relief I noticed the butler having a word with Jenny: Her cue to announce that coffee was being served in the living room, a ploy to allow Jonah and his musicians to set up in the dining room, once the tables and chairs had been cleared away.

Jonah was to begin with "When the Saints Go Marching In," playing softly in imitation of a recording, then building up his volume as the musicians marched into the living room.

The guests were sipping coffee convivially and chatting as Jonah's group began to play, and Shaw remarked that "the records were great." I watched as his eyes grew round with disbelief at the increased volume, then filled with amazement as five musicians marched into and around the living room. Everyone was amazed—there were whoops of delight and general astonishment.

The party was in full swing, with much dancing and laughing, when Jean, quite solemn, called me aside. Shaw's advances were getting to her. She couldn't put up with it and wanted to go home. I drove her to Witch Way, returned to the party, and continued to have a hell of a good time. Jean took off first thing the next morning. "You and your rich friends!" was the last thing she said.

We did have some rich friends, and everyone thought Bette and I were rich, too. But we weren't—not in the way they were. These old Yankee families had it socked away in banks, real estate, or other investments, and a bright accountant watched every penny.

In 1955, Bette went to the coast to make *The Virgin Queen*. It was her first movie since we'd moved to Witch Way, and she decided the premier should be in Portland to benefit the Children's Theatre. There was quite a crowd at the old Strand Theater. It was the first world premier this little city had ever seen. Faye Emerson and Jinx Falkenberg came to Maine, and so did a few other stars of the day, such as Tom Ewell. More than two thousand people attended, and when we got the books straightened out about six months later, we sent the Children's Theatre a check for seven thousand dollars. That's more than we raised at the hockey games passing the hat, but we made the most of our friends on those Sundays by the pond with the fire going and the booze flowing.

I tried to savor the full Maine experience. Two of my hockey friends, Bob Jurgenson and Bob Cooke, were hunters. They thought I, too, should try it. "Well, I'm here in Maine. I see all these guys with their red caps and shot-guns. Maybe I better get a gun and learn to hunt," my reasoning went.

Strolling around the woods and fields near our place were a few pheasant that Bob and Jurgy had been scouting for weeks before the season opened. On the first day of the hunting season, they came to the house to pick me up. We walked just a few hundred yards and Bang! Jurgy brought one down. A few more steps and Pow! There went another. Cooke got him. "These guys have sure done their homework," I thought. With two birds down, we stepped to the side of the road for a smoke. Jurgy put the two pheasants on the hood of the car.

Two other hunters came strolling along and saw the birds. One of them said, "Wow, those are nice-looking birds. Where did you get them?"

I lifted my arm, about to point, and said, "Right ov. . ." when Jurgy's big boot crashed down on my instep so hard I thought he'd broken my foot. I started hopping around, and the other two guys walked off.

"For God's sakes, Merrill," Jurgy said. "Don't you know enough not to tell anyone else where we got our birds? Don't tell anything to other hunters, ever." I was learning how to hunt.

The following week, when I was starting to drive B.D. to school one morning, a pheasant walked across the driveway just in front of us.

"Wait right here, B.D.," I said. "I'm going to the house to get my gun." I trotted back, loaded up, and walked back to the brush where I had seen the bird go in. Sure enough, I flushed him out and shot him. He fell on the road.

He was so lovely. I went over and picked him up. It was the first time I realized that when you hunt, you kill. As I looked down at the beautiful creature limp in my hands, I knew my hunting days were over. I hadn't thought hard enough about what was happening when Jurgy and Bob killed their birds. It was just something Maine men did. I knew I couldn't go along with it.

I didn't mind trapping a few lobsters, though— another Maine activity I got into with Jurgy. He had a license—I didn't. But I had a little skiff to row out to the four or five traps that we tended. There was a lobster car secured to the rocks on shore. Every day or so I'd row out and lift the traps, most of the time with Jurgy along—he made it legal. So I thought.

Generally, we took care to measure our catch, and tried not to take undersized lobsters, the "shorts." But once, when we had a big dinner party coming up, Jurgy and I were keeping just about everything in the traps to feed the guests. On the morning before the party, out we went to collect dinner, lifting and dumping the traps into the boat, and soon the bottom of the skiff was pretty well covered with lobsters—most of them "shorts." I had just started to row toward the shore when I heard a whistle.

"What's that?" I asked.

"It's a warden," Jurgy told me, with this strange look on his face.

"Where is he?"

"He's waiting right on the rocks."

"Shit!" I eased my pace a bit. "What do we do now?"

"Let's tip the boat over," he said. His solution for getting rid of the evidence would have put us into the iciest water this side of the North Pole—and I wasn't ready for that.

"We can talk him out of it," I said, rowing straight ashore.

The warden looked at the boat. "Some of those lobsters are undersize," he said calmly. He measured each one, and put the shorts on the rocks one at a time, counting them.

"Got quite a few shorts here."

"Yeah, okay, now that you know, now that they're all counted, toss them back in the boat," I said.

He gave me a hard look.

"These are evidence," he said. "We're going to have to confiscate every one." Then he asked me if I had a license, and things went from bad to worse. Jurgy just stood there, shifting from one foot to the other.

The warden collected the shorts, the evidence, and walked off with the last we saw of much of the evening's menu. I was in big trouble—no license, short lobsters. It was going to cost me. The only break was that the warden never thought to open the lobster car floating in the shallow water. He had his foot propped on it while he was grabbing the shorts from the skiff. If he had lifted the lid on the car, he would have found about twenty more shorts.

I went into Portland to discuss the situation with a lawyer, Joe Pierce, a Bowdoin fraternity brother. After I'd given him the details, he asked, "Gary, do you want to play this up or down?"

I said we'd better play it down and pay the fine. It was a whopping one, and during the dinner party I kept thinking how much the lobster we had left had cost me— something like fifty bucks apiece.

I did a bit of lobstering once in a while after that, once I got the proper license, and I was always careful about the shorts. After a year or so I realized that I was cutting into the lobstermen's domain. The fellows out there every day were trying to earn a living, and I was just fooling around. And I was encouraging the decline of an important resource. So I stopped.

We did not spend all of our time in Maine during the fifties. Our finances wouldn't allow it. It was always nip and tuck with our bills.

Once, when I was taking off for California for a job, Bette said, "Don't you come back without a business manager." I made the rounds, interviewing several. I remembered that John Wayne had hired a manager who had made so many bad investments that at one time Wayne, who had a tremendous income, was almost broke. So it was not without some trepidation that I approached business managers.

Then I found Alexander Tucker.

After hiring him, I walked into his Los Angeles office with a barracks bag full of old bills, tax statements, cancelled checks. Unceremoniously, I dumped the whole pile on his floor. A day or two later, he called.

"Do you two gamble?" he asked. I said, "No."

"Do you go to nightclubs a lot, use dope?" Again I assured him that we didn't.

"Then you must have a bunch of women on the side."

I said, "No, Tucker, none of that stuff. We spend money more imaginatively. We blow it on a big place in Maine, hiring orchestras, chartering yachts . . . things like that."

"Well," Tucker said, "You're in the hole pretty deep. You'd better get around Hollywood and mingle. Pick up some work fast."

In 1957 Bette, the children, and I left Maine for California, letting it be known we were on the scene. Our professional lives were enhanced by this move, but our personal lives weren't. Our marriage was having a rougher and rougher time. We thought we'd be civilized—have a trial separation, break it gently to the children. We were sure they would understand.

I went back to Maine after a while, but Bette stayed in California with the children and began the search for suitable living space. While she was being shown a house by a real estate agent, she opened a door which she thought was a closet, stepped in, and fell down a steep set of cellar stairs—twenty feet onto a concrete floor. She broke her back. When I heard about it, I convinced her she should recuperate in Maine. That was the end of our trial separation. It was an extremely painful time for her, but she was a tough lady. Six months later she was in New York appearing on a television show.

The following year, we were together again back in California, intent on mingling once more, and again in search of a place to live. Beverly Hills was where the best schools were. We started out in an apartment in the "rich man's tenement district" between Santa Monica and Sunset Boulevards, but, with kids, we realized we had to get a house. While we trailed behind a realtor, going from room to room in one Beverly Hills mansion, I had the eerie feeling that I had seen the place somewhere before. Eventually, as we looked around, it began to dawn on us that indeed we had. Photos of some of the rooms had been in all the newspapers. This was Lana Turner's house, the place where Lana's daughter had shot and killed her mother's lover only three days before! The real estate agency had been so anxious to rent it that the bloodied mattress hadn't been removed before people began to troop through.

"Let's get the hell out of here!" I said.

We looked at another place on Hanover Drive, a great old mansion, done in Art Deco style, which had once belonged to a silent movie actress. Apparently, Art Deco was no longer in vogue, reflected by a rent of only seven hundred fifty dollars. It had a huge living room, a den, bar, and tennis court—typical Hollywood excess. Thomas and Ogletha had come with us, along with the two children, and since we needed a lot of space we took it. My friends were delighted with the tennis courts but wouldn't let me play because I wasn't good enough. They felt no remorse about making me sit and watch. I got in some practice on my own.

But we were here to mingle—something neither Bette nor I had cared about in the past. One night Bette went off to a producer's party and returned about midnight. "They're all fatter and richer and stupider than ever," she announced. So much for her mingling!

Later that week I went to a party at Leon Shamroy's.

He was one of Hollywood's most brilliant cameramen, with Oscars coming out of his ears—a gruff, cigar-smoking man with a crude surface. He had been responsible for shooting *Twelve O'Clock High.*

During that film I'd had trouble finding my "marks"—chalk marks or pieces of tape on the floor that tell the actor where to stand or move or stop. These were positioned for the lighting. After the director and actors had rehearsed the action, stand-ins took over while the cameraman had the scene lit.

There's a knack to playing a scene and hitting the marks without being obvious about it. Later, with more experience, I could hit the marks by feeling the heat of the key light on my face.

But on the set of *Twelve O'Clock High,* Shamroy had said to me, "Get on the mark."

"I'm on the mark!" I yelled back.

Then during another rehearsal, he yelled, "You're not on your mark."

"I'm standing on it!" I shouted.

"Well, toe it then," he instructed.

He gently took me aside. He told me that he lit so tightly that if I didn't toe the mark, I would be standing slightly out of the light. He told me this quietly—his way of saying he liked me and was only trying to help. That started a long friendship of fondness and respect. I found that his gruffness was a front for a warm, sentimental, well-edu-cated guy. One of his best friends was Henry Miller.

So there I was, at Shamroy's party. Among the guests was Henry Ephron, who had become very success-ful as a screenwriter. Henry had begun his career in New York as one of George Kaufman's and Moss Hart's stage managers. Years before any of us had come to California, I was one of a group of actors who had agreed to rehearse a play of Henry's one Sunday night, as a showcase for it. We were all established as performers by then, but we did it as a favor for Ephron.

I found myself in the kitchen with Henry and asked him, "Now that you're such a successful writer and director, why haven't you hired any of those people who helped you all those years ago when you were starting out and needed a helping hand?"

My question, not surprisingly, made him defensive.

"What do you mean? I do when the part is right."

"Crap," I said, and continued to harass him, accusing him of forgetting his friends now that he had become successful.

Then I wandered off. Sometime later Shamroy came up to me and asked what I had done to Henry.

"What do you mean?" I asked, not thinking I had said anything extraordinary.

"He just left," Shamroy said, "and implied that you had called him a stupid ingrate."

Too bad if he couldn't stand the heat, I thought. A few days later, while chatting with a talented writer named Arnie Manhoff, I told him the story of the party and my talk with Henry Ephron.

Arnie said, "Gary, the word is *mingle,* not *mangle!*"

This was one of the scenes which gave me a certain notoriety in Hollywood.

To compound our financial troubles, I got a notice from the Internal Revenue Service. The government told me I owed them fifty thousand dollars in back taxes. Where was I going to get fifty grand? I hadn't paid attention to taxes, thinking the studios were taking it out of our checks. Now the government said that if we didn't pay up they were going to take the house in Maine, the one place I loved, the place I wanted to return to.

My Aunt Marion was ill, and there was a possibility she was dying. I wanted to fly back to Maine to see her and suggested to Bette that, while I was there, I'd visit George Pew to ask for a loan. Bette said, "Geez, if you've got the guts, go ahead." So I took a plane to Portland and after seeing Aunt Marion, who really was quite ill, I went to see George Pew (of the Sun Oil Pews), one of the friends I had made through hockey games and dinners in Cape Elizabeth. He couldn't believe we needed the money. Like everyone else, he was certain Bette and I were millionaires.

"George," I said, "the government is going to take my house if we don't come up with the money before this week is out."

The next morning he took me to his bank, where he sold some stock to cover the loan, wrote a check for fifty thousand dollars payable to the IRS, and said, "Here, Gary, you can pay me back five thousand a year at four and a half percent interest each year."

I flew back to Los Angeles and gave the check to the IRS agent the next morning. And that was the last time I had any of that sort of trouble. From that period on, Tucker took care of the finances until the day he died. His company continues to do the same fine job. I never see my paychecks, just as I never see any of the bills. But they let me know when I have to hustle to keep up.

Our finances improved, but Aunt Marion did not. She died that fall.

7

IT'S A BUMPY ROAD

N ot long after I had moved to Maine, after four years and a fair number of movies, Twentieth Century Fox terminated my contract. I didn't mind. I was living where I wanted to and loving every minute.

In 1953 I made *Witness to Murder* with Barbara Stanwyck and an old friend from *All About Eve*, George Sanders. Early one morning, as we waited around in that endless, boring period before shooting begins, I commented to George, "Don't you wish you were born rich?"

George replied, "The trouble is, I was." His family was aristocratic White Russian.

Typically, Hollywood cast him in to-the-manor-born parts, which really didn't require acting on his part, though he was terrific in his portrayals. On this occasion, he proceeded to bemoan the fact that he was going to New York in August to make a picture.

"How am I going to survive the horrible muggy heat of New York in August?" He stretched out his long legs, crossed them at the ankles, and continued. "Besides, no one is there in August . . . they're sensibly at the shore . . . anywhere but the city."

"Stop worrying, for Chrissake, George. The hotel is air-conditioned, the studio will be air-conditioned. It won't be too bad," I told him, only too aware of how bad it really would be. "Not only that," I droned on, "you'll probably be supplied with an air-conditioned car . . ." George interrupted me with his droll accent, "Yes, but dear boy, how do I get from the hotel to the car?"

George was married to Zsa Zsa Gabor at the time, but he was basically a loner. He had an active, intelligent mind and dabbled with scientific experiments at home—though, when he committed suicide, supposedly it was from sheer boredom.

About that period, my agent got me a role in my first western, *The Missouri Traveler,* with Lee Marvin, Paul Ford, newcomer Mary Hosford, and Brandon DeWilde. I had known Brandon since he was a precocious four-year-old, and here he was, my co-star. I played the role of a newspaper editor who stirred up trouble. In this movie I didn't have to get too involved with horses, but then came *The Black Dakotas,* a real "oater," and I had work a lot more than I wanted on the back of a horse. But since I worked only ten days and made over fifteen thousand dollars doing this second-rater, I figured, "Hell, what an easy way to make a living."

I told my agent, "Get me more jobs like this!"

"One more like this and you'll never work again," he replied.

And then there were the television jobs to keep me going. In New York during the fifties, those TV dramas were all performed live. It was like being on the stage again, though the tension was greater. There was no leeway for the actor. The sinister camera found each miscue, each misstep or wrong pause. We would rehearse for a week or two, depending on the length of the show. And the dress rehearsal took place no more than an hour or two before air time. Since the sponsor and his advertising agency people hovered around the set, the dress rehearsals were as crucial as the live show itself.

When a large company footed the bill, it also claimed the right to make comments and even changes at the last minute, which the producer would invariably be forced to comply with. These changes were sometimes so absurd as to be devastating.

On one show, "The U.S. Steel Hour," I was playing the part of a big businessman named Kaiser, who had nothing to do with steel. But the representatives of U.S. Steel found the name unacceptable—wasn't Henry J. Kaiser a prominent steel company competitor? And wouldn't the use of that name, even in a totally different context, afford their rival a lot of free promotion on a show U.S. Steel was sponsoring? Or was it possible that the ad agency vice president, sitting there in the booth, became afraid that some top executive might think of it that way—which would cause the ad agency, or even himself, to be fired for allowing the blunder?

The result was that the director said, "A small change in the script here, everyone. Gary's name will not be 'Kaiser.' It's been changed to 'Cotler.' Everybody got that?"

This announcement was made less than five minutes before live air time. A sponsor couldn't have found a better way to screw up a production if it tried.

Most of the responsibility for remembering the name change would be on the other actors' shoulders, I thought. But when the show went on the air, I had to answer a phone and identify myself. Of course, I fumbled— and felt like a fool trying to remember my own name!

I played in dozens of such shows, many of them of superior quality, better than most TV fare today. There was the "Philco-Goodyear Playhouse," "Studio One," "Theater Guild of the Air," "Playhouse 90." Plays were performed that would astonish modern TV viewers. No one got murdered, raped, or mangled. The content usually concerned the problems of ordinary people, but transformed to wonderful drama.

Hollywood was losing ground at the box office to this new free entertainment, and finally it had to deal with it. Gradually, the studios began to produce TV shows at the expense of feature films, and studio lots were sectioned off for the production of weekly TV series. Just as gradually, the quality of the TV dramas was reduced to the familiar Hollywood formula. One by one, the successful live shows of the fifties, which took their inspiration from the serious New York theater, gave way to the now-familiar melodramas and sitcoms with their phony laugh tracks. The audience, in turn, became captive to a consumer-oriented hard sell. Underarm deodorant and mouthwash replaced U.S. Steel and Goodyear as sponsors.

I was developing stronger and stronger convictions about what was wrong with our society. I became more and more skeptical about where our leaders, in almost any context, were leading us. This included the movie industry.

In the fifties, there was a lively controversy at the Screen Actors Guild (SAG), my union, about the fact that SAG had no pension fund—probably one of the few unions in the country without one. There were discussions about a strike if a pension fund wasn't pressed for in contract negotiations. Many actors also wanted the union to press for studio payment to actors for TV "residuals." Residuals were basic-scale wages an actor would receive each time one of his or her films was shown on television—a way for actors to get their share of money the studio received for the sale of the films. Ronald Reagan became president of the Screen Actors Guild, passing himself off as a liberal Democrat. In 1960, the negotiations for pension funds and residuals finally broke down. SAG voted to strike. After a couple of weeks of the strike, Reagan came to a meeting and told us that the major studios had offered to give money for the pension fund but wanted to keep the money from all the films made before 1960. Films made after that date would earn residuals. In other words, stars such as Bette Davis, Joan Crawford, Jimmy Stewart, Judy Garland . . . all those major stars would not get a single dime for TV use of the films. Reagan was in favor of the offer. There had to be a vote for or against Reagan's proposal. The majority went along with the studios' offer, because actors are like sheep. The minority, those of us who voted against it, said, "We're being screwed." At best, it was stupid advice from Reagan. Many actors have lost fortunes because of it. I have always thought Reagan sold us out.

But my heaviest political involvement had begun at home in Maine. When Bette and I had first considered making the state of Maine our home, we also considered changing political parties. We were Democrats, but in Maine in the fifties the Democrats seemed beyond resurrection. However, in the end we decided against becoming Republicans. Along with Henri and Kitty Benoit, owners of a Portland men's store, we were among a small minority in the thoroughly Republican turf of Cape Elizabeth.

In 1954 Edmund Muskie was elected governor of Maine. He was the first Democratic governor in twenty years. Bette and I put our hearts and energy into his first and subsequent campaigns. Ed and Jane Muskie became personal friends. In 1958, when Ed was nearing completion of his two two-year terms as governor, and was considering whether to run for the Senate, he and Jane came to Witch Way for dinner. We discussed the pros and cons. They had five children and not much money, and he said, "I can't afford to become a senator." I suggested that, instead of the Senate, Ed should go for president, but Jane brought me to reality with: "I don't think we could afford that, either."

The economics of a move to Washington—having to maintain two homes and five children—was daunting on the small salary, and the campaign would be expensive, too. The basic simplicity and honesty of the Muskies, revealed in this conversation, was what was so attractive about the couple. Once, when I was driving to a meeting where Ed was going to speak, I said to Jane, "Your husband is one of the most honest politicians I've ever met." She replied, "Gary, he shames me daily with his honesty."

These two Mainers, with their basic goodness and clear willingness to do the right thing by the people they represented, appealed to me so much that I decided I would try to help raise the necessary campaign funds for his run for the Senate. It was a chance to put someone in office who not only had the requisite professional qualifications but also the humility that it takes to become a first-rate public servant. So I launched my first big political effort.

To attract a large crowd and raise some money for Ed's Senate campaign, I booked an old friend, the one and only Louis Armstrong, into the Old Orchard Beach amusement park pier, throwing in a personal appearance by Bette and me for good measure. I have always been better at coming up with ideas than with implementing them. This fundraiser was financially a near fiasco. It might have been better if we'd given money directly to the campaign. But we got a lot of publicity and had a great deal of fun.

The next step seemed impractical, but filled me with secret delight. My thought was to introduce Muskie to some of the wealthy, staunch Republicans at Prout's Neck, to prove that he didn't have horns and a tail. Together with Betty Angell, who agreed to host the event, we arranged a cocktail party for Ed and Jane. People from New York, Philadelphia, and Cincinnati, as well as many other places, summered at Prout's. I overheard: "That Merrill—he has the damndest ideas of what we might enjoy!" Though few were able to admit it to me personally, I later heard that the guests had been impressed by the Muskies. In 1959, Muskie took his Senate seat.

Next, I stopped in Chicago to talk to Jake Arvey about Ed Muskie as a presidential candidate. I had heard about Arvey for years. He was the guy every politician came to with questions, money worries, election problems. I'd always wanted to meet him, and asked Frank Sinatra, an old friend of Arvey's, to write me a letter of introduction. I was aware that Arvey had talked Adlai Stevenson into running for governor, and later helped make him the party's presidential nominee.

When I met him I said, "I've got a great presidential candidate for you. He's got all the credentials. He's ethnic, he's Lincolnesque, he's won races where no Democrat has won before. He's a fascinating guy."

"Who is he?"

"He's Ed Muskie, the senator from Maine."

Arvey thought it over a minute, then said, "Too bad he isn't from a little further west."

He didn't follow up on my suggestion, but later on, when he and Muskie met, Arvey reminded Ed that Gary Merrill was the first man ever to mention the Muskie name as a presidential possibility. Muskie was to be the Democrats' vice-presidential nominee in 1968, and a presidential primary candidate in 1972—but, alas, the White House was to be for Ed only a possibility, never a reality.

As the fifties drew to a close, Bette and I increasingly became aware that a big change was on the way for us. Maine was still as sweet as ever, and our home was delightful, but our marriage was opening at the seams. We had tried too hard to take the make-believe of our romance in *All About Eve* and transform it into daily reality. Bette got wrapped up in her roles. When she decided to become "the little woman," she threw herself into it with energy, wanting everyone else to play their parts in her drama. When that didn't happen, her temper would blow everything apart. Some of our arguments were whoppers, the noise level so intense that I'm surprised we could speak the next day. Once, she threatened to call the police, and I told her to go ahead. When they arrived I was sitting at the bottom of the stairs, laughing, while she screamed at them to do something. They said they didn't get involved in domestic quarrels.

Another time, when we were in Westport, Connecticut, Bette and I were walking along a snowy path. Somehow an argument started. I don't recall what it was about, but I do remember that I just got tired of having her scream in my ear. She slapped me, so I pushed her into a snowbank. I am not a wife beater, but ours was not a smooth marriage.

One night, at a time she was in Hollywood doing her next movie, I was staying at home with the children. It was winter and the snow was falling steadily, with the drifts piling up. We were about the last on the route to be plowed out. The men who drove the plow arrived fairly late in the evening. Since it was their final sweep, I invited them in for a drink, a token of appreciation. The two men came in and, as I was rummaging around for a beer, one of the fellows looked around and asked, "Where's your wife?"

"She's in California, working."

He said, "I wish my wife was in California, working."

I concurred. It was peaceful.

Money problems between us cropped up quite often. Bette had made large amounts but didn't save any, preferring to buy things for her family. Jules Stein, the genius producer and agent, had offered to invest some of her money for her, but she responded, "You can handle my jobs, I'll handle my money." If she had listened to Jules, I believe she'd be a wealthy woman today. He had a feel for making money and could see the possibilities from every angle. For example, he was one of the first to see the importance of television when Hollywood was still resisting. Many studios and agencies thought TV was going to be small-time, like radio, and said, "Let the television people have it!" Not Jules. He bought a special studio to begin producing TV shows. He had a feeling that it was the coming thing. Universal Studios is a monument to his foresight.

By the summer of 1959, Bette and I knew, for sure, finally, that we weren't going to stay together. I hadn't been that eager to get a divorce. It had seemed to me we might be able to work out a way to live without blowing the whole design. But tension escalated rapidly during that summer, and finally I moved into the cottage at Prout's Neck, which Aunt Marion had left me. It was as though my aunt had seen the blowup coming and wanted to provide me with a place of my own.

That spring, Norman Corwin, the playwright and producer, had sent along an idea he had for a show. He had been working with Carl Sandburg, the wise, colorful poet, and had put together some theater that was unlike anything I had seen before: a dramatic collage of Sandburg's poetry, philosophy, and comments on the times. Bette and I both read it, loved it, and decided to play it, despite our breakup.

(That same spring, Carl Sandburg had been in California at the same time we happened to be there, and I mentioned to Norman Corwin that we'd like to meet him. He came to the house for a visit and someone took a picture of him and me, with Mike on my lap. The photo looks amazingly like a family portrait of three generations.)

Playing Sandburg was my cup of tea, and Bette did a fine job with the other half—she was the responder, like a Greek chorus, and asked questions. There were just three of us on stage, with three stools (one for the guitar player,

Clark Allen).

The World of Carl Sandburg was a lovely show, a simply lovely evening at the theater. It wasn't exactly a play, and it wasn't just a poetry reading. It created its own form, and was therefore splendid—one of the most enjoyable pieces of work I had ever done. Even the men who were dragged to the theater by their wives ended up having a good evening. It was the high spot in my career.

I insisted that we open the show in Maine, and that it be rehearsed in a grange hall. We had to find a hall convenient for both of us. We wound up using the grange hall in Cape Elizabeth, halfway between Prout's Neck and Witch Way. We'd meet in the morning, rehearse all day, then go our separate ways.

By early September we were ready. There was a three-day tryout at the Pickard Theater at Bowdoin College. Then, on October twelfth, the world premiere took place at the State Theater in Portland. It was quite an evening. The place was packed and everyone loved the show. Ed Muskie and Carl Sandburg attended.

Sandburg came onstage afterwards, settled himself in a big armchair, and stared out over the audience. Suddenly, out came this rolling, sonorous, slow, wonderful voice. "Well," he said, thinking he'd give the Maine audience a history lesson, "There . . . was . . . this . . . man . . . named . . . Fess . . . en . . . den," putting a pause between every syllable, and continued with his story about a Maine Civil-War-era politician. He loved the sound of every letter of every word he said, and pronounced each one clearly. He was quite a ham. Once he took over the stage, he hated to give it up. He went on for so long that I said to him later, "Carl, you keep writing. I'll do the reading!"

There was a party after the show, with crowds of people, and as I moved through the room I heard Carl tell a young woman, "I'm very sorry, my dear, but you bore me, and I don't have enough time left," and he walked away. The remark just came rolling out in that splendid, slow voice, and I was struck by it.

Meeting him, then getting to know him, and reading his work helped me decide what I was going to do with my life. He helped me find a direction, a way of looking at life. It was the example of his forthrightness. I borrowed a part of him. I've not been able to get away with using Carl's candid words, so I think I've been a bit less cruel, but I have managed to keep bores at a distance. The problem is, there are so damned many of them! Perhaps that's why I've become something of a hermit.

During one of our conversations, Sandburg claimed he wrote a four-line novel. I doubted it, so he began:

> Poppa loved Momma.
> Momma loved men.
> Momma's in the graveyard.
> Poppa's in the pen.

It certainly told the whole story.

When we took the show on the road, we traveled by car. Thomas did the driving, and when we got to wherever we were going, he became my dresser. Ogletha came along to take care of Bette. The logistics were tricky, so we didn't commit to a theater more than a day's drive from where we were the evening before.

We went first to Lowell, Massachusetts, where Bette had been born. From there we wandered over into New York State, and then on to the west. Since we had to hire so much space in the hotels—Bette taking rooms on one side of the building, and I on the other, with Thomas—we didn't make much money. But the people loved the show, and that kept us going.

157

The following June we opened at the Huntington Hartford Theater in Los Angeles. This was Bette's town, the place where she had become a star, and everyone turned out for the evening. The initial ovation for her went on for five minutes, and that audience of celebrities, of whom we had been apprehensive, kept applauding through the entire show. It was a tremendous night in the theater for both of us.

After the curtain, Ethel Waters came backstage to our dressing room. She had worked with Bette in a couple of pictures, but I hadn't met her before. I immediately liked her spirit—the way she moved, her presence. She swept into the dressing room with that big smile of hers and said, "Well, I tell you, I nevah saw so much love on one stage."

That broke me up. "Well, you can't say we're not professionals," I laughed.

From Los Angeles, the show moved on to San Francisco, where it closed on the Saturday night before Easter. On Easter Sunday we were invited to brunch at the home of some friends who lived down the Peninsula. I had a few martinis too many, and suddenly I tore into Bette in front of a group of strangers. There wasn't any reason for it—just a case of my being stupid.

That snapped it. She took the next train back to Los Angeles. I screwed around for a few days or so before following. But I couldn't find her anywhere, or the kids. They had just disappeared. I felt lost and was unsure of what to do next, so I rented a small apartment in Los Angeles and considered looking for work at one of the studios.

One afternoon, I came home to find a man standing in front of my door. He was a sturdily built, middle-aged gentleman who looked as though he might be a night watchman at a factory. He had some papers in his hand, and as I approached he shoved them toward me. I realized that he was an officer of some sort, and I was baffled until he explained that he was a sheriff's deputy. "These are the papers for your divorce," he said. "You're being divorced in Maine."

All I could come up with by way of response was, "Well, it's about time."

When Barbara Leeds and I had been divorced, I had agreed to a thousand-dollar-a-month alimony until she remarried. She was smart and lived with her friend, receiving her alimony, until I discovered what was going on and consulted a lawyer. We came up with the agreement that she would receive the thousand for three years, even after she married, and then the alimony would cease. She married her companion.

This time I wanted it simple. If a man is willing to give up his house, control of his kids, and everything else, divorce isn't much of a problem. I let go of it all. There was a clause in the settlement that gave me visitation rights, which I felt was very important; but then I saw the other clause, which said I wasn't allowed to go to Broadway with the Sandburg show—and that really hurt. Bette went to Broadway with Leif Erickson doing my part. It closed in less than four weeks. You can't tamper with the chemistry of shows like that—they're too fragile. We had a well-oiled machine running smoothly, and even a small difference in a production that is finely tuned can change the entire effect. That's what happened. I was sad—sad for the show and sad because we hadn't kept it going together.

After the split, Bette sold Witch Way. I didn't want to be around to see the Maine years end, so I asked my agent to get me out of the country, and ended up making a couple of pictures in Spain. There was no real money involved, but I was away from the scene of the breakup, away from the end of that life in Maine that I knew I would always remember as one of the best times.

One of the major difficulties of our marriage was

that I was Bette's opposite, and there were no grounds for compromise. If it wasn't her way, it was nothing . . . period. With her fierce convictions and uncompromising stubbornness, as a child she would have been difficult for two bright parents. But, since her father left the family when she was only six or seven, Bette pretty well ran the household, including her mother Ruthie and her sister Bobby. When Bette got married, her mother got married, and when Bette got divorced, her mother did too.

In her work, Bette's attitude paid off, but in her private life it didn't. Whatever else marriage means, compromise and an interest in a partner's welfare are basic to it. Marriage is probably the most delicate, fragile arrangement between two human beings, yet they plunge into it headlong—thanks to a glandular disturbance. Nevertheless, it's difficult to come up with pat answers about why a union, begun with faith, dissipates into disillusion and recrimination. Perhaps it's the everyday annoyances constructed into a tower of faults. Unimportant in themselves, when heaped together they create bitterness that can't be overcome.

Joe Mankiewicz said, "Bette, on your tombstone will be engraved, 'Here lies Bette. She did it the hard way'. . . ." And Bette was too much one way, I too much the other. She would empty an ashtray before the cigarette was out, knowing full well there would be another to follow; she had the bed made before my feet hit the floor. Instead of tiptoeing through misunderstandings, we tromped hard with both feet. Her good health might be explained by her ability to get everything out at the moment of anger and frustration, no matter at what decibel. I tried many approaches to deal with this, but usually settled for a try at outdecibeling her— which, of course, failed. I sometimes tried the silent routine. But sooner or later, after a few martinis (*in vino veritas*), the shouting matches began again.

She was a doer and I wasn't. I was a player, she a

worker—so much so that she was unable to relax. She refused to play games, such as golf, at which she didn't excel, because she was unwilling to have others see her doing something imperfectly. She was twenty years old when she rode a bicycle for the first time. Until then, the fear of an injury (and the resulting inability to act) had held her back.

A few years after our divorce, a friend commented, "Do you realize you're drinking a lot less lately?" I had used alcohol when I was younger to loosen my many inhibitions and to overcome a shyness that often blocked communication. Later, I had resorted to booze to avoid a lot of unpleasantness in our marriage.

It's difficult to understand what another person is like, since we are each born with such different qualities. As we know, no two snowflakes are alike—the marvelous design of nature creates an unlimited variety. I knew I was very, very different from Bette. I had never been a competitive kid. If I won this or that, if I outplayed an opponent, it was not because of my need to win. I can remember feeling sorry about winning, lest the kid I bested suffer over the loss. I felt I'd rather lose myself, since it caused me no suffering, than to see him suffer. Then we'd both be happy— right? It's still hard for me to understand, possessing this attitude, how well I've done.

On television, when I see John McEnroe, the tennis star, react to missing a shot, I shudder. He rages at himself and lets his competitive drive turn him into a snarling, racket-throwing tiger. My way is quite different. On the golf course, I sometimes have in hand the club I used for my previous shot, and approach the ball with this same club, even though I know it's the wrong club. I'm too lazy to change clubs. I think, "What the hell, I'll see what I can do with it!" There's a certain nuttiness about this attitude, perhaps, but I find I can just as often make the shot with the wrong club as the right one—and perhaps that reveals the key to my personality: My laziness often pays off. If I'd have taken the right club it would have given me no excuse to miss the shot. With the wrong club, my attitude is "what the hell," and somehow the ball seems likely to get where it's supposed to go. Not being too serious, being relaxed has its advantages too.

I have been very lucky, falling into the good plays, the good parts. I never tried to get the part in *All About Eve*, never called an agent to see if something could be done to promote me. I thought about who might be chosen to play the part, but did nothing about it. I recall that I was lying on the beach in Malibu when the phone rang, and I almost missed hearing it. The call was from Mankiewicz, asking if I would test with Anne Baxter for *Eve*. "Sure! I'd be happy to do that."

For me, how to be something of a success in the entertainment business without really trying amounted to getting by on the least amount of work, being true to my own style, and pushing as little as possible. My laziness did not erase my sense of responsibility, however. When I'm working, I'm always on time, never allowing anything to interfere. I will not allow myself to drink during work periods, miss a schedule, break the discipline.

I'd long had this dream about a splendid place on the coast of Maine, and . . . there it was: the dream come true. It was a dream with a bad ending—but it had come true for a while. Those years in Cape Elizabeth, in that wonderful house, were the most complete years of my life. I'm sure that's true for Bette, too. I bet she would say the same thing. Those years, in spite of our problems, were as good as any she has had.

8

TRAVELS WITH RITA

The divorce rolled along through the legal machinery without a hitch. In the fall of 1960, Bette rented a huge brownstone in Manhattan. *The World of Carl Sandburg* was opening in New York, and I suppose she thought it would run forever. But when it quickly closed there she was with a high rent and no job. That's when she wrote her first book, an autobiography she called *The Lonely Life*. At the time, I didn't understand the title. For ten years with me she had had her family around her, along with the hundreds of visitors who came to Witch Way—all those parties and bright times.

I recalled a surprise birthday party Bette gave for me in Hollywood. She knew I hated birthday parties, but she had invited Ray Middleton, Jim Backus, and a few others for a cookout. The party was in full swing when a huge, intricately decorated cake was brought out: The inscription, instead of the usual "Happy Birthday," read "Fuck You!" And instead of a sweet confection, the cake had been made of cardboard by a prop department. I think that was the party where Jim Backus and I wound up in Margot's playpen.

I remembered the time Eaton Tarbell and I attended a reunion at Bowdoin. I became boisterous, knocking off the marching band's hats, and wound up in the jug in Brunswick. When I got home to Witch Way, Bette had hung a brightly colored banner across the door lettered, "Welcome Home Bowdoin 15th Reunion." She liked "fun." How could she be so lonely?

The advance Bette got for her book saved her for a time and gave her a grace period until she got a part in the remake of *Lady for a Day,* a film first done in 1933. This time around, they called it *Pocketful of Miracles,* and it was a box-office success.

Until Bette's affairs were straightened around, I stayed in New York to take care of the kids. But after her film was completed, which took three months, she moved to California with B.D. and Mikey. I wanted to continue seeing Mikey on weekends, according to the visitation agreement, so I followed them. Walter Rothman, a gentle man and an old friend, had a house off Laurel Canyon, just outside of Los Angeles, and he suggested I move in with him. He was divorced, too, and had been living there alone until I came along. Walter was about ten years older than I, and as we spent some fine hours sitting on his terrace admiring the wonderful view, or just talking, I learned that he had gone to school in Europe and had had a wonderful time going to the small shops, picking up small works of art, a Picasso here, a Utrillo there, and had also found some fine books for his library. He had wanted to be a librarian and, when his schooling was complete, he came back to the States and pursued his own interests. He was at this time a retired librarian, living simply, surrounded by a few of his favorite possessions. He said, "Gary, we're becoming stale. We ought to go out more." But we didn't do much of anything except go out for lunch now and then.

Walter's ex-sister-in-law, Toni Haber, invited us to

her house for drinks and dinner one afternoon, and when we arrived she was trying to get four children organized to make room for the grown-ups. Two of the kids were hers. The visitors were two very handsome girls. The youngest appeared to be about twelve, and the oldest was about fifteen.

"I'm sorry, but I have to drive the girls home. Fix yourselves drinks and I'll be right back. They live just a short distance away," Toni said as she turned toward the door with her charges.

"Hey, don't you leave," I told her. "I'll drive them home. The kids know where they live. They can give me directions."

She thanked me, saying, "Hurry back."

There was no problem. Their house couldn't have been more than a mile away. We drove up, and when the girls got out they ran down the walk and disappeared behind a fence. I walked over to the fence to let the parents know how they had gotten home, and when I looked over the fence, there, sitting by the pool, was Rita Hayworth, talking to an agent friend of mine.

Rita got up, walked over, and said, "Thanks so much, Mr. Haber." I had a beard—not that she would have recognized me, anyway.

"Hey, that's not Mr. Haber," my friend said. "That's Gary Merrill."

Rita laughed, and thanked me again for driving Yasmin and Rebecca home.

As I drove away, the image of Rita sitting by the pool was passing through my mind. I figured she must be about forty, but neither the passing of time nor the troubles she had endured seemed to have altered her appearance, and except for the short wavy hairdo instead of the long, flowing tresses she had worn in her earlier films, she was simply a little older and just as beautiful.

When I got back to Toni's, I said, "That's a very attractive lady, your neighbor. Why don't you call her and ask her down for a drink—maybe she can stay for dinner?"

"Well, sure," Toni said, and went off to make the call.

In about an hour, I was having my first drink with Rita Hayworth. She was charming, lovely to look at, but also very gentle. Walter and I were both enchanted.

I had seen Rita once before, a few months earlier, across the fairway while playing golf in Bel Air. I looked up to see her making her swing—a graceful, flowing swing that was beautiful to watch. I thought to myself then, "Wow! What a lovely golf partner."

The day after the dinner at the Habers, I called my agent friend and asked, "Do you think Rita would play golf with me?" He laughed. "Why don't you call her yourself and find out, you nut?"

I did call, and a couple of days later we played golf. That was the beginning. After that, we started going around together.

She wasn't doing much work in those days. Twenty years before, she and Betty Grable had been known around the world as America's loveliest movie stars. Their two posters—Betty Grable in a white bathing suit, looking over her shoulder, and Rita's, first published in *Life* magazine in 1941—were the favorite pinups of World War II. That picture of her in a black silk-and-lace nightgown with a low-cut bodice hung in submarines, bombers, and barracks all across Europe, the Pacific, and in every basic-training camp in the United States.

In many ways, that publicity hurt Rita more than it helped. Hollywood had typed her as the glamor girl of the forties, a sex symbol rather than an actress. She did what the studios asked, but she never stopped thinking of herself as an actress. Inside, quietly, she resented being perceived as a mere beauty with no real talent. She knew she was brighter and more sensitive than was revealed by the smiling face and perfect body everyone saw in those studio photographs. She was a lost beauty with a fragile psyche, and she spent the fifties trying to break the "love goddess" image, trying to find a good film that would make the studios take her seriously as an actress.

She had just turned forty when we met, and she was still one of the loveliest women I had ever seen. The best part was that she knew how to have fun, wasn't overly serious about life, and accepted whatever the day had to offer. I'd never met a woman I really enjoyed playing golf with, and all of a sudden here was this lady who not only liked golf but seemed able to enjoy being alive. Rita soon became the best companion I ever had.

That first summer went by in a hurry, and in September she was going to Europe to take Yasmin back to school in Geneva. Rita smiled as she said, "Why don't you come along?"

I did what anyone in his right mind would have done, and replied, "Sure, why not?" So the three of us got on the plane together.

Yazzie was dropped off in Geneva, and after she had settled in, Rita and I walked around the beautiful old city. At dinner I said, "Rita, why don't we travel around a bit? I've never been to this part of the world. We don't have to be anywhere, and we could go where we please—stay in the small places, the village hotels, and really see some of this country."

The idea appealed to her sense of adventure, and we immediately rented a convertible. We folded the top down right away, which expanded our sense of freedom. I got behind the wheel and began to drive, not bothering to look at a map. I was almost giddy with the excitement of this "let's pretend" journey.

One afternoon, as we were driving past Mont Blanc, Rita saw a golf course. "Let's play a game," she said, flashing that world-famous smile, her hair blowing softly about her face.

"Sure, let's do that." We played nine holes on that course in the shadow of the snow-covered mountain. This interlude set the pace for the rest of the journey: We gave in to our whims. We rambled through the Alps and traveled south into Italy, stopping in tiny mountain villages where no one recognized us. We stopped at open markets to buy wine and cheese for our meals, and stayed at small country inns. We never made a reservation, but never had trouble finding a room. We felt like kids in a movie romance.

After we got to Venice, not more than one day passed before the *paparazzi* with their cameras spotted us. They swarmed like mosquitoes around Rita—and the more I tried to swat them, the more they multiplied. We escaped by heading back across the mountains to France, driving by the vineyards and again stopping in the evenings at country inns.

Our route took us to the Riviera, where she had been known as Mrs. Aly Khan. She showed me the palace where she had lived during those years, and the memories made her solemn, dimming the happy glow on her face— like a cloud covering the sun for a brief moment. Her emotions always were reflected immediately on her expressive face. But then she brightened again: "I have a friend in Paris who has offered me the use of his apartment whenever I'm there," she said, smiling again. "Let's go to Paris!"

"Gladly," I said.

We drove to a very elegant Paris address, arriving late in the evening. The elevator took us to the top floor, where we entered a fantastic apartment whose windows framed the softly gleaming lights of the city—romantic and beautiful. No one was there except the gentleman's valet.

He welcomed us, even though we looked like a couple of tramps off the street, carrying two weeks of dirty laundry. We were shown to the master bedroom. My shower was wonderful, and Rita had a long bath, unwinding, purring like a happy kitten.

When we awoke the next morning, breakfast was served to us in bed, and if that wasn't astonishing enough—wonder of wonders—every piece of our clothing was brought to us freshly laundered and pressed to perfection. "It's magic!" I exclaimed.

Rita laughed. "I don't know, the croissants are a trifle dry, don't you think?"

Our sojourn ended in Paris, and we flew back to Los Angeles the next day.

Within a week my agent called to ask if I wanted to do a picture in Hong Kong, a film produced in Italy.

"It's fine with me as long as you're sure I'll be paid," I told him.

"Not to worry," he assured me. "This is an MCA deal."

The Music Corporation of America didn't fool around. When you worked on one of their pictures, you got your money up front. One of MCA's staff people called later to say he was glad I was taking the part. "We'll send the script right over," he said.

"Never mind the script, just send me the plane tickets." What did I care about the script! A movie is a movie—when you get on location, the director tells you what to do. I believe this attitude is not universally shared. But this was the attitude I had developed by this time.

There was nothing to do on the plane but drink and socialize. A young couple in the seats in front of me had a small boy, about six years old, I guessed. He and I made friends, and he sat on the seat next to mine. As is usually the case when traveling with children, they wait until the plane is about to arrive at its destination before falling asleep. When the plane landed in Hong Kong, the boy was sound asleep, and, with permission from his parents, I picked him up and carried him into the terminal.

Romano Dondi, the movie's manager, was waiting to meet me. I handed the little guy to his parents, and Romano and I went to my hotel. Later, we were having drinks at the bar. I asked him what he thought when he saw me getting off the plane with a kid in my arms.

He said, "I thought, holy shit, the guy brought his whole family and I only got him a single room!"

Shooting started the next day, and it was the first time I'd looked at the script. I found I really had a tough part to play—a derelict American in the Orient who drinks too much! I hardly had to look at the script again! (And I have not been able to remember the title of the movie!)

At the end of each day, I called Rita in California. As the movie began to wind down, I could see free time ahead, so I asked her to meet me in Hong Kong. "We can play in Asia the way we did in Europe," I said. Two days later, she was there.

It took another week to finish the movie, but in the meantime we made plans. Our first stop would be Bangkok. Before we left, the American consul in Hong Kong got word that Rita was in town and invited us to lunch. What better way to launch our new adventure, we thought, so we accepted.

The embassy was quite imposing, a beautiful building. The air-conditioned living room was cool and lovely. As we sat sipping drinks, the consul's wife played American songs on a grand piano. When lunch was announced, we all moved into the dining room, and, as we sat there, I noticed a remarkable difference in temperature. It must have been fifty degrees hotter in the dining room—I mean, it was *hot*. This was puzzling. I asked the consul's wife, "How come you don't have air-conditioning here as you do in the living room?"

"That piano in there," she answered, "is U.S. government property. The air-conditioning is to keep the piano from rotting in the heat and humidity—not to keep us cool. We don't belong to the government. We just work here, and we don't make enough to afford air-conditioning!"

The next day Rita and I were off to Bangkok, where I had my first taste of Thai food. We stayed at a tiny hotel run by a tiny Chinese woman. Her dining room served rather bland Chinese food, but when I told her I loved spicy food and had heard that Thai food was the spiciest in the world, she said she could arrange an authentic Thai meal for us.

She went over to the headwaiter and had a fairly lengthy conversation. Then both of them disappeared into the kitchen and we could hear all kinds of chatter and rattling behind the door. In about fifteen minutes, out comes the headwaiter carrying a tray laden with bowls of different sorts of food. And it was the hottest food I've ever put into my mouth. I thought my tongue would be scarred for life! But I loved it.

I asked the woman how she had prepared such a variety of food so quickly. She told us the food belonged to the kitchen crew—the cook, the busboys, and the other help. We were eating the lunches they had brought for themselves in brown paper bags! That's one way to make sure you're getting the Real McCoy!

From Bangkok we took a train to Penang, on the Malay peninsula. The ticket agent said our car was air-conditioned—which meant that we had a window that actually opened. It didn't matter. Rita never complained. She was a good scout, a fine traveler.

The train stopped about every half hour and, even when it really got going, it never went very fast. But we got off to walk through the village at every stop, to see the local temple. Kids ran alongside the train holding food on sticks for us to grab. I ate everything, though I had been told never to touch anything that wasn't washed, boiled, and sterilized. "You'll kill yourself," people had told me.

Well, I consider that kind of remark an overstatement. I am convinced that to capture the full atmosphere of a place, the real life of its people, you must sample the local food. My other theory is that if you drink enough local booze, the germs are properly taken care of. The stuff we got in Bangkok could have probably killed germs that hadn't been discovered yet. We made sure we were well stocked.

Rita had an introduction to a young Chinese couple in Penang, and we called upon them. They were handsome people in their early twenties, with two children. They were very courteous and solicitous of our needs. The young man worked for his father, a trader in the import-export business, apparently a successful enterprise, as we were to discover. The father had sent all his children to attend schools in England, and they were given many advantages; but the young people said that they were limiting their own family to two, since they couldn't afford to educate more than two children in the manner they themselves had been.

We were taken to meet his father and mother, and we learned that the older gentleman gave his wife a new Rolls Royce every year. It was apparent that he was generous: His wife was wearing a beautiful, wide golden belt. Rita remarked on how lovely it was, and, as she was admiring it, the lady took it off and handed it to her, saying, "Would you like to see it more closely?" As she placed it in Rita's hands, Rita almost dropped it. It was solid gold and heavy as lead.

We also met an English couple who were in the automobile business. They offered us a car to use, saying we could drop it off in Singapore. The Englishman asked us to their English club for dinner one day, and as it was on the way to the club, I suggested we meet them at the home of the older Chinese couple. He agreed to the arrangement. In the course of our conversation I found that, although the Englishman and Chinese man had been doing business for years, it was the first time the Englishman had been to their house. This was typical of the way the colonial British behaved, living totally separate lives, a world unto themselves. The Chinese were so courteous to us that I was almost embarrassed.

While in Penang, we were given a tour of a rubber plantation, a very impressive operation. This is my kind of business, I thought: Tap a few hundred rubber trees, send some men out to empty the buckets, ship the stuff to the States, and get the check in the mail—while you sit on the porch sipping a drink and watching the rubber trees drip.

We had decided to head farther south, to Singapore, but everyone we met in Penang said, "Oh, no, you can't do that. The territory between here and Singapore is full of Communists."

We hadn't given that much thought, but Rita and I discussed it. "Well, what could the Communists do to a couple of dusty Americans driving a beat-up car over jungle roads?" I said. Rita wasn't sure, but didn't object to finding out. So off we went, south, along the Malay peninsula. We stopped in little towns to walk around, and the people, who might have been Communists for all we knew, were always polite. They lived in wonderful houses which were built on three levels: The first was a dirt-floored, shaded area, and the next two were balconied on all four sides. No matter how hot it might be, there was always a cool spot to sit on one level or another, open to the breeze.

In one village, we called on the local doctor, a Scotsman, a fine fellow we had met in Penang. Some of the villagers said he was a Communist because he treated people from what was supposed to be a Communist hamlet. While we were talking, I said to him, "Hey, they tell me you're a Communist."

He looked straight into my eyes and said, "I'm a doctor. They bring me broken people, I try to mend them. I don't ask about their politics before I begin. What's more, I could care less."

We traveled on and eventually got to Singapore. We checked in at Raffles, the famous hotel. A few years after we'd been there, someone wrote a book about Raffles, and in it is a photograph of their guest register. There, in the middle of the register page, are the names Gary Merrill and Rita Hayworth.

We stayed in Singapore only a day or two, and did the usual tourist bits, having fun. Then we flew to Japan. Near Mount Fuji we spotted a golf course and played nine holes in the shadow of the mountain, just as we had done near Mont Blanc in Switzerland. I think we eventually played on half the courses in Japan—but we never got used to the tiny female caddies, and constantly worried that one of them might collapse under the weight of the bags that seemed as big as they were. I wanted to carry my own, but they wouldn't allow it.

We kept wandering, spending little time in the large cities, instead roaming the countryside. We came across a temple, a former palace in Kyoto, made with as much attention to detail as a piece of cabinetry, each bit of wood chosen for its grain and the way it would interlock with the next. We were told that the wood was fitted to sound an alarm: No one could sneak up on anyone inside. I took off my shoes and tried to tiptoe in from every possible approach. I crept slowly, carefully, but couldn't take a single step without making a sound—the wood squeaked or groaned. Though I shifted my weight, tried to make myself lighter, nothing worked. There was simply no way to make a surprise entrance.

Then this delightful trip, too, came to an end. I'd never had such an unassuming, sweet, cooperative companion.

We returned to California and stayed in Malibu until Rita went on location for a film. I packed my bag to travel again, too, because my agent had found a movie for me to shoot in England. After Rita's job, she moved on to do a film in Spain, so we met in London and explored England together for a few days. Then we flew to Los Angeles, where soon we were to be propelled back to grim reality.

In L.A. I was seeing Mike as often as I could on alternate weekends and sometimes after school. *The Sound of Music* had just opened, and though neither Rita nor I was excited about seeing the play, we thought the children might have fun. I picked up B.D. and Mike, and Rita collected Yazzie and Rebecca, and off we went. We had fine seats, right down front.

The children were delighted, their faces bright with enjoyment, and when the curtain came down I suggested we go backstage. I knew some of the people in the show and thought the kids would be interested in meeting them. Because our seats were so close to the front, we got backstage pretty fast. There, in the center of the bare stage, was a gathering of nuns and the boys' choir that had been part of the last scene. They were crowded together and one of those Simon Legree stage managers was yelling at them at the top of his lungs: "If one of you little cocksuckers gooses another nun on stage," he screamed, "you'll be out on your ass so fast you won't know what hit you!"

We were standing on the side, listening to this, and I thought, "Oh my God, what will this do to these four kids? They've been entranced for two hours and now every illusion is out the window." I learned a lesson—never go backstage too soon after a performance.

We hurried to the dressing room, met some of the

performers, then it was time to take the kids home.

When I dropped Mike and B.D. at Bette's, the upstairs window flew open with a bang. Bette leaned out, saw Rita with me, and commenced to scream and yell, using language a hardened sailor would have thought music to his ears. "That's not a fit woman for my children to be with . . . You and that whore shouldn't be together with young children . . ." and on and on.

She kept it up for about five minutes. I thought, "Isn't that just like Davis! She wants everything her way. She doesn't want me, but she doesn't want me to be happy with anyone else either!"

I yelled right back and told her to shut up. But the shit had hit the fan again.

The following day, Bette went off to see her lawyers to try to get my visitation rights with Mike revoked. And she did. All of a sudden, I was barred from seeing my own son. So I made an appointment to see my lawyer. I had "reasonable rights" to see Mike: That's what the divorce agreement stated. B.D. then wrote me a letter saying that she no longer wanted to see me, and though I wrote back to let her know that I loved her and would be available if she ever needed my help, she had basically divorced me when her mother did. So now all I had, in addition to Margot at the Lochland School, was Mike.

Bette had previously gone so far as to call the mother of one of Mike's friends, telling her that Mike couldn't visit if Rita was there. That was pretty heavy-handed, but we had done our best to ignore her edicts. When Bette refused to let me see Mike at all, however, when she tried to say she alone would decide when and where I could see Mike, that couldn't be ignored.

"What does 'reasonable rights' mean legally?" I asked my lawyer. He launched into an explanation and suggested Bette and I get together to work out a friendly arrangement. "It would save going into court, with all the ensuing expenses," he said. We composed a letter. But the Queen did not like it.

Mike was only nine or ten at the time and I didn't want him dragged into court. Also, Rita had had enough trouble in her life, and I didn't want to add to it. I was tempted, in despair, to drop the whole thing. But a good friend advised me to make the effort. He said that if I didn't go to the wall, for the rest of their lives Bette would tell the kids that their father had never given a damn about them. I decided to go to court.

Bette and I were both working, which made it difficult to find a suitable time for us to appear in court simultaneously, so during that fall of 1961 there was a series of no-shows in court. I'd appear with my lawyer and Bette wouldn't, and the case would be postponed. The domestic relations courts were in Santa Monica, and, because of the many postponements, five judges heard the case. Ed Mosk, my lawyer, asked what I wanted for a judgment. There was no problem answering that. I believed every parent should spend as much time as possible with his children, and when the mother had custody the father should at least share half of the child's free time—which meant that I wanted to see Michael every other weekend and half of all vacations. Ed doubted that the judge would agree to my demands, but I pushed for them.

Because it was so difficult to get us together, one of the judges finally made a temporary ruling, until both Bette and I could appear simultaneously. He stipulated that I should have Mike every other weekend; and that I could pick up Mike at eleven o'clock in the morning the day after Christmas, and he could spend the remainder of the Christmas vacation with me. This was what I wanted, but it was not to Bette's liking. Each time I arrived to pick up Michael, the front door would open and he'd rush out—almost as though he'd been ejected. I'd wrap him in my arms and away we'd go to Dodger games, or to his Little League games, and sometimes to dinner and the movies. And, as I now lived again at a beach house in Malibu, we swam a lot.

I realized that he must be getting a third degree each Sunday night when he returned home—about where we'd been, what we'd done, and whom we had been with. I reassured him that if things were too rough, I'd be willing to forgo my visits. He assured me that it was okay. To me, this meant that he was willing to take some guff so we might have our times together. Over the years many people remarked on what a handsome boy Mike was, to which I always replied, "Yes, and he's just as beautiful inside, which is more important."

During one of our times together, I had come across a little hotel called the Newporter Inn, at Newport Beach, about sixty miles south of L.A. It had a great nine-hole, par-three golf course laid out around it, which was ideal for a child golfer. When anyone was available, we'd pick up other couples and play for nickels and dimes. Mike had had lessons during the summers in Maine, so he was familiar with the etiquette of the game. On one occasion, two men were standing idly by so we asked them to play with us. But they were singularly inept and they wouldn't play for nickels. I told Michael we'd do gamesmanship, which meant that all the etiquette would be reversed—dropping putters, talking on back swings, and so on—and this delighted Michael. We later discovered that these two fellows were detectives Bette had hired to follow us.

During a party, the detectives took a picture of Mike in my room at the inn. It showed a bottle of scotch in the foreground. This was later used in court, "evidence" to prove that I was a dissolute father. They also testified that I'd turned left on a red traffic light, and that I'd gone out one evening and left Mike alone at the inn. I had had an arrangement with the person at the front desk, who acted as a baby-sitter—a point overlooked.

My weekends with Mike were going along beautifully, but on the day after Christmas, when I drove up to Bette's house at eleven o'clock in the morning to pick him up for our holiday together, I noticed a Bel Air patrol car parked in front of the house—a disquieting omen. I went over to ask what was up and the patrolman said he had been told to be there, that was all he knew. I thought that strange, but went over to the house. A maid came out and said, "You wait here."

"What?"

"You're to wait here, that's all I know."

This was strange! I waited. A few minutes later a young lawyer from Ed Mosk's office drove up and said that Bette, B.D., and Mike were at court in Santa Monica, had been there since nine o'clock that morning, and that Bette had gotten some warrant or writ. He went on to say that Ed had been trying to find me for a couple of days, to let me know what was going on.

All I could think was, "What a lovely Christmas present for Michael." I guessed Bette had been plotting this little surprise all during the Christmas holidays. When I reached the court, Ed greeted me and explained that Bette had planned to take the kids to Palm Springs for a few days and had brought the whole thing to court to get permission. Ed suggested that we let Mike go to Palm Springs and have him spend time with me later. I was appalled—hell, she'd known that Mike was to be with me! She was always rough when she didn't get her way.

"Ed," I began, "the last judge said that I was to pick Mike up and have him for the rest of the vacation. Bette's had her time and now it's my turn. Now, where's the court? Let's go."

I walked into the chambers, and, as I passed a door,

I saw the name of the judge—Judge Lynch! I thought, "Oh, shit. Here we go!"

This was the first time Bette had appeared in court. When being sworn in, she was asked to state her name. "Bette Davis," she said, and took her place in the witness box. The judge looked at the papers in front of him, then at her, and finally said, "It says here that your name is Mrs. Gary Merrill."

She was a bit startled, turned crimson, but restated her name as Bette Davis. There had been a lot of ink in the papers—some that very morning—about how she was her own woman, going her own way, and about how she hated men. At this point, I believed it all. (When I later discussed her anger with my business manager and said I couldn't understand why two years after the divorce she had gone on such a tear, Tucker said, "Look Gary, she's probably still in love with you. Here you are, going around with one of the world's most beautiful women, and it probably hurts her pride.")

The judge, for some reason preoccupied by the issue of the way her name appeared in the papers, told her she was still listed as Mrs. Gary Merrill, and it was then I began to think I might not get lynched after all.

Judge Lynch continued studying the papers in front of him and asked Bette about Palm Springs. He then asked me what my wishes were, studied the papers on his desk again, and said to Bette, "It appears that you and Mr. Merrill have joint custody and you don't like the rulings. Do you think I'm an oracle, that I can decide things of this sort to please everyone equally?" He shuffled the papers around and then said, "Do you have any objections to my having a little talk with Michael?"

There were no objections, and he looked right at Bette as he said, "There will be no discussion with Michael as to what is said in my chambers." He nodded to me, "The same goes for you."

Michael marched down through the courtroom and into the judge's chambers. After a few minutes the judge came out, looked at me, and said, "Would you like to talk to Michael?"

My first inclination was to say no because I thought Mike had been through enough, but then I realized that this might be misunderstood. I said yes, and went in to Mike.

He looked so vulnerable sitting there. "Jeez, Mikey, I'm sorry to have to put you through all this. How are you doing?"

"I'm okay."

"Would you be heartbroken if you didn't go to Palm Springs with your mother?" I asked him.

"Nope."

I went back into the courtroom and told Ed, my lawyer, I wanted to stay with the original ruling. He presented my request to Judge Lynch, who thereupon proclaimed that I would pick Mike up one hour from the time court was dismissed.

I had regained my rights and learned a lesson about lawyers. Your lawyer is your employee. I said to Ed, "You lay out the cards. I'll play them."

But our session with Judge Lynch was hardly the final match between Bette and me. She hired Murray Chotiner, the toughest lawyer in Hollywood, and went to court to prove that "reasonable rights" meant I would see Mike only when she said I could, and at no other time.

The custody trial came up several months later. It began at nine o'clock in the morning and continued, with an hour out for lunch, until five o'clock that afternoon. It was the longest, toughest day of my life—to sit for all those hours without being able to cry or laugh, to act completely emotionless all day long.

During the previous months, I had asked myself

many times if I was doing this for Mike or to get at Bette. I had decided I really was doing it for both Mike and me.

As I drove into the courthouse parking lot that morning, I ran into Jean Leon, the owner of La Scala Restaurant in Beverly Hills. "What the hell are you doing here?" I asked him.

"Hey," he said, "I got a subpoena."

Murray Chotiner had apparently arranged for this. Good old Murray, the man behind Richard Nixon's entry into the political arena in California; the same fellow who had backed Nixon with his attack on Helen Gahagan Douglas—some lawyer. Now he had subpoenaed Jean Leon and I couldn't figure out what the hell for. After two hours of back and forth between Bette and me, Jean took the stand, and I realized what was going on.

Months before, Rita and I had been at La Scala for dinner. It was the night of our visit to *The Sound of Music* with the children, when Bette had launched into her tirade. Upset with Bette's insults, Rita had made a scene in the restaurant, waving her arms and talking pretty loudly while I tried to persuade her to leave. My attempts at persuasion got fairly spirited for a while, because Rita definitely had not wanted to leave.

A newspaper columnist had been on the premises, and, as is usual in Hollywood, the story ballooned once it got out of the restaurant and into the papers. Eventually, the item made *Time*, with a gossip item about Rita being drunk and me falling on my face, also drunk. The way Chotiner saw it, the incident demonstrated my unsuitability as a father.

Jean took the stand and Chotiner began boring in: "Did this happen? Did that happen?" And Jean kept saying, "No, that's not the way it was." Chotiner's frown deepened, and he repeated the same questions—rephrasing, but asking the same questions. Jean consistently gave the same answer: "No."

Carried away with his performance, Chotiner stormed over to his table, picked up a copy of *Time*, opened to the People section, shoved the magazine under Jean's nose, and exclaimed: "Read this!" Jean complied and told him one more time, "That is not what happened."

Then Chotiner put his face right into the witness box and asked Jean if he was telling the truth. That tactic upset the judge so much that he leaned over the bench and said, "Counselor, are you trying to impeach your own witness?"

Finally Jean gave his version. "This is what happened: Miss Hayworth was having a problem and Mr. Merrill was trying to solve it. He tried to quiet her—tried to avoid trouble, not start it."

Chotiner could see he wasn't making any progress, so Jean was excused. But then he brought out his other "evidence."

I had been dabbling at monologues in San Francisco at a nightclub, the Hungry i, where beginning performers sharpened their skills and had a chance to sing, dance, or do comedy routines before a live audience. It was owned by Enrico Banducci, who became a good friend. Many now-famous performers got started at the Hungry i, including Mort Sahl, Woody Allen, Barbra Streisand, and Robin Williams. One night Vaughn Meader—whose name became familiar to many Americans because of his ability to imitate so closely the speech and mannerisms of President John Kennedy—was due to play. He didn't show up, so I volunteered to replace him: talk to the audience, read poetry, tell stories, find a way to express my ideas, and get some response. I had thought it would be nice to have a TV talk show of my own, and the Hungry i was a terrific proving ground.

I lasted two or three nights. While I was sitting at a table one evening, I noticed a woman at a neighboring table whose companion had obviously passed out from booze, her head resting in her folded arms. Her friend was trying to waken her. "Here, let me help. I'll show ya how to do it," I said, and thought the heat from a lighted cigarette, held close to her, would get a reaction. Like a fool, I went too far. I burned her. She woke up all right, and was so wide awake that the next thing I knew she had contacted Melvin Belli, the famous San Francisco lawyer. Fortunately, nothing serious came of it, because I also contacted a good lawyer, my friend Jake Ehrlich.

But during the custody trial, Chotiner brought up that episode along with the driving infraction (the left turn on a red light), and the bottle-of-scotch picture with Mike in the room. It was getting tough for me. If you want to have all your sins paraded before the world, have a court battle with Bette Davis.

I countered their evidence by introducing a photograph of my own.

As a U.S. senator, Ed Muskie had come to California on behalf of his antipollution efforts. I decided I would have a party for him at the Newporter Inn and introduce him around, in case he wanted to go further with his political career. So I flew in some clams and lobsters from Maine, and invited about forty or fifty people, including some well-placed Republicans.

An old friend, Phil Stern, was one of the guests; he is a photographer with enormous talent. During the party, Phil took pictures—at the same time Bette's detectives were skulking about taking their pictures. The photographs I showed the judge included Senator Muskie, State Senator Phil Burton of California, and Mike. Same party, different scene.

It was around this time that Teddy Newton, my first actor friend, whom I had known since my Loomis days, was dying of cancer, and Mike and I had gone to visit him.

Chotiner brought that up, saying he thought it was terrible for a father to take his son to visit a man dying of cancer.

By the time the long day had ended, the judge appeared to have had enough of Chotiner. The court decided in my favor, granting all that I asked for: visits with Mike every other weekend, plus half his school vacations.

Two weeks later, at my house in Malibu, I got a phone call from Ed Mosk, who had been instructed by Bette to tell me that Mike would be delivered to me in two hours. I couldn't figure out why. When Mike got there, I learned he wasn't just coming for the afternoon, he was coming to live with me. Bette hadn't gotten her way in the trial, so she threw Mike at me like a loaf of bread. The limo drove up, and there was little Mike with his bags.

Instead of leaving for New York as I had planned at that time, I stayed in Malibu for four months until Mike finished school, I drove him to school every morning and picked him up in the afternoon. About the time school ended, Bette had pulled herself together and took Mike back to live with her.

Rita and I generally weren't bothered by Bette's shenanigans, but played golf and kept seeing each other fairly steadily for the rest of 1962. That year, Herbert Bayard Swope, Jr., came to me with a play called *Step on a Crack* . There was a rather small part in it for me, and I felt that Rita was right for the part of the mother, a lead character, and asked her to read it. Swope was delirious. Any play with Rita Hayworth would pull in an audience, no matter how bad it was. He went to talk to Rita, she agreed to do it, and off we went to New York.

Swope had been a half-assed producer, and had seldom directed, but he was determined to direct this play. Joey Heatherton and William Hickey were going to be in the cast, as well as Donald Madden. (Bill Hickey finally won recognition playing the godfather in the movie *Prizzi's*

Honor.) I didn't have much to do at the time, and neither did Rita. "Let's give it a try," I said.

After a couple of days of rehearsing, Rita realized that Swope couldn't direct a two-car funeral. She pulled out of the show then and there and went back to California.

I stayed with it as it went on the road and Swope kept trying to fix things, rewriting during the rehearsals. "Herb, this mess isn't going anywhere," I finally told him. "Why don't we pack it in?" But he wouldn't quit. "We're going to take this show to New York!" he said, and that was that.

We did make it to Broadway. Rita's original understudy, Pauline Flannagan, was now the lead, poor girl. The show opened and what a turkey! The critics were rightfully merciless—it was a supreme flop. I went to the theater the next day to pick up my things, convinced the play would close with a whimper, but the stagehands appeared to be getting ready for another performance.

"What the hell? What's going on here?" I asked, unable to believe what I was seeing.

They told me Swope wanted to keep the thing going for another week. "To hell with that," I said, and called everyone together—got the stage manager, the cast, and everybody else on the stage. "This thing is a disaster! It's not going to make a cent. We've got to close this fucking calamity!"

Everyone agreed. Swope was called with the message that we weren't going to make believe another day—enough was enough. One night! That's how long *Step on a Crack* lasted. It was the worst—actually, the only—flop I was ever in. Rita was right to have left when she did.

Ah, Rita . . . She had been born in New York City, her father a Latin dancer. His dance studio failed in the Depression, and he had Rita dancing in Tijuana at twelve years of age. She said, "He had me dancing before I could walk." At first she was just a member of the family dance group, but by the time she was sixteen Eduardo Cansino had made his daughter Margarita his partner and had her dye her hair black so she would appear more Latin. They did twenty performances a week. She had no life of her own. She was constantly under the watchful eye of her father. When she was eighteen, she eloped with an older man—mostly to get free of her father.

It didn't help. Her new husband had plans for her, too. He recognized the potential of her special beauty and talent and now had her hair dyed to strawberry blonde. He changed her name to Rita Hayworth (a form of her mother's maiden name, Haworth), and introduced her to Harry Cohn of Columbia pictures. From small parts in B movies she quickly rose to become America's number-one glamor girl. By the time I met her, she had been through five marriages. All her life, she had had someone telling her what to do.

With me she let go, and for the first time in her life did what she wanted, when she wanted to, and seemed to revel in her sense of freedom. Evidently, she thought I was responsible for this change, and felt that if she were to lose me her freedom might disappear. So, paradoxically, she clung to me quite tightly.

However, our work continually took us our separate ways such as in 1963 when I was called to England to do *The Woman Who Wouldn't Die*, a spook movie. (In it, my character tries to drown his wife in a bathtub, only to find that she is absolutely indestructible.) On this job I lived in Shepperton in a pub called the Ship. At my insistence, MCA got me a motor launch, which was tied up across the street. Most American actors lived in big hotels in London and spent an hour driving to work at the studios, but I was ten minutes from the studio. Ten minutes after work I'd be on the boat going through the locks to a fine inn for dinner.

The pub had a moderate trade with the local people. About a week before Thanksgiving I was sitting in the Ship having a drink when someone mentioned that he had heard that President John Kennedy had been shot. The man was rather vague and suggested it might have been a radio drama that he'd heard.

Shortly after, two of the local constabulary walked into the pub to talk to the publican. I overheard that the word was out that Kennedy had been gunned down in Dallas and priests were in attendance at the hospital. As soon as I heard that priests were on the scene, I realized that something serious was going on. Only later did I discover that the constables' visit to the pub had to do with the publican's wife. She had been missing for two days, during which time the Thames had been flooding. The woman's body had been found along the banks and, since there was no contrary evidence, it was decided she had committed suicide. This was what they came to report to her husband.

The following day, a London television producer called me to ask if I would take part in a memorial show for President Kennedy. I readily agreed. I was one of several Americans rounded up for the program. When I arrived at the BBC studio I found Eli Wallach and Anne Bancroft. Eli and I had known each other slightly because we shared a great dentist in New York, Archie Epstein. I hadn't seen Anne Bancroft since we'd had dinner at Sardi's years earlier, when I was being considered for a play by Fred Coe, *Two for the Seesaw*, which had only two characters. Anne had been set for her part and I wanted to meet her to see if there was rapport. I found her absolutely lovely, with a gamine personality. Her appearance in that play made her a star, but unfortunately for me, Henry Fonda, not I, was chosen to play opposite her.

The other member of the memorial cast was Laurence Olivier, whom I hadn't seen since that wonderful

Sunday when Bette and I had visited at the Abbey. He too recalled the visit with pleasure, and we reminisced until rehearsals. Each American had a piece to read, and, as I recall, the Gettysburg Address was one of them. Sir Laurence was the narrator. He used a teleprompter, but during the actual broadcast he stumbled over his words several times. We couldn't understand why he made these mistakes. We knew it couldn't be attributed to emotional upset—he was much too professional.

When the show ended, it was obvious that he was disappointed by his performance. Fuming, he walked over to me and said, "Me and my goddamned vanity. I didn't wear my glasses and couldn't read the teleprompter. Stupid!" I did what I could to calm him.

During this London visit, I also saw Jean Simmons one weekend. I'd met her in Los Angeles. She had recently divorced Stewart Granger. I envisioned the possibility of forming a closer friendship with Jean. I rang the bell and introduced myself to the maid, who was just taking a breakfast tray to Jean's room.

"Allow me," I said. "This will be a little surprise."

I carried the tray up to the room, knocked, and when she answered, went in. She was delighted. We had an enjoyable visit—but the next surprise was mine. She told me she was about to marry writer-producer Richard Brooks, and wasn't I pleased? Of course I said I was, but my heart wasn't in it.

One day during rehearsals at the BBC studios, a writer friend from New York tracked me down and asked if I'd be interested in making a pilot for a television series to be called "The Reporter." Harry Guardino was to play the reporter who got the stories, and I would play the city editor who sat behind a desk.

As soon as I could, I returned to New York to make the pilot. The show was picked up by CBS and the series was to start in late May or June, directed by my friend Tom Gries. The producer, Keefe Brasselle, was an actor friend of Jim Aubrey, a CBS vice president.

I'm not sure what I had anticipated—perhaps that the pilot might not be picked up or that the job wouldn't last—but I suddenly had to think about what I would do with my son Mike when I had to work all summer. He would be coming to spend half his vacation with me, and I felt I couldn't ask a kid to sit around in the city in the summer heat.

When I had arrived in New York, my writer friend Eliot Asinof had kindly opened his guest quarters to me. He lived at Seventy-second and West End Avenue, and I remembered that there was a marina on the Hudson at Seventy-ninth Street. The solution became obvious: I'd charter a cruiser for the time that Michael would be with me. It would be berthed at the marina, and Mike and I could live on it, and spend the weekends cruising, or whenever my schedule allowed.

One of my requirements was that a captain familiar with the coast of Maine be provided, as well as a first mate who could cook.

When Mike arrived he found that his summer home was a fifty-foot yacht moored at Seventy-ninth Street, with all the necessary comforts and the power of mobility. We'd sail off on Saturday morning and return in time for the next shooting day—Monday or Tuesday. We traveled down the Jersey coast to visit friends, out to Fire Island, or simply around Manhattan. When I was free for a stretch, we cruised through Long Island Sound and on down to Maine. Often, we stopped in isolated bays to chase around the rocks and have cookouts on the shore.

Maine still felt like our home, so when we got to the Portland Yacht Club we stayed for a while and invited some of Mike's old friends to go cruising with us. I kept in touch with New York by phone, flying down when I had to. Once, when I'd been away for a week, I got a message telling me I had to work on Friday. I returned the call, saying there was a storm and I couldn't get out by plane. Tom Gries responded, "Okay, you only had a couple of lines—forget it."

The days were particularly lovely during that summer of 1964, and nothing mattered but that Mike enjoy it. One day I chartered a seaplane. We were late for a party to which Mike had been looking forward, so what better way to get there quickly? We flew over Cape Elizabeth, and Mike gave directions to the pilot, as though he were in the back seat of a taxi. As we circled the shorefront house, we could see the kids on the lawn looking up in surprise. Then we zoomed in to land on the water and taxied to the beach. As the kids stood around gaping, out stepped Mike—they whooped and laughed, Mike most of all.

Before Mike's summer visit, Rita had come to New York. Keefe Brasselle had asked at one point if there was anything else I needed, and I had said, "Yes, I need a chauffeur-driven limo with a phone." Rita wanted to look at a house up the Hudson at Nyack. I provided the limo and the real estate agent guided us to the house by phone like an airport traffic controller. That phone was useful—and well used—for setting up dental appointments, calling in to the studio, or simply calling friends. Later, Keefe told me that the phone bill had cost more than the rental of the car.

Through this period, "The Reporter" show was in constant chaos, although never from lack of talent. It lacked cohesion. Its characters were not as fully developed as in a later version, which starred Ed Asner as Lou Grant. Keefe got bounced through the maze of network executives who didn't quite know what to do, and "The Reporter" was cancelled after thirteen weeks.

I went back to California, where I got parts here and there in some of those horseshit movies of the sixties. Each time I'd stay with Rita. There were a half-dozen or so memorable celluloids such as *Around the World Under the Sea, Destination Inner Space, Ride beyond Vengeance,* and *The Last Challenge.* I was now doing character parts—sleazy businessmen, card cheats, half-mad scientists, and reformed drunks. The jobs were a snap, and usually enjoyable because of the company or the travel involved.

During this period I also did a movie in New Orleans titled *Clambake,* in which Elvis Presley played around with at least fourteen beautiful young girls while I ran an old boat along the Mississippi. The movie was terrible, but I liked Elvis.

"Success is wonderful," he told me. "I never knew there were so many Presleys in the world, and they all turn out to be kin."

In the fall of 1964, when Michael was just thirteen, he entered Loomis, much to my pleasure. Bette had thought he should go to Choate, a more prestigious name, but I had gone to Loomis and had played against Choate in hockey. Choate was the only school whose players weren't strictly clean. Mike had no real feelings pro or con about Loomis, but I knew the headmaster, an old friend who wouldn't require that I go through formal channels when I wanted to check up on Mike's progress. Besides, I was footing the bills.

Despite thirteen years of turbulence, he was a fine, intelligent, normal boy, ready to begin life as a teenager in the company of his peers. Our relationship was firm and steady. On one vacation in Maine, when Mike was eleven, we had been visiting friends who lived just a short distance from Witch Way. As we were leaving, we looked across the cove at our old house. I glanced at Michael and saw tears in his eyes. It really got to me and I said, "Let's cry together." We cried our way to the main road and then pulled ourselves together. We shared a basic trust in each other—not only could we laugh together, we could cry together as well. I think we had an intimacy unusual for father and son.

When Michael was settling in at Loomis, I was in New York, where I had leased a small penthouse apartment overlooking Central Park West, just large enough for me. Although Mike and his friends would arrive once in a while, and we'd go to the theater, essentially I was alone. Rita was ever on my mind. I became engrossed in contemplating my capacity for self-delusion, not just in my two marriages, but perhaps now, with Rita. I wanted to make her happy—but she wasn't. I had heard her history of pain, and I had thought, "Well, let me make it all right—I'll make everything turn out right for her." I had tried, but failed. Now I was forced to deal with the reality of my limitations—which, for the first time, I felt with great force. My self-confidence, I discovered, lay over a bed of quicksand.

Rita came to New York and settled into a hotel within walking distance of my apartment. We went to the theater and to restaurants, but now there was something missing: The mysterious, vital ingredient necessary for real joy was no longer with us. We began to see less and less of each other, although neither of us could cut the cord completely. We telephoned back and forth for almost a month, as if talk could resolve our mutual anxieties.

One winter weekend I drove alone to Connecticut to see Mike at school and take him skiing. When I got back to the city on Monday I learned that Rita had left for Los Angeles.

9

LONELINESS
TO COMMITMENT

I n my small New York apartment, I was completely alone for the first time in my life. I'd
always had a family, or roommates, or a wife. I wasn't even
alone in my mother's womb, but a twin. I was at a cross-
roads. I had no idea which path I should take or what life
might present to me. I didn't care. I sat on my terrace for
days, doing nothing, seeing no one but the pigeons I fed. I
sent out for food or cooked myself an egg, drank coffee, and
ate raw vegetables. I had no desire for alcohol—or anything
at all, really.

After a while, I felt an enormous, intimidating anxi-
ety. I looked at my past performances with the women in my
life, and at my career—all of it. I hadn't tried hard enough,
or I had allowed others to push me around, I concluded. I
berated myself for my lack of drive. When I thought of Bette
and the children, my memories horrified me. And then I
began to feel as though my few talents were disappearing.

I kept telling myself, "Okay, it's over. You're rid of it.
You have a wonderful son, now get on with your life."

But, like people who have been in an automobile
accident, the expectation of future disasters hung over me. I

couldn't think clearly or make decisions. I was so unable to cope with my thoughts that I seemed to be paralyzed. I didn't shave, answer the phone, or go out, and I couldn't even lose myself in reading. I just sat around feeling sorry for myself. I'd had lows before—my life had been a series of ups and downs—but this was a deeper depression, one by which I could gauge the insignificance of all the rest.

I spent some time on the terrace tearing up strips of toilet paper, watching them float out and around, wondering how far they would go before settling on another terrace. One morning just before dawn, I stood on my terrace, sixteen floors above the street, and leaned over the four-foot wall. I looked down to the street below and saw no one, not even a pigeon. Well, Jesus, I had been feeding those birds every morning for days! Where the hell were they? I was so depressed that I imagined flinging myself over the side, envisioning myself splattered on the sidewalk. I could see my body floating out like the strips of toilet paper. But there would be no one to witness the event—not even a goddamned pigeon. I remained leaning over the wall for quite a while.

Then the idiocy of it all came over me—to think I had to have an audience when I committed the final act! It made me back off. I was drained. I didn't have the energy or the courage to climb up and over the wall. I felt the chill of the morning and went inside to get warm. I put some water on to heat for coffee and thought, "Well, why not really warm it up?" I hadn't had a drink for days, but I splashed some scotch into the cup and, as I drank it, a warmth radiated through every fiber.

Galvanized by the booze, the shifting layers of thought bubbled over, and I began to give voice. The first word that came out of my mouth after days of silence was a shout: "Shit!" It echoed around the room and out the window, followed by a stream of invective. It helped: I felt a little better. The knot in my stomach seemed to dissolve as I became angry. And my anger had a definite focus: It was Davis.

I spent days in that apartment reliving our years together, one scene after another, yelling out my rage to a chair, as though it could absorb and transmit to Bette all the words I should have said, all the things I should have done. The futile rage reverberated inside me as I paced up and down the room, stepping out onto the terrace only long enough to chase the pigeons away, the same ones I had befriended. I now refused to give them so much as a crumb.

"Jesus," I thought. "Maybe I'm going crazy! I ought to get some help, visit a shrink."

I used the bottle as a substitute, but instead of having a calming effect it filled me with energy and more anger. I poured another drink and ranted on.

One night, tired of hearing my own voice, I turned on the television, twiddling the dial until—"Jesus, that's a familiar voice!"

I stopped and waited for the picture to become clearer. I knew what I was about to see. There was Davis, and—Christ, there I was. *All About Eve* was playing on the late show. I sat and watched it unfold. I hadn't seen that movie since it had first come out, fifteen years before. There were Gary Merrill and Bette Davis as Bill Sampson and Margo Channing, playing lovers at the very beginning of what had been our real-life romance. Life imitating art, by God!

There was Margo Channing, the ambitious, resourceful, self-centered, and beautiful woman—the epitome of the aging star, accustomed to the fawning of writers and producers, now having to rethink her role in life. And Eve Harrington, younger, even more ambitious, slyly wrenching Margo's star from the door. As for the loyal Bill Sampson, when he went begging to make a lover's peace, all

Margo could cry out was: "I demand unconditional surrender!"

Never in the history of motion pictures had an actress been so perfectly cast! Only after Eve stole the prize role did Margo decide to give up the theater for the man she loved, and lovable, creative, sympathetic Bill Sampson was finally accepted.

Bette Davis had played out the role in our marriage—and Gary Merrill had gone right along. Then she had shattered all his dreams, with her disdain for everyone's feelings but her own, her insensitivity, and her often humiliating insistence on having her own way. She did not care who was cut down with the sharp scythe of her tongue, she was self-righteous in her desire to be the queen, and she demeaned everyone who opposed her will. She had totally cut herself off from others. I finally understood why she had chosen *The Lonely Life* as the title of her book—and she was welcome to it. I began to laugh at the marvelous joke. I felt a sense of liberation when I realized that Bette had been as big a fool as I.

It was indeed time to get on with my life, and the first thing I decided to do was to return to Maine to live. Carl Sandburg had taught me that life ought to be spent doing what felt right, not what one thought he ought to do. I was always happier in Maine than in New York or Hollywood. What felt right was to "go home" to Maine—to lie around and do nothing. I would travel to do a movie or a show, but Maine would be my home base.

So I went back to Maine once again. I also decided to see if I could convince Rita to live in Maine, too. I did persuade her to try it on a visit.

We played golf at the country club just down the road from the house I rented in Falmouth. One day I called Hank Payson to ask if he and his wife, Joan, would play a round of golf with us. By the time we got to the last hole near the clubhouse, a huge crowd had gathered, mostly women. I said to Hank, "What's happening at the club today?"

He looked at me as though I'd turned simple: "You idiot! They found out we're playing golf with Rita Hayworth."

It was a good weekend, but when it came to an end and I drove Rita to the airport, she told me she didn't want to live in Maine—she was a California girl, she explained. As the plane took off, I knew the affair was thoroughly over. But I also knew that from now on we would be friends. It was a good feeling. A big improvement over my despair in New York. I felt that already Maine was mellowing me.

I went to California some months later to make another movie, and stayed with Rita. She asked me to live with her, and I truly made an effort to picture myself in California on a permanent basis, trying to imagine what that would again be like. It didn't work.

"I'm a guy in his fifties trying to make some sense out of his existence," I told her, "and Maine is the only place where I think I've got half a chance." I once again left California and returned to Maine—home.

I had never thought about what the future might hold when I had first seen Rita sitting near her swimming pool that afternoon when I'd driven Yazzie and Becky home from the Haber's. All I knew was that I had to see more of her—I couldn't have held back if I'd wanted to. I'd felt the same way when I'd first met Bette on the set of *All About Eve*. I had always followed my cock, not my head, with the ladies. Now, I thought, at my age, I should use my brain.

Another thing I'd picked up from Carl Sandburg was that a person had to go his own way, and if someone didn't want to follow—good luck. I loved Rita, but I couldn't sell her on my way of life. So, sadly, we said good-bye. Maybe I was wrong: She was the best companion I'd ever had. Maybe I was just no good at female relationships.

At this time in my life, I hoped, too, that the long battle with Bette was finally over, that we could retreat to acceptable positions that would make reasonable sociability possible. But this assumption was short-lived. Margot, our little girl in the Lochland School, was the catalyst for another battle.

I had often visited Margot at the school over the years, and she had visited both Bette and me for holidays. Her condition had become more apparent as she grew more mature in appearance. We all loved her, but it was Miss Stewart who had given Margot her real home. Over the years, Miss Stewart had become a good friend with me, too. She had helped me in dealing with Bette's attitude toward Mike. When Bette had been too hard on him, I'd give him a wink—Miss Stewart told me to keep on winking. One day she said, "Keep that little boy away from his mother as much as possible."

I returned from several weeks in Europe and, as usual, called Miss Stewart to find out how Margot was doing. "She's not here," I was told. "Bette came and took her away."

When this bit of information finally sank in, I realized how typical it was of Bette to wait until I was far away, then take it on herself to make decisions about Margot. I was told that Bette had consulted a psychologist, who, without any real understanding of the matter, had convinced Bette that Margot would be better off living with a family. So Bette had found a family on a farm outside Philadelphia and had taken Margot there.

"They didn't even take any of the records we've kept over the years," Miss Stewart noted.

They had just spirited Margot away. I asked for the address and set out immediately. I didn't call. I just went. This was my daughter. I didn't want anyone putting on an act in anticipation of my arrival.

I knocked on the farmhouse door and asked for Margot.

"Oh, yes, that poor little girl . . ." the lady said. "She left a month ago."

"Left?" My heart sank. "Where did she go?"

The woman said she was sorry, but she didn't know. What the hell was I to do now? I called Miss Stewart. She, too, was stunned. She asked around the school. One of the teachers mentioned a former employee Bette had thought well of, who had moved to a place near Pittsburgh. The former teacher's name and address were given to me.

I drove west and, the next day, found the place on a country road. There was no one at home, but on the back porch I saw a familiar trunk with a tag, TWO'S COMPANY, on it. I was at the right place.

I waited, and after a while a car drove in. There was Margot—she was fine. I introduced myself to the family and they became somewhat frightened, as though I had come to kidnap her.

I took Margot for a drive on back roads and got her talking. She liked living in the country, and she liked the family she was with. "All right," I thought, "perhaps it wasn't such a bad idea. Perhaps the change was good for her." So I told her that I was glad she was there and that I would call her and come again soon.

But when I next went to see her, Bette had again changed her mind! With neither consultation nor warning, she had taken Margot out of Pennsylvania and this time put her in the Devereux Foundation school near Santa Barbara, California—against the advice of the same psychologist who had inspired the move from Lochland in the first place.

A short while later, Bette called to say that Margot was unhappy. I had had it with her. "What the hell are you doing?" I shouted at her. "What's going on in that head of yours? First you want to give your own daughter away for adoption, and now she's unhappy in that school. Margot doesn't need all this upset in her life! She should have stayed at Lochland—we agreed that that was to be her home."

Bette shouted right back. "If you're so set on Lochland, all right! You take her back there, and *you* pay for it!"

"What were you looking for," I yelled, "a bargain?"

She hung up on me.

I called Miss Stewart and took Margot home to her. From 1965 on I have paid the entire cost of keeping her there. In recent years Bette hasn't even seen her; and, sadly, she hasn't seen her grandchildren, either.

In a book about Bette Davis, I read a remark attributed to her about Margot: *I owe everything to Miss Stewart for the disciplined way Margot has been brought up . . . She is a beautiful, loving child, able to cope with her limitations. It, of course, has been a heartbreak for all of us, but thank God we found the Lochland School, for her sake and for ours.*

Thank you, Bette Davis!

Margot will never progress beyond the mental capabilities of a seven- or eight-year-old, though she is now almost forty. Miss Stewart once said that she was the most pathetic child at the school because she was just bright enough to know what she was missing. She wanted to have babies, hold a job, get married—all the things normal people do—and she knows she can't. A recent Christmas was one of the best for her because she was in a workshop and was able to make some boxes that she gave as gifts.

As I got into my fifties, my interest and activism in politics increased. It was a way of getting outside myself. My purging in that apartment in New York had been more thorough than I had realized. I was changing in a variety of ways. For the first thirty years of my life I had remained blissfully unaware of the world outside my most immediate needs. Now I was making up for lost time. The effort would help fill the empty places in my days. I had taken over the care of Margot and Michael, so it was necessary to work when it became available, but during the off-hours I continued to read a great deal: newspapers, magazines, books of all kinds. I became aware of the troubles in the world as my personal troubles began to recede. I began to question what I read. It wasn't that I'd been totally ignorant in the past. But now, it seemed, I had to understand much more about what was happening, and why.

I became increasingly involved in the who's, the why's, and the how's of the political system. I read everything available on a subject, digested it, and came up with my own conclusions.

In the spring of 1965, I reflected on a confrontation between blacks and police which I'd just seen on TV. Martin Luther King and his followers had been treated brutally at the bridge between Selma and the highway to Montgomery, the capital of Alabama. The protesters had been forced to cancel the march because of continual violence. There had been a tremendous uproar across the country against the bullying tactics of the police. President Johnson had ordered federal troops to Alabama, with orders to guard the route to enable the marchers to proceed. I suddenly realized that there was nothing to prevent me from joining the marchers.

This was a time of ferment. Medgar Evers had been shot to death in the doorway of his own home in Mississippi. In Birmingham, Alabama, police dogs, electric cattle prods, and fire hoses were used against blacks demonstrating in the streets. A bomb blast killed four black children attending Sunday school in a church. Three young men in Mississippi, working to implement the Federal Voting Rights Act, were brutally murdered—and it seemed the local police were involved. I was not alone in being moved.

I called a few friends to say that I was driving down

to Selma and wondered if anyone wanted to join me.

"What? Are you mad? Going to Selma in a white Mercedes?"

They were afraid of getting killed—a real possibility. And I was afraid, too. But I drove to Selma alone.

As I drove slowly along Selma's main street, what came to mind was Gary Cooper facing the menacingly empty streets in the movie *High Noon.* I drove through this surrealistic scene, the town seemingly empty, no one on the streets. I kept an eye out for the church that was the headquarters of Dr. King's Southern Christian Leadership Conference. As I approached the west end of town and saw the run-down housing, I realized I was entering the black section.

I saw a taxi whose driver would certainly be able to direct me. So I drove over to him and stopped.

"Where can I find Dr. King's headquarters?"

He looked me over carefully before he said, "Follow me. That's where I'm going."

As we turned into the street where the church stood, I saw that the area was the center of great activity, and tremendous interest on the part of the law—there were many sheriff's and state trooper's cars lined up directly opposite it. I pulled in under a tree, just in front of the church, and went in. A friendly but harried individual explained that I wouldn't necessarily be marching because many more than the allowed three hundred had arrived, but that there were other ways of contributing. The march was to be treated like a troop movement, with the logistical effort involving food, shelter, and protection to be sustained over a forty-five-mile walk expected to take four days. At the end of each day's march, there would be bivouacs with food and tents.

I was told to report to a group across the street. There I found several seminarians who had bussed from

California. Our responsibility was to truck a huge tent to a specified site, set it up in time for the arrival of the marchers, and dig slit trenches for latrines. The tent had to be taken down the following morning for trucking to the next stop. For a bunch of ministers and one all-thumbs actor, this was no simple matter.

But, the second night of the march, we felt like old hands in a traveling circus. We were instructed to remain close to the march—two marchers had strayed and gotten badly beaten by local rednecks.

"Christ," I thought, "this is just like a war. Out there is No Man's Land." I stayed at a black woman's house that night, with the shades drawn.

On the third day, the bulging clouds finally burst their seams. Rain came down drenchingly and turned the camp into a sea of mud. Bales of straw were brought in to spread over the mud, but this only made it slightly less treacherous. It was a miserable night, and the next morning the canvas was almost unmanageable. When we finally got it folded and packed into the truck, we wondered how we would ever get it up again.

Reporters were swarming all over the place. One of them caught up with me: "Hey, Mr. Merrill, what are you doing in Alabama?"

"Well, I was too young for Lexington and Concord," I replied. Harry Belefonte later told me he'd gotten a big laugh out of this quote when he'd seen it in the newspapers. But, to me, this was a revolution.

As the march continued, we were followed by the sheriff's cars and state troopers. I observed that the cops had more cameras than the reporters—to record everyone involved, I assumed. Finally, we reached the outskirts of Montgomery, and here we set up the largest camp. Those who hadn't been able to spend days marching drove or flew in from all over the country for a huge rally and entertainment with star performers Dick Gregory, Harry Belafonte, and Godfrey Cambridge, as well as NAACP leaders, church spokesmen, and people from all levels of the economic scale. To construct a make-do stage, we had to rely on wooden boxes originally intended for shipping coffins.

The next day we entered Montgomery. We were in a long line of twenty-five thousand souls. As we marched, jeers and abusive remarks flowed: "Fuckin' nigger lovers! . . . Commies! . . . Yankee bastards!" All along the route, we were surrounded by Confederate flags. There was not one American flag to be seen. I couldn't understand how the mass of onlookers could stand there, so mean-hearted and mean-spirited, proudly displaying their hatred for another race of fellow human beings—and for those of their own race. Hundreds of armed federal troops had been stationed along the route to protect us, but the special danger was to Martin Luther King himself.

A year or so earlier, I had realized that King was always in danger. I'd been on my way to Carl Sandburg's farm, because Carl was in poor health, and when I checked in at the local airport an employee exclaimed, "What a pleasure it is to have a celebrity come through!" On my way back, he said, "It's a big day for celebrities—Martin Luther King has just arrived and will be taking the same plane to Atlanta."

I climbed aboard, but as we taxied down the runway, the plane suddenly stopped. The pilot's voice came through the speakers: "I'm sorry to inconvenience you, ladies and gentlemen, but we will have to vacate the plane. Please leave in an orderly fashion, but with some haste. We've been informed that a bomb has been placed somewhere on board."

A shocked murmur rippled through the plane as people snapped open their seat belts.

The ramp was placed at the exit, and as soon as the

door opened everyone rushed from the plane to the terminal. From there, we watched fire engines, airport employees, and policemen make their way to the empty plane.

I went over to Dr. King and his group and introduced myself. "I wanted to meet you and tell you how much I admire you and what you're doing, not only for your people, but for everyone," I told him. He was extremely gracious, and, as we talked, waiting for the authorities to go through the plane and the luggage, he explained that nothing would be found.

"It's just another example of harassment," he said. "It seems I must go through this sort of thing everywhere I go, no matter what transportation I use." His voice was calm, matter-of-fact, and I was struck by a certain serenity, an acceptance of whatever life might hold for him. It occurred to me that people whose lives are repeatedly threatened come to accept the fact that they may be killed while standing up for their beliefs, and therefore they spend little time worrying about it.

I had seen that same sort of serenity in Miriam Makeba, a woman from Namibia, South West Africa (controlled by racist South Africa). Her politics made it impossible for her to return to her homeland for fear of arrest or death. Once, when Louis Armstrong was playing a gig at the St. Francis Hotel in San Francisco, I introduced her to him. For years, Satch had been sending his old horns to Africa for young people studying music, and Miriam knew a young man who had received one. I thought Satch, and the rest of the people attending the performance, would be interested in the story, so during the show I went onstage and asked him if I could borrow the mike for a minute. I told the story and then brought Miriam up. They had never met, and, I must say, it was a touching meeting. Later, in his dressing room, Mrs. Armstrong said, "Satch must love you—he's never allowed anyone onstage during a performance."

Now, as I and many others stood with Martin Luther King in this extremely dangerous situation in Montgomery, I once more saw in him that clear serenity. He spoke of his endless faith in brotherhood—he was a man blessed with enormous persuasive powers—and, as I listened to him there under those sinister Confederate flags, I felt a strong sense of hope. Only three years later he would be assassinated and a powerful force for human rights would be extinguished. But that day it was immensely inspiring to be one of the thousands who had congregated in this southern city. All week I had been reminded of the spirit of our country in the example of the people I'd met who had had the courage to be counted among those fighting racism. And with much risk: A woman from Michigan, who was ferrying people back to Selma at the end of the march, was murdered.

I returned to Selma on a crowded bus. People were singing vigorously, to ease the nervousness we all felt.

The next morning, as I walked to the church to see if my car was still intact (it was), I was hailed by one of the deputies parked across the street.

"Hey, Merrill," he said. "Come here."

I approached with trepidation.

"Yeah."

"I jest wanted to tell ya that I seen all yer pictures," he said, "but from now on, I ain't gonna see anuther fuckin' one."

I thanked him and left Selma. I didn't feel easy until I had crossed the Alabama state line, going home to Maine.

That week, living with the blacks in the South, for the first time I had an inkling of the fear in which they had lived all those years. Fear! What a monstrous pall over the spirit of man. To be forced to live with it throughout life is to warp one's sensitivity to all things.

Although my social awareness was awakening, I had to keep on earning money. Yet, more and more, all my experiences—perhaps reflective of the times—seemed to have political tones to them. I did a sci-fi movie with George Hamilton at the time he was romancing Lynda Bird Johnson, the president's daughter. The Secret Service was always around. I discovered she was one of those rare people, a considerate person, when I overheard her tell the guards assigned to her that they could plan on taking off a certain night in Washington for their personal lives.

Later, when I met Lady Bird Johnson at a Democratic party in Maine, I mentioned the thoughtfulness her daughter had displayed. I also showed her how to crack a lobster claw. Stuart Udall, the Secretary of the Interior, noticed how well I got along with her and turned to Ed Muskie: "Say, why don't you run this guy for office."

"Because we want to win!" Muskie exclaimed.

Around this time I went to the Philippines to film *The Secret of the Sacred Forest*, a yarn about dope smuggling. The leading lady was the wife of President Marcos's Secretary of State, Ponce Enrile, and it was through her that I got to see how the rich lived in the Philippines. Mrs. Enrile's role grabbing was typical of the way the movie business works all over the world, but it was especially typical of how it worked in the Philippines. The oligarchy owned and ran everything. I saw the mansions belonging to American businessmen who made their millions from mines and plantations while those they employed earned sixty cents a day. The mansions were surrounded by soldiers—not government soldiers, but private armies. At this period in the Philippines, elections were a form of warfare and hundreds were regularly slaughtered in the process.

Years before, while I was touring with stage plays, an interviewer asked where I lived. I said, "On the train."

But in the sixties, I just about lived on planes. One summer, en route to Spain, I thought I'd save some money by changing the ticket to tourist class. There were very few people on the long flight so I was able to remove the armrests from three seats, making a bed for myself, and curled up with the small pillows the stewardess gave me. I found it quite comfortable. As the stewardess passed my seat on her way down the aisle, she mentioned that Samuel Bronston—the internationally famous filmmaker—was in first class. Bronston was responsible for the epic *El Cid*. I went up to say hello and the first thing he asked was, "What are you doing flying tourist?"

"It's slightly more expensive," I told him, "but I find it much more comfortable."

His eyebrows shot up. "More expensive?"

"Yeah," I drawled. "I buy three seats and make a bed."

To be sure of having a comfortable seat, a private plane is best. I remember once when that luxury was made available by a friend, Jean Gannett Hawley, the owner of a chain of Maine newspapers. She had invited Senator Ed Muskie and me to appear at one of her pet benefits in Maine and had sent her private plane to pick us up. After going to Washington for Ed, the plane made a brief stop in New York for me, and with the drone of the motors as background, the opportunity to press Ed about important issues was too good to pass up.

During the sixties, my interest in Maine's favorite son had persisted, but as the decade wore on, with our country's continuing insane involvement in the Vietnam War, I found myself reassessing my opinion of him. I took advantage of the flight to present him with a barrage of protest. Ed had taken the loyal party position, supporting the war, year after year, and was using all the usual rationalizations to justify the carnage. I suggested that he should have stood up in the Senate to oppose LBJ's ignominious Tonkin Gulf Resolution along with Senators Morse and Gruening, the only two with the courage to register a protest. Muskie observed dryly that he was still in the Senate, while they were not. However, as a staunch anticommunist Catholic, he really believed in that war, I concluded.

I asked if he wasn't aware of the feelings of a growing percentage of the American public, if he hadn't felt the power of the peace movement. I had been on a recent peace march in Washington and had never seen such a crowd of truly distressed people, who had come from all across the country. I even tried to get through to him by talking about his love for his own children.

"Well, it's like a poker game," he said, rationalizing again. "We're committed there, Gary. We've got to see it through."

"With your kids, Ed," I replied. "Not mine."

After that flight, I no longer felt the same about him: He seemed in many ways to be just another pol trying to get as far as he could. A nice man, certainly, and no doubt superior to his colleagues in many ways. But for me, he had lost his appeal.

The Vietnam War was never out of mind, and became part of my luggage. When I had returned to California in 1965 to shoot a western, in San Jose I met Phil and John Burton, two liberal young politicians who later became congressmen. They were then in their first campaigns for the state legislature and asked me to speak at their rallies, to bolster their antiwar protest with fifteen-minute diatribes of my own. Apparently, it came out pretty strong. They came up to me afterward and said, "Christ, you're so avid on the subject you made us sound like Goldwaterites."

Other people suggested I run for Congress.

Instead, in an effort to get the message across to the people of Maine, I worked in 1966 for Thomas Maynard, who ran for Congress in the First District, where I lived. He ran as an Independent on an antiwar ticket. He got twelve percent of the vote, the highest percentage of any New England peace candidate that year.

The news stories coming out of Vietnam were getting bleaker. In 1967 I was asked by the USO to travel there as an entertainer. I refused because of my antiwar convictions, but when I was approached the second time I decided to go to see for myself what was happening. The visit didn't mean I approved of the war, but that I wanted to do something for the boys who were being forced to fight it.

My mission was primarily to talk with the soldiers, give them some personal contact with the home front. It didn't seem to matter that I wasn't a singer, a celebrated comedian, or a dancer. The GIs appreciated the chance to sit around and chat with a football or basketball player, or an actor. Of course, to see an American girl again, particularly one as attractive as my traveling companion, the actress Susan Oliver, was especially stimulating for the troops.

The USO had found that dropping a small group into outlying bases was as good as or better at building morale than staging large entertainments.

Susan and I had done a television show or two in New York prior to this job, and we got reacquainted during the long flight. As we disembarked, we were presented with papers that ranked us as full colonels for the purpose of guaranteeing us VIP treatment.

I had just finished making a movie in which I played an old sea captain, and had grown a full beard for the part. I had no definite plans about what I might do in the way of entertainment, so I was pleased and surprised to find my beard become a constant topic of conversation. The soldiers were so intrigued that they wanted to feel it. Some of them said, "Boy, when I get home, I'm gonna grow one like that!"

(They had to shave every day because of the steamy heat of the jungle—and to discourage lice.)

We visited a few Vietnamese villages, and wherever I walked children gathered, giggling and pointing. I couldn't understand all the attention at first, but then I was told that with them, too, my beard had become a conversation piece—a beard is a sign of an elder, someone full of sagacity, someone highly respected.

That would have been a fine part to play, but instead my routine evolved into that of court jester to the queen (Miss Oliver), with a good deal of buffoonery.

We were flown in and out of many bases, some quite close to the fighting. Our transportation was a wide-open "bird," a helicopter with no doors. It was exhilarating to be able to hang my legs over the side and look straight down from a height of several thousand feet, held in by no more than a seat belt. The wind and cooler air at that altitude was a wonderful respite from the torrid heat at ground level.

Susan Oliver, who had flown her own plane across the Atlantic, enjoyed flying in the helicopter far more than our "baby-sitter," the captain who accompanied us night and day and who would always sit in the middle. The pilots were kids of nineteen or twenty, and I often saw a glint in their eyes when they saw Susan. They became jocks at the controls, turning the flight into a roller-coaster ride. It was the poor captain who suffered. Susan enjoyed it immensely.

At one point we were flying almost below tree level, following a river. We were not more than fifty feet above the water.

"Why are we following the river at such a low altitude?" I asked the pilot.

"The enemy are down there," I was told. "We're flying fast and low so they can't zero in on us."

Once or twice we were fired at, but never hit. When

we could gain altitude and fly at one to two thousand feet, we could see countryside which had been devastated by bombing and the defoliant Agent Orange. The landscape sometimes looked like a moonscape with craters. We flew from the Mekong Delta in the south to the DMZ, the "demilitarized zone," in the north, making numerous stops along the way.

My first hospital visit was dreadful. I saw a nine-teen-year-old kid in a traction device, with multiple casts. He was the first casualty I came to on the ward. I was struck dumb. What can anyone say to a kid like that without bursting into tears? I felt stupid, and wanted to run to the nearest telephone to call the White House and scream at the insanity of all this. But I didn't. I looked at this boy and, to regain my composure, tried to smile.

"You okay?" I asked.

He shrugged, nodded, and he, too, tried to smile. I wanted to leave, but I stayed there. It was my first confrontation ever with a crippled soldier, and I thought that if I could get through this ordeal maybe I could go on and face the others.

"How'd it happen?" I asked, and saw, in my mind's eye, that he'd probably stepped on a land mine or been hit by a mortar shell.

He looked embarrassed, pathetic even. "It happened in Saigon," he began. "I was riding my cycle with a bar girl . . . the damned thing skidded . . ."

I didn't know if he was kidding or not. It didn't matter, I suppose. I was so attuned to tragedy, it was all the same to me. In the next ward, it got much worse. I was especially appalled by the number of Vietnamese children with lost arms and legs from our mines and bombs.

We went to a Green Beret base. An officer handed me a piece of shell that had been lobbed in that morning. I could see the Chinese writing on it. This was one of our overnight stops. After dinner we were taken to the NCO club. It was like entering another world—a miniature Vegas. There was a long bar, slot machines, a stage, music, lights, and a large sign over the bar which read, FUCK COMMUNISM.

A talented group of young Australian men and women danced, sang, and told jokes. They were part of a regular troupe that toured Vietnam, rather like the vaudeville circuit in the United States before movies and TV knocked it out. After the show, our baby-sitter captain tried to herd us toward a car in an effort to take us to our quarters and be rid of us for the night. But I'd been talking to a couple of young Green Beret captains who vouched for my safe return, so I was allowed to stay on. We spent the entire night drinking and talking.

In Saigon I had met someone who worked for Air America, which was a CIA airline. He had flown the Green Berets to their destinations on occasion. Now, as my two Green Beret friends talked at the club, they brought up the subject of Air America and said that when their tour of duty was up they would not reinlist but join the CIA instead.

"Hell, we're doing CIA work but we're not being paid their wages! We might as well join and get the benefits," they told me. "The risks are about the same."

As we flew off the next day, the soldiers, as usual, waved their "V" signs at us. We were used to seeing that. It was the peace sign at home, and the victory sign here. But this time I did a double-take and noticed that these soldiers were waving three fingers. I asked the pilot what it meant. "That's the sign for 'Fuck Peace,'" he said.

So, Russia and Communism were the bogeymen. But my impression was that what was really at stake was American oil rights and gaining economic advantage in Southeast Asia. I recall the words of Smedley Butler, Major General, United States Marine Corps, 1931:

I helped purify Nicaragua for the international banking house of Brown Brothers in 1909-1912. I helped make Mexico and especially Tampico safe for American oil interests in 1916 . . . I helped make Haiti and Cuba a decent place for the National City [Bank] boys to collect revenue in. I helped in the rape of half a dozen Central American republics for the benefit of Wall Street . . .

We were invited to stay at a magnificent three-bedroom house on top of a hill overlooking Cam Ranh Bay. The general who escorted us said that it had been built by the army in less than a week, to house President Johnson on a brief visit. Well, why not, I thought, it was his war, wasn't it? There it sat, cared for by an orderly or two. Other VIPs stayed there—congressmen, Pentagon officials, and entertainers. But not Bob Hope, we learned. He always stayed in Bangkok, flew in with his huge troupe, did his show, and then got out.

We lived royally that one night, and then found ourselves plopped down within a few miles of the DMZ at the northernmost American outpost. As we were talking to the colonel in charge, distant booms could be heard, followed by plumes of smoke that dirtied the horizon. A sergeant came up to the colonel as we stood there and suggested that it might be better to talk inside the bomb shelter. The colonel led the way, and we had been inside for less than a minute when several shells landed near where we had just been.

The colonel appeared tired and jumpy—very understandable, I felt, since he had spent far longer at this outpost and at others along the lines of fire than was usual, and without being relieved, I learned. As we talked to the men, I gathered that the colonel was extremely competent. Apparently, if you were good at your job, you were made to stay too long.

As we trooped from place to place, one of the tasks I had set for myself was to seek out boys from Maine who might want to send messages to their families back home. I was able to locate a few, and when I got back I called their families. One boy's grandfather answered and I told him I'd just seen his grandson a few days before. When he realized I had actually spoken to the boy, he began to laugh, then to cry. Soon, I was crying, too.

Toward the end of our expedition, we were asked to dine with a general in Saigon. We made an appearance at the Armed Forces Radio station after dinner, and the general asked us to return for a nightcap. Susan was tired and went off to bed, but I didn't want to waste a chance to learn more about the war.

The general and I were sipping our drinks when an aide appeared and announced that two Vietnamese commanders were there to see him. He immediately excused himself saying, "They're among the ablest of the Vietnamese, and it's crucial that I speak to them."

I wasn't sure what to expect and thought I'd be waiting for a while, but the aide returned to ask if I wanted to observe. Of course! I followed him to an adjoining room where a fairly large table was spread with maps, the men leaning over them, like doctors around an operating table. But this operation was a battle plan for the following day. During the discussion, the general constantly referred to the overworked colonel we had seen earlier, and I knew the poor man was in for another hellish battle.

In those three weeks, what I saw was more devastating than anything I could have imagined. The grunts—as the soldiers were called—were cynical, disgusted with the war and with the men who commanded them. Day after day, I witnessed more resentment toward the army than toward the enemy. And, from generals on down, the majority feeling was that we were wrong to be there.

One morning, we talked with a group of men who were waiting with their gear to be helicoptered out for a ten-day patrol. Susan and I soon left on our job, but when we returned to the base later that day, several of them were still waiting. One man, with whom I had talked that morning, had been jumpy to start with, and waiting all day long had made him more so. He had only two weeks to serve before returning to the States, and the possibility of being killed during the patrol—within days of returning home—was horrifying to him.

The idiocy of sending a man out under those circumstances was clear: In his extreme apprehension and need to protect himself, he would jeopardize the entire outfit. I suppose that in any war there are myriad occasions of this sort.

On the day of our departure, I remembered a request from some friends back home. I went over to the captain with some timidity, and asked quietly, "Do you think you might get me some pot?"

He nodded his head and yelled to the sergeant: "Hey, Sarge! Get Merrill some grass!"

Back home, the news reports had suggested it, but I hadn't seen any evidence in Vietnam of the prevalence of drugs. The captain's reaction made it pretty plain that it was everyday stuff. Bringing it back, I was nervous as a cat.

As soon as I got home, I went to a Portland TV station and asked for some time. I wanted to share my experiences with Mainers, to let them know what I had seen and heard. But I was turned down.

"Sorry, we've had enough of Vietnam," I was told.

Everyone had had enough of Vietnam. Why, then, was the war still going on? Martin Luther King, in his speech *Beyond Vietnam*, had said, "Vietnam is a symptom of a far deeper malady . . . and if we ignore this malady this time, and unless there is a significant and profound change in U.S. foreign policy, we will begin organizing a decade from now around Guatemala and Peru, Thailand and Cambodia, Mozambique and South Africa."

I have always believed that it was because of Vietnam that Dr. King was assassinated. King had dared to come out against that war—saying it was evil, racist, and had to be opposed. To speak boldly for the right to ride in the front of a bus was one thing, but to stand for peace in time of war was quite another.

By 1968, the country was polarized. Thoughts of the war had become, for me, such an obsession, there seemed to be nothing more important than to work for its termination.

The notion that I could get elected to Congress from Maine on an antiwar platform took hold of me. Elected or not, just to campaign for what I so strongly believed was for me a joy as well as an obligation. I felt sure that the people of the First Congressional District in Maine would readily respond to my message, and that I could persuade many of them with the rightness of my cause.

I had always been a Democrat, but this time I felt it would be smarter to register as a Republican for the June primary battle. A case could be made for rejecting the Democratic party and its president for their commitment to Vietnam.

I knew that joining the GOP would no doubt shake up the local Republican bigwigs, who were just as committed to the war as the administration in Washington. But by running against their pro-war candidates, perhaps I could prove that sensible Americans, regardless of party, shared my position.

I wasn't naive, so I realized how difficult it would be. I was a novice, with a history of eccentricities and a habit of being outspoken. My chief opponent was an established Republican winner, State Senator Horace Hildreth, Jr., who was being groomed for a career in national politics. He was the son of a former governor. I had no funds and no important backing, and I didn't talk like a respectable Republican—and looked even less like one.

Nonetheless, I felt I could go from a considerable disadvantage to a real foothold in politics. I didn't have to win this nomination—just make a substantial dent in the vote. Of course, everyone running for office feels there is a chance to win, but I planned to use this race to develop a constituency and become known as a serious politician with an important message.

So I plunged ahead with press conferences, local radio and television interviews, and luncheon speeches.

"I renounce the War Party that has put this country in Southeast Asia!" I said at my first press conference. Thus, I let the Republicans of the First Congressional District know exactly what I was campaigning for.

In order to have one's name placed on the ballot in Maine, one had to gather two thousand signatures on a petition. I had no organization, no one working for me, so I bought a used card table and a high-backed rocking chair at a junk shop and positioned myself in Monument Square, in the very center of downtown Portland. It was February, but the weather gods were kind—and so were the citizens of Portland. I got the two thousand signatures.

A television news department was also kind. Their office just happened to be near where I sat. It could not have been too difficult a decision for the news director to feature my rocker and me on that evening's news.

It became a three-way race: Besides the front-runner, Hildreth, there was a young newcomer, David Ault. We were off and running.

Maine's First District is fairly compact, but I traveled

around to all the nooks and crannies for our nightly debates. Though Ault was young, he was well-connected—and extremely reactionary. He delivered the same super-patriotic speech every night. Hildreth followed the traditional, moderate Republican line, secure in the backing of the party machine. I tried to get the feel of each audience, varying my approach, though always stating my opposition to the Democratic administration, LBJ, and the war. Both my opponents supported the war, especially Ault.

Throughout the campaign, I tried to deflect any show of patriotic emotion, but one night as I finished my diatribe a little old Republican lady stood up to challenge me, with fire in her eyes.

"Mr. Merrill, are you telling us that if your son decided against going to war, you would allow him to be a draft dodger?"

"Yes, ma'am! I certainly would."

She glared at me. "If it were my son, I'd beat him!"

I could almost feel the pull of the audience toward her position—and I set myself the task, working doubly hard, to make them understand what they were actually saying. Wars, I said, are not always worth the sacrifice of one's children—of anyone's children. Simply because the political leaders of one's country endorse a war does not necessarily make it morally right or historically justified.

"But that's downright unpatriotic!"was the little lady's reaction to my reasoned exposition.

"Why?" I asked, hoping for a reasonable reply. "I'm not giving secrets to the enemy . . ."

"But you're speaking against your own government!"

"My dear lady, during a Democratic administration, Republicans do that every day!"

This line was followed by a substantial amount of laughter.

But the issue was war, not party, and it didn't matter to many which party had provoked it. They saw war as respectable, ennobling, and—*sub rosa* — good for business. Young men died in wars, but elderly Republican ladies knew of no time in history when this was not the case. It was as if war was simply part of life, an obligation that all young men were duty-bound to endure.

The questions followed a pattern.

"Mr. Merrill, do you really believe you know more about the security of our country than the generals in the Pentagon?"

"Certainly they know far more than I do. But they're generals—they're trained in warfare. They see the security of America through war-colored glasses. You have to consider that every country has these experts—and they all love their countries, don't they? But in any war, in every war, half of them have to be wrong!"

With these remarks, I could see I had gained their attention. Now they were listening, so I could take another step.

"Let's face it—we're losing this war. Our generals are wrong this time. I also happen to think that the security of our country in this instance is not at stake—win or lose."

Well, all right! I'd shocked them. That, too, served a political function: presenting them with a point of view they had never before encountered.

Afterwards, over coffee and cake, a number of people would offer me kind words. "Very interesting," or "I disagree, of course, but you made some telling points." Or "I thought you handled that very well."

I wasn't sure how my message would be received— but they seemed to like me, by God. I was the rebel who justified the democratic process. They could all go home and say, "Hey, wasn't that exciting!" Perhaps it made them feel broadminded, even virtuous, to listen to a man who spoke from the heart.

There were many outings, many not controversial, some of them fun, and I got good press coverage. Newspapers were sympathetic and took me seriously. I made jokes about myself, and on the week before primary day, the *Maine Sunday Telegram* ran a big picture story about me in which I was allowed to speak my mind. They referred to my nonconformist reputation. This was precisely the time for a nonconformist congressman, I told them.

Many friends wrote, some with contributions. The most memorable was a note with a ten-dollar bill enclosed. The writer said, "I was on the march with you in Selma. Good luck!" That could keep a man going for a while.

Michael spent his Easter vacation on the campaign trail with me, rallying his friends to help pass out leaflets, do door-to-door solicitations, address and seal envelopes. Because ours was such a small, independent venture, it made Michael and his friends wince when they witnessed the political professionalism of my rivals.

A lot of ground was covered in those four months before primary day, and I saw many new faces. When I considered my chances, I kept telling myself to be skeptical. But I wanted so badly to help end the war that I was convinced I had a real chance to do something good, something worthwhile. Wasn't I speaking about what the American public really wanted to hear? And wasn't this in fact the optimum time in our history for the likes of me?

Then June 17th was upon us. When the results were finally in, I stared at the figures like one reading his own obituary.

Horace Hildreth, Jr.	23,594
David Ault	6,448
Gary Merrill	5,674

I had never been one to suffer much when I was defeated, but this was a crusher. My friend, John Cole, editor of the weekly *Maine Times*, assured me that I had not done so poorly, that I was bucking a machine politician, a man with established political family connections—and that every vote I got was purely for me. I had to win every one of them by myself. And I'd got one out of six votes—not bad for a beginner.

10

MANY CAREERS

P olitics, politicians, and the ins and outs of their decisions have become as much a part of my daily fare as breakfast or the morning mail. Though I no longer think of running for office, democracy in action is like a long-running play in which I have a small part.

In the sixties and seventies, I spent a lot of time in Washington, D.C. These visits always sparked my hunger to participate in some fashion in the political process. Sitting in the gallery in Congress whetted my desire to be on the floor below. I sometimes took Mike to see the action, and once even sat him in the Speaker's chair, with permission from the famous "Fishbait" Miller, the head doorkeeper of the House of Representatives at the time.

"Now take me to Westminster Abbey," Mike quipped.

Fishbait was a warm, ebullient, archetypal southern gentleman, full of blarney, and a lover of people. He would do anything for anybody.

I had first met him in the mid-sixties when I had gone to D.C. to co-host some pilots for a television series to be called "Perle Mesta's Washington," with Perle Mesta her-

224

Above: Bette and Gary at home, Witch Way.

Below: with Barbara Stanwyck in *Witness to Murder*, 1954.
"That movie wasn't a bad picture. George Sanders was in it. I never thought much about it, though. I'd just do it. I went in and said my lines and went home — back to the beach."

Above: *The Black Dakotas*,
1954.
*"I never learned to ride a
horse. I'd just get on 'em and
off 'em. I hate horses. But I
loved westerns. You didn't
have to do anything: somebody
else'd do all the riding, and
then they'd fight, and you'd sit
down and watch them."*

Left: *The Missouri Traveler*,
with Brandon de Wilde,
1958.
*"I was dispensing a little
discipline here, I guess."*

SHOCKING! VIOLENT! RAW!

GARY MERRILL · JAN STERLING
in
'THE HUMAN JUNGLE'
with PAULA RAYMOND · EMILE MEYER
AN ALLIED ARTISTS PICTURE

The Human Jungle, with Jan Sterling, 1954.
Below: "*All the fighting was done by stuntmen. Then you'd go in and they'd take a closeup. This was just a pose.*"

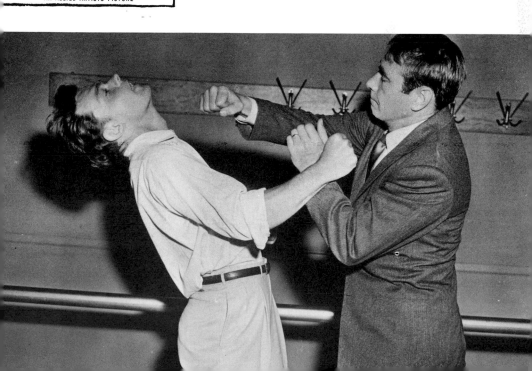

THIS IS THE STORY of our daughÌ
By calendar computation, Margot is eigÌ
In all other ways, except for her size, Ì
four. She is one of the unfortunate Ì
every one hundred children who are boÌ

I have taught myself to accept thÌ
Margot is as she is, and to be as franÌ
disability as I would be if she sufferedÌ
matic fever or a broken leg. This is notÌ
But until it is done, a retarded child,Ì
the stimulation and the competition ofÌ
has an unhappy time.

Margot came to Gary and me throuÌ
who knew we wished to adopt a child.Ì
child of an unmarried mother, and caÌ
world with the easiest possible birth.Ì
examination left nothing to be desireÌ
was so beautiful that Gary and I scÌ
believe our good fortune.

We brought her home, from the hoÌ
she was born, when she was five days cÌ
I said to our three-year-old daughter, ÌÌ
down in a chair, please, and close youÌ
have the most wonderful surprise!"

We put Margot in her lap. I canÌ
her joy.

Margot cried a great deal as a baÌ
cried differently than I remembered ÌÌ
But, as we all told each other, knÌ
enough, children differ. We were toÌ
more and more frequently and with Ì
conviction that it was an adequate exÌ
what went on.

I remember the first time MargotÌ
away. Gary, B. D. and I stood lauÌ
children's governess overtook her in aÌ

MARGOT seemed to be a normal as well as a beautiful
baby, but the doctors later
found that she had been born
with serious brain damage.

BETTE and GARY make fre-
quent visits to their 8-year-old
daughter, who has made much
progress in a private school
with other retarded children.

"Ou

By BETTE DAVIS
AS TOLD TO ADELE WHITELY FLETCHER
PHOTOGRAPHS BY JAMES ABBE, JR.

ow fast Margot runs!" said Gary, with ride.

mber the day I left Margot in the car pped to say hello to a neighbor. When I f the house, Margot had taken off all her

en often strip," friends told me, laughing, run away." But there was something way Margot did these things, and the with which she did them, that worried seemed driven.

nd fears moved up and down in a crazy d at night, when I was half asleep and censor was off guard, all the disturbing had pushed away during the day would ing to the surface.

Margot did not have much of a vocabu-nds used to ask—in what I'm sure they as a casual, off-hand manner—"How's department?" However, she made up k of words with reiteration. "Hi," she day after day, "Hi, Hi, Hi, Hi, Hi, Hi. " while I prayed that I would keep my d my sanity.

were something to dread. Five minutes had put her to bed she would be up crib bars and screaming. We would take ing her down, telling her it was time to es and go to sleep. Within five minutes be up again. By two or three o'clock in ng, exhausted from lack of sleep, she n a nervous rage. And sometimes, I am were, too.

mber the day she tried to choke her

orry," I was told. "It doesn't mean a

thing when children are cruel to animals. They have no moral sense until they are older."

I treasured such reassurances. And sometimes Margot herself would offer me fresh hope that things were not as bad as I feared; especially when she was dressed for a party, in her white dress and blue sash, her black Mary Janes, all tubbed and shiny, the customary perplexed look in her eyes dissipated by her excitement.

Too often her brother, Michael, was her victim. The competition he, a normal child, offered frus-trated her to a point of fury. More than once she pulled out his baby hair in tufts. And one dreadful day, when she was two and he was one, realizing they had been gone from the room for several min-utes, I began, fearfully, to look for them. I found them at the bar. Broken glasses were on the floor. Margot was standing watching Michael, who, view-ing the bleeding nicks on his hands and arms, was crying.

Finally, because I could not control Margot, I announced to our household, "No one is to correct Margot today—whatever she does. I think I have been overdoing the discipline a bit, making her nervous and rebellious. Let us see."

Within two hours, half of the things in her room were hopelessly broken.

"We need professional help," I said to Gary. "For Margot's sake. For all our sakes." Gary agreed.

We took Margot to the Presbyterian Hospital in New York. During a week's stay she was examined thoroughly, mentally and physically. We were told that our adopted daughter was a brain-

injured child and that her IQ was only 60.

An IQ of 60 meant, of course, that she was an "in between." If your child has an IQ of only 40 you can say, "This is my tragedy. My child always will have to be cared for like a baby and never may emerge into society." But with care and training a child with a 60 IQ can be equipped for a life within the limits of his, or her, mental capacity.

For an emotionally disturbed person there is hope. Deep anxieties and emotional blocks some-times can be cleared away or lessened. Brain damage is irreparable.

I wonder about Margot's brain damage, whether it was caused perhaps by the abortive drugs her mother may have taken. This is only my personal thinking. But those with whom I have discussed this theory find it reasonable. And I am hoping tests will be conducted along this line some day.

The doctors of the examining board assured us, for instance, that Margot really wanted to stay in bed at night, but that she couldn't put on her own brakes. She couldn't cope with herself.

They recommended that we get her a jacket which would permit her complete freedom in bed but make it impossible for her to get out of bed. This we did. And she seemed grateful for it. For the first time in two years she slept through the night.

One of the doctors served us well when he told us: "Just remember that the frustration of retarded children when they are subjected to normal life throws them into a permanent rage. They should be with others like themselves."

The National Association for Retarded Children tells us there *(Continued on following page)*

WITH HER older sister, Bar-bara ("B. D.") at the wheel, Margot, with Gary and Michael, made a tractor tour of their estate on the coast of Maine.

THIS IS the school where Margot is getting the expert care that helps "in-between" children make the most of their limited mental powers.

PHIL STERN

aughter"

Above: Bette and Gary with Carl Sandburg, 1959.
Below right: *We were rehearsing a scene from* The World of Carl Sandburg *in the Cape Elizabeth Grange Hall.*

AGEBILL
Chicago's Theatre Magazine

BETTE DAVIS and GARY MERRILL
in
"THE WORLD OF CARL SANDBURG"
CIVIC THEATRE

FIRE EXIT

(Continued on page 69)

Ella
rsons
ngs you
he truth
about
the new
and zany
romance
that
has set
all
Hollywood
on
its ear

Rita Hayworth
&
Gary Merrill

FOR LOVE
OR
LAUGHS?

28

Above: *Modern Screen*, 1961.
Right: *Photoplay*, 1961.
*"You couldn't believe these
goddam magazines! I never
read any of them. The studio
publicity people fed them."*

24

Rita Hayworth a
are burning with

Rita and Merrill In Hong Kong— About to Marry?

Looks Like It

GARY MERRILL met actress Rita Hayworth at Hong Kong airport Wednesday with a big kiss and a hint that their globe trotting romance was about to culminate in marriage.

Merrill told newsmen a Chinese fortune teller had predicted his third marriage would be his last.

"Rita is the third," he said. He walked away without answering further questions. Miss Hayworth had nothing to say to reporters.

Merrill is working in an Italian-produced movie being filmed in Hong Kong.

Merrill said Miss Hayworth would spend about a week in Hong Kong and that the two then plan to visit other parts of Asia in June.

MERRILL   **RITA**

ณะบินกลับไทย
สะพานพุทธ

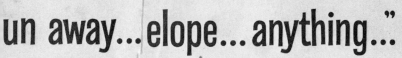

you   marry him,
un away... elope... anything..."

very happy. The girl stretched out her lovely and called out so everyone could hear her. "Oh, o wonderful to be out seeing people again. It's onderful to be free."

girl was Rita Hayworth. The boy was Gary

Her second husband was Orson Welles, then a Hollywood-styled and self-styled genius. Orson was brilliant; Rita was inarticulate. Orson was worldly; Rita knew only one world—the private, closed world of backstage.

went to Europe in 1948, she took four-year-old Rebecca with her. Remember that year—1948—for that was the year Rita met Aly Khan—one-quarter Persian, one-quarter Iranian, one-half Italian and all charmer. Since Aly's father was then the Aga Khan

Gary and Rita on the Grand Canal, Venice, 1961. *"The paparazzi found us."*

Left: at a friend's house, California.

Opposite: playbill for *Step on a Crack* , 1961.

ROGER L. STEVENS and HERBERT SWOPE, Jr.

present

RITA   GARY
HAYWORTH MERRILL

in

STEP ON A CRACK

A New Drama by **BERNARD EVSLIN**

also starring

MARGARET HAYES   MAGGIE McNAMARA

with

BARBARA MATTES   BILL HICKEY   JOEY HEATHERTON

and

DONALD MADDEN

Scenery and Lighting by   Costumes by
GEORGE JENKINS   PATRICIA ZIPPRODT

Staged by **MR. SWOPE**

"Phil Stern and I were just fiddling around, taking some pictures. The ball was leaning against the wall, so it'd look like I was balancing it."

Gary and Ed Muskie
(next to Gary) at a benefit,
late 1960's.

USO SHOWS

in association with

THE HOLLYWOOD OVERSEAS COMMITTEE

presents

GARY MERRILL
and
SUSAN OLIVER

VIETNAM
COMING SOON!
CONTACT SPECIAL SERVICES OFFICER FOR DETAILS

Program for USO tour in Vietnam, 1967.
"Susan Oliver was a better pilot than an actress."

DON JOHNSON

Cape Elizabeth, 1967.
Gary telling Lady Bird Johnson how to get the most meat
out of a Maine lobster. Secretary of the Interior Stewart Udall
on right. *"I saw all those cameras."*

Actor quits Democrats over Viet Nam stance

FREEPORT, Maine (Reuters)—Actor Gary Merrill, who is seeking the Republican nomination for Congress here as a "peace candidate," says he believes that an unconditional bombing of

the Democratic party over the Viet Nam issue and w seeking the Republic nomination for Main Democrat-held first elec al district "because J son has to be gotten rid "I'm just so ada about Johnson bein

Toronto Star,
1968.

"If Reagan Can Do It, Why Can't I?"

GARY MERRILL

FOR CONGRESS

Ken Foster

...nning for Congress, 1968.
...ght: *"I said, 'Why don't you ...n me? I'm a better actor ...n he is!'"*

...low: on the campaign trail.
...his was at a great place in ...rtland, with the greatest ...h chowder."

I thought Gary Merrill was very good. Also, I thought he was the most ~~fanatic~~ fascinating man I ever have seen before

I thought it would be very boring, but it was. Quite surprised, how then it was. The way he read made you sit up and listen. He read poems so they had meaning to them.

I didn't like it I would have rathe[r] had science.

Left: a poetry reading.
Above: a few student reviews of Gary.

Above: Gary and Amy Carter, 1976.

Right: Gary as Captain Hull, with George Hamilton in a television special, *The Seekers*, 1979.

"That was just a couple of days' work. I told them afterwards, 'Why didn't you just send me the money?' You're in a thing like that for just a second. You know— they load it with all these people. Who's gonna know whether I was in it or not? Dummies! . . . I had the best suntan because I was out of work more often."

Above: Gary, on left, in Hirschfeld caricature of *Morning's at Seven*, 1980.

Left: picketing the release of B.D.'s book about Bette, 1985.

Below: Gary's ad

PLEASE Boycott My Mother's Keeper

No Mother Deserves This

ANYTHING FOR A BUCK . . . Greed was B.D. Hyman's guide when she wrote "My Mother's Keeper", the scurrilous new book about B.D.'s mother, actress Bette Davis. Anything for a buck is what William Morrow & Co. must have said when they published it

SUPPORT YOUR LOCAL LIBRARY . . . Don't fork over almost 20 bucks for this book. Visit your library, or buy one copy and pass it along.

AND SUPPORT BETTE . . . Write her* and wish her well. Tell her you are boycotting the book. You'll both feel better.

A message from Gary Merrill, Bette's friend and former husband.

Thornhurst Road
Falmouth Foreside, ME 04105

*Write: Bette Davis, c/o Harold Schiff, 455 East 57 St., N. Y., N. Y. 10

Margot at 35, 1985.

Gary with his son Michael,
a lawyer in Brookline,
Massachusetts, and grandsons
Matthew (left) and Cameron,
1986.

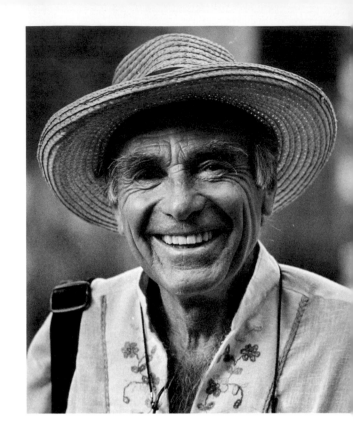

At home in Falmouth
Foreside, Maine.

self. Perle was known as the "hostess with the mostest," and had inspired the Broadway musical *Call Me Madam*, in which Ethel Merman starred. The premise of the TV show supposedly was that we would interview leading politicians in such a way as to provide the viewer with the man's or woman's human side.

We were to do three pilots—three half-hour shows done on speculation—in the hope that one of the networks would pick up the series. I was excited by the prospect because I thought there was great potential for entertainment as well as information about how our government works, and about the people involved in it. Selfishly, too, I envisioned visiting various embassies and offices around the world.

I asked one of the producers, "Why me?" He said that when he had approached Mrs. Mesta, she had been interested but had professed a complete lack of knowledge about television and interview shows. She had asked for a professional co-host, someone who wouldn't overshadow her but who would help keep the show on a professional level. I had been involved with television, was politically curious, and somewhat gregarious.

We were expected to complete three half-hour pilots in one day! Knowing the problems of filming for television, particularly for color television at that time, I doubted that even one show would be completed. But that was before I met Perle Mesta.

The evening before the shows were to be taped, the producers, the director, and I met Mrs. Mesta for dinner, where she impressed me tremendously. At that meeting, I began to suspect those shows could indeed be done in one day. As we said our goodnights, she reminded us that we were to join her in her box the following evening at the Washington horse show, a gala social occasion, and following that, we would be expected to attend a black-tie dinner.

Arrangements had been made for us to meet at the studio the following morning at eight o'clock.

I thought: "She's impressive, but this is pushing it! An entire day in a studio, then a horse show and a formal dinner—and she must be well into her seventies. She'll collapse!"

At eight o'clock the next morning we greeted our first two guests, not exactly political types: Jeane Dixon, the prophetess and fortuneteller who was also a successful real estate developer (an unbeatable combination, I thought); the other woman was a writer of books on the subject of the occult. While we were shaking hands, Miss Dixon assured me that I had the heart of a young man, and that I'd live a long time. It was a fine way to start any day, and particularly the one ahead.

It was almost unbelievable to me, but we had the first show finished in a comparatively short time, and we began preparing for the second before lunch. For the second pilot we interviewed two ambassadors' wives, Madame Herve Alphond of France and a beautiful young woman from Kuwait, whose name meant "smile." (I asked whether her smile or the name came first, but have forgotten the answer.) While we were taping the second show, Mrs. Mesta was informed that her guest for the third show, Vice President Hubert Humphrey, had been forced to cancel. He'd been called to President Johnson's ranch in Texas. I didn't worry about it and figured that the two shows we'd done were enough. Perle emphatically disagreed. She'd promised three shows, and there would be three. "I'll get Fishbait," she said.

We all looked at each other and said, "Who the hell is *Fishbait?*"

When she described the man and explained what his job was, we agreed immediately that it was a great idea. As soon as he arrived, we knew everything would be just fine. Nothing flustered him; he was as natural in front of the camera as in person. He gave us a shot in the arm at the end of the long, hard session.

One of Fishbait's more exciting jobs was to introduce the President of the United States when he addressed a joint session of Congress. "Mr. Speakuh, the President of the United States," he announced. That was his line, and he delivered it clearly and proudly, in stentorian tones.

With the exception of Dwight Eisenhower, presidents from Harry S Truman on had been members of Congress. Fishbait had known them all as freshman congressmen. He was in charge of the practical matters of Congress, from toilet paper to pages, and he had helped everyone in their struggle to find their way around the maze of the Capitol. He thought of them as "his boys." I asked him how he felt when he announced them as presidents. "Gary, ah get goose bumps all over me ever' time ah say it," he answered.

A stranger visiting the Capitol for the first time might be lost for days without the help of someone like Fishbait. It never happened to me after I became his friend. I'd go directly to his office for information. I can hear him now, calling to an assistant, "Get Gary a page or we'll have him here forever." And off I'd go with my guide.

I was intrigued by his nickname. He explained that when he was a boy growing up in Mississippi he'd been very skinny, so small and thin that he seemed no larger than fishbait. The name just stuck, and his proper name— William—was so seldom used that he might not answer if it were.

Our taping of the show with Fishbait wound up by dinnertime, just as Mrs. Mesta had promised. We all left the set for our hotels to dress for the horse show and dinner. Perle Mesta was indefatigable. We arrived at the show to find her resplendent, as radiant as she had been at eight in the morning, sparkling with some of her fabulous pieces of jewelry. She was as friendly and open with everyone who greeted her as if she had spent the afternoon lazing in a warm bath.

After the horse show we moved on to a hotel. Mrs. Mesta's dinner party was sprinkled with notables, and it was after one in the morning when the guest of honor retired. Protocol being satisfied, Mrs. Mesta was finally free to say, "Goodnight and thank you." It had been a seventeen-hour day, and she had remained graceful throughout.

The show never sold, and no reason was given. It might be too pat to say that it was *too* good, in comparison with other TV fare—but I tend to believe it was. It reminded me of another aborted TV production I had been involved with, in Boston in 1959. There were practically no "talk shows" in those days, and I had what I thought was an interesting idea. I would assemble several specialists on a particular subject; after each expert was introduced, I would give him an opportunity to discuss his views and expertise; after this, there would be a general discussion about a current social problem—usually one that was much in the news.

For the first show, I had cajoled a medical internist friend from Pennsylvania, an architect from Maine, a writer from Italy, and the dean of the Harvard Business School to appear for our first "Round Table" discussion. The set consisted of a round table surrounded by a few director's chairs, a rocking chair, and a revolving bookcase.

Mary Harding, my writer friend from Italy, in America to promote her book *Dear Friends and Darling Romans*, really zeroed in on our subject for the afternoon, juvenile delinquency. Mary said there was very little in Rome because Italian parents felt a kick in the ass is love, too. The discussion was lively, intelligent, and thoroughly enjoyable—which came across on the tape. But the station manager decided to drop the program. I later asked if I could take the tape to New York, but it had already been erased. I was heartbroken.

That same fall, David Susskind launched his talk show, and I dropped my idea. There was nothing I could have done about the Mesta show, but, in retrospect, I think I should have fought harder to realize my Round Table.

During the sixties I took Michael on many of my travels. He once visited me in Rome, where I was working on an Italian production. Several years before, the production company had run out of money before the film was completed, but now we had returned to finish the picture. When the shooting was done, Michael and I planned to extend our trip and go on to Israel.

An amenity I specified in Rome was a swimming pool at my hotel. American production companies on location there used the Hilton, or several other hotels known to cater to American tastes. But our company knew of a new Italian hotel, the Parco. It was a wonderful surprise. The floors were covered with cool tiles, the pool was beautiful, and because of the hotel's location I was able to walk to work every day. Michael found some young friends, and he enjoyed our stay as much as I did. One day we ran into Godfrey Cambridge, the wonderful black actor and comedian. He was on a roll, and I'd never heard Mike laugh so completely.

It was just a year after the Six-Day War when we arrived in Israel. I thought it would be fascinating to visit the Suez, so upon our arrival we got in touch with a colonel from the public relations office of the Israeli Army. He suggested we go north, where we could at least see the Golan Heights. Although there had been considerable action there, he thought it unlikely that we would be turned back because of the military situation.

I would rather have rented a car and wandered

about on our own, but neither Michael nor I could decipher the road signs, so we hired a driver, Michael Gal. He was a godsend who did a wonderful job of showing us a bit of everything during the short time we had—from diamond cutters to the old Roman ruins at Haifa. At the Golan Heights, as we clambered over rusting tanks and poked around the parapets and trenches, we understood why the Heights had had to be taken with very close combat. I was chilled when I realized that the soldiers had to look into the eyes of those they were shooting.

We traveled to Nablus, in Samaria, then on to Bethlehem and Jerusalem. While we wandered about Jerusalem, seeing holy places of three of the great religions of the world, we found ourselves wondering why it couldn't become an international city, belonging to all the people of the world. In Jerusalem and many other places, Arabs and Israelis lived side by side, behaving as neighbors do in any other town.

I carried a letter of introduction to Meyer Weisgal, the producer of *The Eternal Road,* one of the first plays in which I had a part (as an extra). He was on a visit to Israel. Because of the hundreds of extras in the cast, there was no reason in the world why Meyer would have remembered me, so I felt the introductory letter would be useful. We knocked at his door one morning and found him just finishing a late breakfast, still in his pajamas and robe. But he was a gregarious fellow who welcomed us warmly.

He looked at Michael's blond hair and blue eyes and said, "Who's the goy?" (I later had to explain "goy" to Mike.)

One of the high points was a night we spent in a kibbutz. This way of life seemed very civilized. Children were brought together during the day and supervised by the members of the kibbutz who specialized in child care, and went home at night to their parents. Everyone held a job in his or her field of expertise, but once a week all were required to share in the scullery work. At the kibbutz it wasn't just the women who were responsible for it; everyone shared the drudgery. Women on the kibbutz were actively involved at all levels of planning and establishing the new community. They were also required to spend a period of time serving in the Israeli Army, doing whatever was necessary as soldiers. In my opinion, it was this successful example set by the kibbutz society that gave the women's movement in the United States its model of what might be accomplished in liberalizing women's roles in modern America.

All too soon we left Israel, and my son Michael had to leave me in Rome to go back to the States. I planned to visit Michael Craig, an English actor I'd met in Spain while filming *Mysterious Island*. Craig was about to leave England for Ireland to begin making a picture with Peter O'Toole. Since I had a free week or two before I was due in Philadelphia to start another picture, I decided to travel with him. I had long been an admirer of Peter O'Toole, and looked forward to meeting him. I flew to England.

As it turned out, my timing was perfect. Michael Craig's driving license had been suspended, so I offered my services as a chauffeur until we reached the ferryboat to Ireland. I hadn't driven on the left side of the road for quite some time, but, with only a few exclamations of "You're looking the wrong way!" from Michael, I managed fairly well.

When we arrived in Dublin, I found Peter O'Toole to be even more vivid than I had expected—a tall, reed-thin, extremely handsome man, as wild and spirited as a thoroughbred horse. He was so thorough, in fact, that he'd managed to have *his* driving license suspended for life! Wonderful, mad Peter decided there were certain things I should see in Ireland.

"Let me mark your chart," he said. "You've got to see Dr. Johnny Walsh in Ballybunion. You'll run into a fellow who works for Dr. Johnny who's going to build my house—right here." He made another mark where his house would be.

We went off to a rental agency to get a car for me, and I discovered that Ireland had a law prohibiting the lease of cars by actors! Apparently, we weren't considered sufficiently responsible people. It took some time to cut through the red tape.

When I finally got the car I set off and drove south on lanes skirting the seacoast whenever possible. The landscape was brooding, rocky, quite treeless, and I saw real poverty. Only goats or sheep could survive on this land, and the small farmhouses had rock walls surrounding struggling vegetables and flowers, an attempt to protect them from the relentless winds rolling off the sea. The effect was a beautiful but poignant timelessness.

As I turned west and drove inland, the countryside changed to a lush greenness, punctuated by fishing lodges along the many streams. This is the Ireland visited by tourists, and I suppose most remain unaware of the poverty that exists a few stone's throws away. Whenever the driving began to lull me to drowsiness, I pulled off the road to take a short nap in a field. Once I awoke to find the face of a very large sheep staring down at me.

Along the route to Ballybunion, I passed a number of pedestrians, and some of them waved as I went by. It dawned on me that the friendly, waist-level wave was not that of a person out for a walk, but a way of asking for a ride—they were hitchhikers! Their gesture was the most refined variation I'd ever seen, a suggestion so subtle that a driver need feel no guilt for not stopping. And the hiker had an out, too. He might feel that if his request hadn't been acknowledged it was because it hadn't been seen. In the

United States, I'd always felt guilty about not stopping, and knew the person with the high thumb was saying to himself, "You selfish son of a bitch." But in Ireland everyone could save face. It seemed very civilized.

Ballybunion is a summer resort about six miles west of Listowel. It is a lovely place on the Atlantic. After washing up in the bridal suite of a hotel—the only room available with a private bath—I called Peter's friend, Dr. Johnny, to ask when I might visit him.

We went out to dinner the next day. Dr. Johnny was a robust, jovial, witty man, and his wife, Peggy, a charming, gentle lady. They told me about their life and their family, and answered some of my questions about Ireland. At one point during dinner, Dr. Johnny said, "Would you like to know when I first saw Peter? He was brought to me from a Boy Scout camp, and I was looking at a boil on his arse."

After leaving Ballybunion, I had to drive through part of Northern Ireland. At the border I drove up to a bridge and saw a gatehouse. But there were no guards. The gate was up, so I went on through. An hour or so later I came to the border again, on my way back to Dublin, but this time there were guards on duty. I had no papers with me and the guards asked how I'd gotten in. I explained that I'd come through the northern gate around seven o'clock that morning, but as no one was there, I'd just kept on going.

"Oh," said the guard. "We don't open till eight."

Imagine not opening one's country till eight o'clock! Again, a civilized attitude. I doubt, however, that, with the increased violence in Northern Ireland, such a border crossing exists today.

Back in Dublin, I found Peter O'Toole and Mike Craig, and we had a wild night together. The next day I flew to Philadelphia. The script of the picture I did in Philadelphia was so bad that the movie was never released.

That fall of 1968, my son entered the University of North Carolina at Chapel Hill, his first step toward adulthood. In due course he attended Boston University Law School and became a lawyer. Michael is now married to a woman named Charlene, who is known as Chou-Chou, and they have two children, Matthew and Cameron. When in law school, Michael became close friends with another young student, and they got on so well they decided to open their own law office together. Eventually, Michael was elected a selectman in Brookline, a suburb of Boston. He was the youngest selectman ever to be elected in the community—a first step into the political arena. His original law partner left to open his own office, and Mike now has a new law partner, a bright young woman.

During Michael's college years, I was living in a converted stable just minutes away from Portland. I learned to live alone, but I fought my tendency to become a hermit not only by continuing to keep in touch with the political climate of the state and the country, but also by making forays into the business world. I began by investing in an automobile agency. Ernie Viveirous, a Maine automobile dealer, called to see if I would be interested in a Florida Fiat franchise that he had heard about at a convention. The Fiat was a dependable little car, perfect for economy-minded Americans, and, as it dominated the Italian market, it had to have a lot of quality going for it. The extent of my knowledge of cars was to drive them to either Bothel's or Jonesy's garage in Cape Elizabeth, but the business opportunity Ernie described was made to sound as though heaven had opened to show me the way—and double my money. I was reluctant at first, insisting I didn't know a thing about business, but Ernie was enthusiastic, and eventually the opportunity began to appeal to me. I took the plunge and made a plane reservation to St. Petersburg, to meet with other investors in the fledgling corporation.

There were only a half-dozen people in the first-class section, and before long we were all talking together, becoming a chummy little group. I found myself talking with a gentleman who gave his name as Cody Fowler, a lawyer from Florida. It soon became apparent that he was in love with his home state, because he began selling Florida as eagerly as I promoted Maine. The more we talked, the more I liked him, so I took the next step.

"Well, Christ," I exclaimed, "I'm going down to your state to make a business deal with a man I never met. I'm getting involved in a business I know nothing about. Why don't you come along to help me out? I need a lawyer, and it might as well be a lawyer I don't know."

He picked up on the suggestion and it was only later that I was told that Cody Fowler was "the biggest fuckin' lawyer in Florida, and how'd I ever get him?"

Before the week was out, we formed Gary Merrill Import Motors, Inc. I was the backer and promoter.

If everything about a business were as simple as setting one up, more than half the people of the world would be running corporations. The underlying cause for the decline of my car-import business was the unavailability of Fiat parts. The Fiat franchise was controlled by a company in New Jersey, through which all cars and parts were processed. Unless a local dealership is stocked with parts, or at least has ready access to them, who would buy the car? For us, in Florida, it was difficult to obtain Fiat parts when they were needed. In three years we were washed up. I managed to get a bit of my investment back by spending a few weeks in Florida during the winter at the homes of my fellow investors. However, I was never one to anguish over money lost.

Not all my business investments have been failures. My very first venture did extremely well. This was way back in 1937 when I replaced José Ferrer in *Brother Rat*. A lot of us in the cast found ourselves with little money at the end of the week, usually because of a poker game or "games" with women. The actor George Meister devised a way to tide himself over until payday by putting together sandwiches to sell. He was doing pretty well, so I asked if I could get in on the action. "Hell yes," he agreed. "We can expand." Together, we bought lox, cream cheese, ham, salami, rye bread—all the stuff that makes a good sandwich. We didn't forget about dessert. We'd buy a whole cake and sell it by the slice. Every night was a sellout. Because there was no overhead—just a table to set up—George and I made out like bandits.

In the late sixties, I fell into another successful venture. Bob Jurgenson opened the World Travel Agency in Portland. He needed the relatively small sum of five thousand dollars for operating capital, in addition to what he and his wife Betty put up. I was able to come up with the funds, and there has been a return on my investment ever since.

Once, when I was living in California, I tried unsuccessfully to persuade Eaton Tarbell to join me. He did come out to look things over, but he wouldn't move from Maine. At one point we walked the expanse of a beach south of Los Angeles with another friend, Nick Katchedoorian, who grows grapes for raisins. (He sends me a package of them now and then, usually at Christmas, and they are the best. When I first got some I noticed the vine was still attached, and I complained. "For Chrissake, Nick, this is pretty messy with all the sticks still attached." He explained that the longer they stay on the vine, the fresher they remain. That ended my protest.)

At the time of Eaton's visit, as the three of us walked along the beach, we noticed that it was sparsely populated, with entire stretches of beautiful, unspoiled land along the oceanfront. Eaton said, "Why don't you pick up some of this land. Prices are pretty reasonable." Well, of course, that would have been the thing to do, considering the development of California, but lacking in foresight I let it ride.

The idea of real estate development stuck with me, however. When I moved back to Maine after my divorce from Bette, I went so far as to take a real estate course to obtain a broker's license. I had to take the test twice to pass it, and then went out and bought a lighthouse on Cape Elizabeth, which, with Eaton's creative assistance as an architect, was scheduled to become my home. The structure had been abandoned for some time, and had been vandalized, but it was basically sound. I looked forward to the remodeling with enthusiasm, and the local newspapers were also enthusiastic. On a trip out to show the place to my friend John Cole, we came across a bird's nest on one of the stairwells at the top of the lighthouse. He became quite excited about it. "Wow, Gary," John shouted, "those look like osprey's eggs! You've got ospreys nesting in your lighthouse."

Ospreys are large, beautiful eagle-like birds. John advised me to find someone to positively identify the eggs, so on another trip I took along an ornithologist—who positively identified them as pigeon's eggs! Eventually, the idea of redoing the lighthouse became more of a bother than it seemed to be worth. It was on a rise of land that overlooked the ocean, but was not on the shore. Many small houses had been built up around it. So, after owning the lighthouse for four years, and after it had consumed a fair amount of my energy, I sold it.

Actually, I have long been involved in a business in which I have become quite successful: television commercials. For many years I had as my agents Noel Rubaloff and Harry Abrams, whose firm was a spin-off from Jules Stein's MCA. Back in 1948, they had found me the Lucky Strike cigarette commercials to do, as well as a few other things on radio. Jim Daly, who had been my understudy in *Born Yester-*

day, was doing well with commercials, and through the years I ran into him now and then in New York.

One gray day in the late sixties I was staying at the Plaza Hotel in New York. Clouds hung low over the city, bouncing off the skyscrapers, and it was raining like hell. I had been set up with an appointment for an audition at the Cunningham and Walsh advertising agency, but I was reluctant to join the sodden streams of humanity on the streets below. Instead, I called a friend to come over for a drink, thinking we might have a cozy afternoon inside. She insisted on keeping a late-afternoon appointment, however, and couldn't be convinced otherwise, so I offered to accompany her there.

Since I was out, I decided I might as well keep my appointment at the agency. I sat in the waiting room, in a cocoon of boredom. I looked up to see my old friend from *All About Eve,* Hugh Marlowe, who had just completed his audition. We exchanged greetings, then I went in to do mine. This kind of audition consists of reading material for the commercial—the same material that at least twenty others may already have read. Then somebody decides if he or she wants you. For this particular commercial, it was only the voice they wanted.

I went in, was handed a script, read it . . . and got the job. To my pleasure, it amounted to a ten-year run, giving me a solid financial base! It was my first TV commercial for Old Milwaukee beer—"Old Milwaukee . . . Tastes as great as its name!" It was great! Only a few hours work, lots of time for play.

Another turning point in my commercials career occurred not long after. I got a call in Maine on a Saturday from another advertising agency. One of the first questions was, "Do you have blue eyes?"

"No, mine are brown."

"Good," said the voice. "Can you be in New York to

do a commercial on Monday?"

"I'll have to get back to you," I replied. Then I called my agent to tell him about the offer. The company involved was doing a commercial which was to be shown during an NBC show of Richard Nixon's trip to China, which was big news. I would get twenty-five thousand for one day's work. My agent agreed that the offer was sound.

Other jobs followed: I did TV ads for airlines, automobiles, cereal, books, and newspapers—*The Wall Street Journal*, Sears, Volvo, IBM, etc. In order to ease my conscience about selling people things they don't need and might not want, I refused to do commercials for toys that feature guns or bombs or anything else that might confuse children into thinking that war is just another game.

I have my father to thank for my voice. It's a slow, lazy sort of voice that conjures up a certain integrity—very like his. All his life, my father had toiled in an insurance company, wanting to make enough to keep up with the neighbors. He sang in a choral group, but he could have owned the whole damned neighborhood if only he had known how to use his voice to earn a living.

I had never had voice lessons in my youth. I did not even realize that there might be a proper or improper way to use my voice. But as I began doing more TV commercials, I hired a coach. He helped me learn to project from the diaphragm, deepening my tones, using my vocal chords as a singer does. I had never done a thing to help in the past—I shouted myself hoarse at football games and smoked cigarettes! The few times I became hoarse or had laryngitis, a shot of vitamin B-12 cleared the annoyance in a few hours. But now I am conscious of my voice's value. It has been my bread and butter, like a dancer's feet or a pianist's hands. My voice teacher, Keith Davis, said that I was capable of performing in musicals if I worked at it. Not, of course, as a great singer. But I can carry a tune, and the natural quality of my voice would do the rest.

Keith Davis taught me that using the voice is a science as well as an art. He encouraged warm-up exercises: speaking at various levels from subdued to excited; he taught me how to handle the sound as the tone rises. When I become excited, I automatically control my voice to avoid damaging it, even when I am not acting.

During my radio years I had met a short, unprepossessing actor who had a beautiful, seductive voice often heard on soap operas. He became quite well known. When I asked the secret of his success, he said: "I think 'cock!' with every line."

As my career diversified, I discovered another use for my voice, one that has given me profound enjoyment—reading poetry to an audience. The Sandburg play was the catalyst, or maybe it was simply his lovely poetry. Even though Bette prevented me from performing in the Sandburg show in New York, I didn't want to be deprived of continuing in this—for me—new and exciting medium of expression. Over a period of time I worked out a small program of poetry that I thought children might enjoy, selecting a few poems of Carl's and some by Robert Frost. I cooked up a plan to take it to the schools. I wanted to introduce children to poetry in a way that would make sense to them.

This was in 1965, and I was in New York City. I called my agent and asked if he would organize this for me by calling some schools. Although he thought I was crazy, he came through. My fee was one dime, at that time the subway fare. So, eventually, I found myself in a high school auditorium before an assembly of kids ranging from fourteen to seventeen.

"When I was your age," I began, "I didn't like poetry, didn't understand it. It was thrown at the class by teachers who didn't understand it. Certainly, they didn't really love it. But things have changed for me—I've come across two American poets who spell it out so beautifully. Carl Sandburg, for example, who could look at a person and write a poem about him."

I was considered quite a character around the New York City schools—in Brooklyn, the Bronx, in Queens, all over. For me, sharing the poetry was a complete joy. The kids' response convinced me that they would feel differently about poetry as a result of my readings. The teachers were enthusiastic too. I felt like Johnny Appleseed, dropping a few seeds here and there, hoping some would sprout and flourish.

When I would leave New York to return to Maine, I continued my efforts there, beginning with the Falmouth schools near my home. In Maine, what I was doing became newsworthy. Photographers and members of the press were sprinkled throughout the audiences. I read a report in which a teacher was quoted as saying that I had done more for poetry in that one day than the school had been able to accomplish in the entire semester. When I went to Florida one winter, I met with members of the state education association to see if I might do the same there. Their enthusiasm for the plan was so great that I was booked by over forty schools. By this time, I had picked up a lot of poetry that kids themselves had written. Here's one written by a young person:

PEOPLE

Some people are fat
Some people are skinny
Some people are tall
Some people are small
I am just right!

Petra Franklin, 7 going on 8

Another poem I use was written by Janet Neuman, a friend who is in her nineties:

I LOVE YOU DARLING

I love you darling,
I love you dearly;
But let's talk turkey
While we still think clearly.
You have a home
And a yacht to boot;
And frankly I want
Some of that loot.
Ere we are wed,
Please make a deed,
A document toward
My future need.
If you should stray
Or wander elsewhere
I'll be assured
I have my fair share.
My love is clear
As is my head;
So off to the lawyer
Before the bed.

Poetry has been written through the ages to fit every mood, every occasion. It can be extremely simple or positively cryptic. But if it's a good poem the message always elicits a clear response from the reader: laughter, reflection, melancholy, or even patriotism. Some of the most poignant writing I have seen was written by kids spending time in a juvenile detention center where I had been invited to read. Their poetry contained the essence of what was missing from their lives—love and freedom.

Under the auspices of the army and the USO, Mercedes McCambridge and I made a trip through Europe in 1970, visiting GIs at various bases. Our previous infatuation was ancient history, and our relationship had been cemented by friendship and respect. Mercedes was campaigning against drug and alcohol use. She was appalled that there was so much readily available to the servicemen. As she visited the hospitals and clubs, doing her work, she discovered that it was the army's policy to set the price of drinks in the clubs so low that they were almost free. "What's the good of being against it, talking about its effects, when it's being thrown around so freely?" she moaned.

While she was speaking to her groups and meeting soldiers and their families, I went to the schools the servicemen's children attended, to give poetry readings. The trip was a huge treat for me. One of our stops was an Eighth Air Force Base in England which had been a strategic location during World War II. The base had been cut out of the king's forest to supply the best possible landing strip for limping planes returning from forays into Germany. One of the runways pointed directly toward Germany. Although *Twelve O'Clock High* had been filmed in Florida, it was this air base and the men of the Eighth Air Force that the film was all about. I found that England was still proud of its alliance with the United States and what we had accomplished together in World War II. But in Spain I noticed a difference. At the Torrejon Air Force Base outside Madrid, there were signs instructing personnel to refrain from wearing uniforms off base.

I had contact with American kids at every base— and on eloquent terms. I was meeting them not only as myself but also through Frost and Sandburg. Their responses were warm and accepting.

One day, back in Maine, I happened to pick up two

hitchhikers. One of them looked at me curiously and I could almost see him thinking, "Do I know this guy?" But he was too shy to ask. Then, suddenly, his eyes lit up.

"Say," he said, as he looked at me intently, "aren't you the man who read us poems a few months ago?"

He had been at one of the base schools in England. He smiled, pointing to a beautiful stand of birches along the road, and said, "I liked that poem." He was referring to Robert Frost's *Birches*.

Frequently I'd walk into an assembly to overhear kids mumbling to each other, "Oh, it's just some guy gonna read poetry . . . Jeeeezus . . ." But when I began to read and the thing got rolling, I could feel enthusiasm and interest replace the apathy. They discovered poetry wasn't inevitably dull.

In New York, I would read Lord Buckley, a comedian, a minstrel, and a poet—a zany character who was a literary hipster and the founder of the Universal Jazz Church. In New York the cadence of his language went over well. But in Maine Buckley's words sounded like a foreign language. I'd look up to see faces with question marks. The less urbanized kids were unable to understand this amusing and colorful "hip talk."

When I went back to New York in 1980 to play in *Morning's at Seven*, I recommenced poetry reading in the schools. I found the experience just this side of disastrous. Now the kids were impolite and unruly. They continued their conversations with their seatmates, paying no attention to the reading. They obviously did not care about school, poetry, or anything else. It was a bad experience— something of a shocker—and left me wondering if the educational system had gone completely awry, or if this inattention was an indication of what was happening to all of us. At these schools, assemblies had been discontinued because they so easily got out of hand.

After breathing the fetid city air for a while, I decided it was time to return to Maine, breathe in the sea air, and consider, refreshed once more, what I might be able to do to help create a saner world.

11

INTO THE SUNSET, PROTESTING

T he studio star system of Hollywood's heyday has disappeared. The new movie star is the most recent television personality, maybe someone who first made it big on TV commercials. From selling improved nasal congestion sprays, the next step is perhaps a star role in a series. If the series appeals to the public, it's only another small step to a star role in a movie. The crowning irony is that these performers are then sought after to play lead roles on Broadway. This is a *reductio ad absurdum* of the manipulation of the American public. Everything is ass-backwards. Starring on Broadway has become a fringe benefit of making your million as a face on a soap commercial. The recognition factor—that's the thing.

Talent doesn't count much when an actor becomes bankable. In Hollywood, actors were cast the way kids in Maine read menus—look at the price first. Producers would say, I want a hundred-thousand-dollar actor in this part, or let's go with a five-hundred-thousand-dollar actress here. It was their way of packaging for promotion, for creating the proper level for a picture.

For many actors, how they ate it up, struggling for

the next level of money-making! The parts didn't count, only the salary. When the contract-player system was abandoned and the actors left the studios, when the star actors became larger that the studios and could control what they did in pictures, have scripts written for them and even choose their own directors, the money factor won out totally. It broke the best actors. The agent, the producer, and the studio itself with its banker mentality, and the bankers themselves were usually more guileful and manipulative than any actor. Very few actors were also good at business.

In the sixties I was in a movie, *The Incident,* which was filmed in a New York subway, one of those hostage stories where a pair of hoodlums terrorizes subway riders. Ed McMahon—Johnny Carson's sidekick on television's "The Tonight Show"—was cast for a role in the movie, for whatever mileage could be gotten out of his name. The trouble was that Ed couldn't act his way out of a box of Kleenex: He's an announcer. When Ed's role required that he express fear, he merely appeared bored. Larry Peerce, the director, was forced to resort to extraordinary techniques to provoke an adequate reaction from Ed. Between takes, he took Martin Sheen and Tony Musante aside and asked them to fake an argument with one another in front of McMahon. They did, going at each other with really violent personal hostility, which built to a ferocious, almost murderous, tension. It came so unexpectedly that McMahon was terrified, and when the camera began rolling again the proper reaction was recorded on old Ed's face—fear!

In spite of my criticism of the medium, let it not be thought that I have eschewed television. I found satisfaction in the role of Ernest Hemingway for one show, a Maine sea captain in another. I was even given the part of the older doctor in a failed attempt to rekindle the "Young Dr. Kildare" series.

One of the most gratifying acting experiences in my

older years was, unexpectedly, in summer stock.

One day I received a warm letter signed by two fans. The writers wanted to know what was the most important career advice I had ever received. The answer came quickly to mind. I recalled a letter from Walter Huston, John's father. When I was offered parts in two different summer stock plays, I couldn't decide which to take, and had asked his advice. He said, "I'd take whatever keeps the stomach fullest."

His advice was extremely practical, and I followed it again when I was asked, later in life, to appear in a number of summer stock productions. One of these, ironically, was *Born Yesterday*. In the original Broadway production, I was the young, idealistic, and romantic journalist. Thirty years later I was playing the heavy, Paul Douglas's part. It was a difficult transformation despite the intervening years, but I managed it with my voice, using a strident, harsh, surly, and arrogant quality.

Summer stock productions are quickly produced, whereas really hard work goes into a Broadway production, with shifts in casting, with subtle day-to-day changes—all sorts of corrections made along the way. An incredible amount of energy is spent developing the right nuances. There is a dedication to proper timing, so that every line is perfectly balanced.

Sandy Dennis played Judy Holliday's part in the *Born Yesterday* summer stock production. She has real talent but little stage discipline, and subjected the brilliance of the play to her own whims. This play is marvelously constructed: a one-two- three laugh, which leads to another one-two-three laugh—like clockwork. Unfortunately, we would go one-two—but there was no three. Sandy would be over in a corner making a face or playing with the drapes. I could imagine her thinking, "I'm being very imaginative. I'm creating new concepts of acting the part . . ." Nevertheless, we traveled the circuit from Ogunquit, Maine, to Falmouth, Massachusetts, to Westport, Palm Beach, Atlanta, and Milwaukee.

Into the seventies and eighties, I continued to visit Washington, D.C. Maine's William Hathaway, a liberal Democratic senator during the seventies, became a valued friend. I would occasionally play golf with him at the illustrious Burning Tree Country Club. Its membership includes the most highly placed and powerful people in government. Everyone has heard stories about insurance agents who make their little deals during a round of golf with a prospective client, but at Burning Tree I literally gasped at the conversations overheard along the fairways. There were senators, diplomats, lobbyists, business tycoons, Pentagon officials, cabinet members, labor union VIPs, and so on. Sometimes I got the feeling that governments rose and fell as a result of what was said between golf shots. The club was staffed with a hundred caddies, all black, most of whom had worked there for years. I wondered what parts of the history books would have to be rewritten if some of the caddies had been wired.

One day, as a guest of Hathaway for the weekly Sunday Breakfast Club tournament, I was to join him at eight o'clock. A bit confused at that early hour, I arrived at the Grill Room dressed in the only golf clothes I had available on that visit to Washington: a worn, faded denim shirt, old shorts, and less than whole sneakers. I imagine I also needed a shave, not to mention a haircut.

To anyone inside the clubhouse, looking out from the huge picture window at the green, I might have appeared to be a construction worker, there to do some Sunday digging. I can only imagine the shock of these extremely well-dressed golfers when I casually walked into the clubhouse.

Some fellows were standing about. "Has anyone

seen Hathaway?" I asked them.

"Not here yet," someone said.

Bill had said he might be late and suggested that I look up a playing partner, John Walker, a lobbyist for Air France.

"Is John Walker about?"

They were all staring at me as though I had arrived from a distant planet, especially Walker himself.

"I'm John Walker," he said, as he moved toward me. "Who are you?"

After I introduced myself, Walker began to laugh and the others relaxed too. Walker had seen a TV movie the night before, the one in which I'd played the dissolute drunk.

"Well, Mr. Merrill," he said. "I see you haven't changed a bit!"

Hathaway, now a highly paid Washington lobbyist himself, insists he has heard this story repeated at the club at least twice a year.

During the fall of 1974, Hathaway invited me to attend the state Democratic convention in Maine. Since I was self-conscious about the effect my appearance at the golf club had had, I thought I should ask about proper attire. "Do you mind if I dress in a white suit with a string tie?" I asked.

He laughed. "No, it's going to be a dull affair anyway."

On the plane from Washington, Hathaway introduced me to a new political face, the governor of Georgia, Jimmy Carter. Carter was dressed in a routine business suit, which made me laugh.

"Say, Governor," I said. "It looks as though I've got on your costume and you're wearing mine."

Carter was slated to be keynote speaker at the Maine gathering. His presidential campaign was just getting under way. He was quietly going around the country meeting all the Democratic pols, ostensibly for the unification of the party. Bob Strauss—the new Jake Arvey—was behind him even then.

I sat with Carter on the plane, eager to point out the features as we flew over the Maine coast and countryside. Alas, the cloud cover was too thick. I had recently bought the unused lighthouse on Cape Elizabeth, and at that time still hoped to create a residence within it. But I could only describe it to Carter, and told him about the magnificent view I had from it. I could see Mount Washington in New Hampshire, seventy miles to the west. But I had no idea, I told him, how far, perched atop the lighthouse, I could see across the Atlantic. Trained as an engineer, Carter explained triangulation for the measurement of such distances and, in fact, was so lucid that I could almost understand the theory myself.

Upon our arrival in Bangor, the convention city, the governor, Ken Curtis, Senator Ed Muskie, and a host of local celebrities greeted us. I realized I was among friends, knowing most of them on a first-name basis. In the airport I was whisked into the press conference. Reporters, TV cameras, and photographers were all around. They surrounded me as though *I* was the person for media attention! Naturally, I took advantage of the situation, speaking out with the quiet modesty that characterizes my appearances:

"I would like to announce that I plan to run for the presidency in 1976. I know that Ronald Reagan is planning to do the same as a Republican," I said in my clearest, roundest tones. "As I see it, I'm a better actor than he, and with the Democratic Party behind me, I would be certain to win by a landslide."

The local papers ate it up, and gave this "announcement" as much front-page attention as the opening of the convention. I fantasized: If I made enough of a stir, maybe I would get picked up by some political bigwigs and be propelled into becoming a contender.

I was fully aware, however, that I might not be the type to be exploited by Democratic power brokers. Actors are not highly respected as role models. We may be thought of as glamorous, but most people also think of us as something other than normal. One's credibility is constantly questioned. It is difficult to reverse this image. You must come across as Ronald Reagan did—Mr. Clean, the All-American Boy. Bore everyone to tears, but allow them to trust you with the silverware.

I could never fit the mold, but I continued to fantasize: I saw myself as a potential mover and shaker. In my dreams, I would soar to high places, reform the whole country, by God, and turn everyone into a community-oriented, peace-loving, nonpolluting, public-spirited citizen. It was an adult form of masturbation, of course. Although my ability at free-form flight held me aloft for a short time, not much came of my "campaign"—except a lot of good publicity. So before long I threw my energies into Jimmy Carter's camp. I still feel he was a fine president, hampered only by his inability to form a staff who understood the ways of Congress. He was basically a humanitarian who couldn't get his programs across. Now, as a retired president, he is still trying. In an attempt to get attention to the need for low-cost housing, he rolled up his sleeves and did some on-site carpentry, working along with the low-income group he was trying to help. I consider him an honorable man and I'm proud to have known him and Rosalynn Carter, as well as the great lady, Miss Lillian, who was his mother. I have been to visit them in their Georgia town of Plains, a community so small that newsmen and camerapeople who go down for an interview are forced to stay in the nearby town of Americus.

As my political feelings grew stronger, I found

myself less and less able to tolerate what I saw as the stupidity and arrogance of the political right.

Flying home to Maine from a visit to Nova Scotia in the mid-seventies with Phil Stern, my Hollywood photographer friend, I celebrated on the plane and was in fine spirits when we touched down at the Portland airport. Carrying the brand-new Irish shillelagh I'd bought on the trip, I strode into the small airport and heard a page for William Buckley.

For years I'd been rankled by this conservative columnist and commentator. I especially despised his haughty manner. As soon as his name rolled from the airport loudspeakers, I told Phil I'd find the SOB and give him a piece of my mind. With shillelagh in hand, I began the search. In those years, Portland's airport was not much larger than a good-size living room, and I soon found Buckley in a phone booth.

"Come on out, you fascist," I yelled, rapping on the booth with my new Irish weapon. "Come on out and defend your politics."

Buckley stayed where he was, his eyes wide with alarm at the sight of a stranger with a shillelagh. He quit the call he was making and called the Portland police who, in turn, got in touch with airport security. "Security" turned out to be an elderly guard I'd known for years.

"Take it easy, Gary," he said, while Buckley yelled instructions for my arrest, "give the poor guy a break." I did, and Phil and I left to find our luggage. But I've felt better ever since when I remember the incident and think about Buckley's discomfort.

By the late seventies, I was spending most of my time in Maine with the exception of lucrative television commercials, which, fortunately, continue to this day. In 1980, just before I was to leave Maine for my usual wintertime jaunt to Florida, my agent at the time, Bruce Savan, visited me with a request that I do a play in New York. I resisted strongly. I didn't want to stay in New York for any length of time. But he insisted.

"You've got to let them know you're still alive, Gary," he urged. "Besides, even though it's a pretty good play, I think it will have a modest run. Rehearsals will begin in March. It'll probably open in April, run two or three months, and you'll be back in Maine before you know it."

The words "modest run" loomed large. When *Morning's at Seven* was first staged in 1939 by Josh Logan, it had lasted for only forty-four performances. That, in itself, was encouraging. How could it hurt? I could let everyone know I was still kicking, and be back in Maine by August at the latest. "Okay, I'll do it," I said.

I fell in love with the cast, especially Maureen O'Sullivan, Nancy Marchand, Teresa Wright, and Elizabeth Wilson. Maurice Copland, Richard Hamilton, and David Rounds were also talented, but I was bowled over by the women. I played Maureen's husband and the other ladies were her sisters; the men, her brothers-in-law. In my role, I saw the in-laws as dumb and boring and enjoyed telling them as much.

Morning's at Seven, authored by Paul Osborn, opened at the Lyceum Theater, where I had first appeared thirty-four years before in *Born Yesterday*. I found a small apartment in Greenwich Village and was able to walk to work. *Morning's at Seven*, about backyard family intrigues, proved irresistible to theatergoers this second time around. The ensemble clicked, and here I was, stuck in a hit play. I was the only one complaining! After six months I was ready to go home, but I couldn't leave until the next April, when my contract expired.

The gossip columnists hinted that my *Morning's at Seven* co-star, Maureen O'Sullivan, and I were hitting it off especially well—but that was another instance of columnists not having much to write about. In latter years, I have been wary of the love disease. Falling in love is wonderful, but it's also debilitating. It's a tender emotion that unsettles the day with an alternating sense of urgency, elation, or despair, with an occasional infusion of helplessness—but then holds out a promise of ecstasy.

A few years following my definitive return to Maine in the mid-sixties, I met a young woman with five children whose husband had been stricken with a crippling disease that required him to be in a wheelchair. When he had first been ill, she had virtually lived in a motel near the hospital while bearing the responsibilities for the children. For a variety of reasons, a divorce became imminent, and she decided to move to Washington with the kids. I offered my help in getting them settled and drove with her and the children to the new house. By the time I got back to Maine, I was helpless. I had fallen in love with this strong, capable woman who filled me with compassion, and, though she was years younger, I decided she should marry me.

Claude Rains had married a lovely woman twenty years his junior, and I'll never forget the anguish he went through when she asked for a divorce. On a visit to Witch Way, he announced to Bette and me, with tears in his eyes, "Frances has left me." "Well, of course," was my response, just barely commiserating, "when little girls grow up, they leave home."

Now I was confronted with the possibility of marrying a much younger woman. To press my suit, I told her that she should marry me so that she could get her life together. Five years was all I asked for. I went off to do a job and, by the time I returned, she had found someone else. That affair ended as abruptly as it had begun.

About four years later, another young woman, this one with two children, loomed large in my life, but some thoughts of marriage were all that occurred.

Eventually, my past romances seemed to be revisiting me. In 1985, while searching for reading material one afternoon in a bookstore, I came across a volume, *My Mother's Keeper,* which had just been released. It was written by B.D. Hyman, Bette's daughter from her marriage to William Sherry. This was the same little girl I had adopted when Bette and I first married.

When I read it, I was astonished. This was not just a bad book, it was unbelievable. My initial reaction was that B.D. was low on money again, and this was her way to get some extra change. It was such an outrageous exploitation that I decided to raise hell about it.

Bette hadn't been well. She'd had a mastectomy a few years back, then she'd had a stroke, and then she broke her hip. With all her troubles, I didn't think she should have to put up with the outrage of having people believe some of the things her own child (for whom she had a deep and abiding love) had written about her. The book's release was timed to coincide with Mother's Day, of all things! B.D. had portrayed her mother as a drunk and a child abuser. How could this drivel be anyone's idea of a Mother's Day gift?

All her life, B.D. had accepted her mother's money. Bette had bought a farm for her and her husband, had paid the bills at a private school for the grandchildren, and continued to give until there was little left for herself. I surmised that B.D. must have wanted something Bette couldn't afford. The result was this outpouring, patterned after *Mommie Dearest,* Christina Crawford's book about her mother, Joan Crawford.

Perhaps, as a family, we were more volatile than most, with turbulent disagreements on occasion, but by and large we were fairly ordinary. As a boy growing up, I was constantly being spanked, or threatened with spanking, for some misdemeanor. Sometimes my behind glowed as I tried to find a comfortable position in order to go to sleep at night. As a result, I determined early on not to subject any child of mine to this sort of treatment, opting for discussion first. But there were a few quick spanks and slaps used as exclamation points when repeated reprimands were ignored.

Although most of the time Bette was too permissive with B.D., I was a gratified witness once to a good slap she administered to B.D.'s behind. It was Christmastime and we were on a shopping trip in Portland's big department store, which was crowded. B.D. had fastened on an item on display which she thought she must have, but Bette refused to buy it. Aware that people were noticing her famous mother, B.D. decided a tantrum might help change Bette's mind—and proceeded to perform. Bette yanked her around, gave her a good one, and marched B.D. out of the store. It was a mother's appropriate reaction to an embarrassing scene created by a manipulative eight-year-old. For this Bette was crucified.

Upset by the book, I placed ads in *The New York Times* and in the Portland newspaper, urging people not to buy it. I made a placard and marched up and down outside a Falmouth bookstore, and explained to anyone who asked what I was up to: "If you feel you must read the book, please don't buy it. Visit the local library instead."

This generated a certain amount of publicity, which I hoped would make B.D. and her publishers the losers. *Parade* later chose my newspaper advertisement as its "Best Ad of the Year." And Bette sent a postcard thanking me. After all those years, this was my only contact with her.

Becoming a "senior citizen" has not diminished my protesting. I continually find more to protest about. In recent years, I have been increasingly upset with American policy in Central America. By 1986, I decided to go there to see for myself what was really going on in Nicaragua, as I had done in Vietnam. So I called a group I knew was active in this issue, Clergy and Laity Concerned, and asked for advice.

"Well, you could go as an individual, but I think you ought to go with a group," I was told.

I was put in touch with members of a group called Witness for Peace. They sponsored people in my area on trips to Nicaragua. For me, the name was apt. I wanted to be a witness, and I wanted peace. There were Witness groups all over the United States, but the Northeast group wasn't planning to visit Nicaragua until months later.

"I'd like to go now, if I could," I told them.

"The Southeast group is going. I can put you in touch with the person running that." I was given a name and phone number. The Southeast group welcomed me as a fill-in, because someone had cancelled.

"We'll meet in Miami for introductions and a little background about what you can expect," said Gail Phares, the leader, when I called her.

We arrived in Miami on a Saturday afternoon and Gail started the indoctrination right away. The first meeting was held in a little church, and we spent all day Sunday going through the paces. We were given pieces of advice— don't wear shorts—and told how to protect ourselves. When it came to the church stuff, the singing and holding hands, she said, "Anyone who gets a little uptight about this, just walk away." So when that started, I'd go out and have a cigarette until the singing died out.

It was hot in Miami, the kind of heat that people from the Northeast can't even remember, come March. The humidity was heavy. As soon as I arrived at the airport I took off my jacket, loosened my tie, and tried to make myself as comfortable as possible.

On Monday, the plane was to leave at two o'clock in the afternoon, and I packed up my things. I discovered my passport was missing! I went through all my bags with no success. It had been in my jacket pocket. I figured it must have fallen out when I took off my jacket at the airport.

I called Gail, and she said, "You get yourself into Miami to the government center and then get to the airport as fast as you can."

I had never gotten a passport so fast in my life! It only took about forty-five minutes. I had told the cab driver to wait for me while I went into the passport office, but when I returned he'd driven off. I missed the plane.

At the airport I found that all my luggage had been put to one side and reservations made for me on a later flight. Gail had told me that sometimes the plane stopped overnight in Tegucigalpa, the capital of Honduras. It turned out that the plane I should have been on went straight through, but the plane I eventually got on did stop there. Now what? I went to a small hotel in Tegucigalpa, giving the man at the desk my credit card, certain I would have to speak in sign language. "Ah, Maine," he said in English. "I spent a year up there. South Paris."

South Paris, Maine! I didn't feel like such a lost puppy after that. We talked about Maine for some time. The next morning I took a plane to El Salvador and, after some delay, got on the connecting flight to Nicaragua.

In Nicaragua, they did the baggage search, passport inspection, all the rest—and then I was standing there at the airport feeling rather lost. No one was there to meet me, and all I knew was that the group had a base house in Managua. Well, better get a cab to the nearest hotel, I thought, and I walked over to the head cabman. I discovered a message had been left for me with him to go to a Witness office.

By now it was nine-thirty at night. I got into the cab and he drove me to a place that resembled a seminary. There was no one around, no action of any kind. We walked in and saw two or three priests comfortably ensconced before a television set. I explained in English what I was doing, said I had instructions to go there, but got no response, except for a shrugging of shoulders.

Wondering what my next move should be, I decided to call the embassy, thinking someone there would know where I could find the group. No answer! I turned to the cab driver. "Take me someplace, I'm tired! There has to be someone around who knows something."

He drove me to a hotel. The people at the front desk said they had no rooms, but, since they spoke a little English, I tried to tell them what was going on. They knew nothing. "Call the consul," they said. "You must call the consul."

I called, and an American voice answered.

"Witness for Peace," I said.

He had never heard of the organization. He wanted to know what country I'd come from, who I was, and so on. But he was no help, so I turned to the cab driver once more. "I don't want to be a bore, and I'm sorry for being chauvinistic, but can you take me to a hotel where everyone speaks English, please?"

He whisked me to the cab and in a very short while we wheeled up to a big hotel, the Inter-Continental in Managua, a huge pyramid-shaped structure with balconied windows on each level. As I walked out the next day and looked up at this building, I said to myself, "I'll be a son of a bitch."

I remembered a story from the early seventies, about Howard Hughes living in Central America. I asked the fellow behind the desk, "Is this the hotel where Howard Hughes lived?"

He beamed. "Yes," he said. "He took over the entire ninth floor. But that was also the year the earthquake hit. It leveled the city, except for one American bank, right up to the hotel. It didn't touch the hotel! Hughes sat in his Mercedes most of the night, obviously uncomfortable about being on the ninth floor, and took off early the next morning."

Since most of the buildings in the downtown area had been destroyed by the quake, President Luis Somoza and his government moved into some of the hotel's space. When the Somoza regime was replaced by the Sandinistas, many of the top political and military leaders of Somoza's gang sent their families abroad and moved into the hotel. The place teemed with generals, journalists, and, it was said, an American who was thought to be the head of the Central Intelligence Agency in Managua. He supposedly carried on his day-to-day intrigues in the lobby.

Immediately after the Somoza government was overthrown, some of the Sandinistas, too, made their headquarters at the Inter-Continental. Before they took office, Daniel Ortega Saavedra and Sergio Ramirez Mercado shared a room on the third floor, and the Interior Ministry was once located on another.

The Somoza family had owned fifty-six percent of the shares of stock in the hotel, which the Sandinistas confiscated when Somoza was overthrown. So now the Sandinista government shares in the profits of the hotel, but only forty percent.

A great many of the guests were American journalists, I was told, though I saw nearly every nation in the world represented there. I talked with a fellow from the American press to see if he had any ideas about how I might find the Witness for Peace group. If anyone knew, I felt, a journalist certainly should. And he did. He gave me a name and number at the embassy, saying he was sure they'd be able to help. Nevertheless, it took me a good two days to track down the group. In the meantime, I just wandered around.

When the Witness group I was supposed to be with had arrived in Nicaragua, they had talked with embassy people, Nicaraguan government people, businesspeople, and the press. When I finally caught up with them, they were heading into the countryside, and I finally got an opportunity to talk to the Nicaraguan people.

The Contras, I discovered, were terrorists, a bunch of ragamuffins bound together by their desire to bring back the old order. One of the leaders is a man who had the Coca-Cola concession during Somoza's years of power. As I visited a hospital and saw kids with a leg or an arm blown off from a Contra (U.S.-supplied) mine, I was reminded of the kids I'd seen in Vietnam.

I also found that twelve thousand students were enrolled in the university. Education is high on the list of Sandinista priorities. Few Nicaraguans, before the present time, were able to go to school. I looked up a film department where documentaries were made, and saw educational television commercials whose purpose was to convince peasants to have their kids inoculated and to teach them basic hygiene, such as brushing their teeth and washing their hands.

Redistribution of land was also moving ahead in this country where the Somoza family and its business friends were the dominant landlords for so long. Nicaragua has the land and other resources to feed its population, but in the past the wealthy landowners—who comprised less than five percent of the population—concentrated production on export crops. Thousands of acres were taken over by sugar cane, cotton, bananas, or coffee—crops to be shipped out of the country. In the Somoza economy, the workers were not allowed to grow the food they needed, nor did they have the money to buy it. This system kept the majority of the Nicaraguan people at a standard of living lower than that of the slaves of the old American South—one major reason why Somoza was finally ousted. The new regime is trying to bring about land reform so farmers may soon be able not only to feed themselves and their families but grow enough extra to help feed the rest of the inhabitants of this small nation.

Other countries have admired this effort and have sent people to help, but the United States government, *my* government, has for years been giving arms and money to the Contras, the terrorists who have put the entire country in deep depression for years.

But I met some Americans who had come to help, to assist in bringing about agrarian reform and to help implement the medical programs started by the Sandinistas. One group of young people from the Lake Tahoe, Nevada, area had been working on the construction of an agricultural cooperative. The day the Americans left, the Contras hit the town, destroyed two tractors, and burned down a couple of the buildings. They terrorized the local people. But when the next American group arrived, the rebuilding process began all over again.

So this is where I am in my seventies: still a protester, political and otherwise. Some people see some of my activities as deviltry, but it's just that I have found a lot of gratification in sticking up for my rights—and in sticking up for the rights of others.

My most recent protest began as an innocent outing with a Maine friend, Richard Greeley. We had been visiting down east and were returning to my house, but hadn't had dinner. It was getting late so we stopped along the highway near where I live at a restaurant of no particular style, just a convenient place to eat. Luckily, they were still serving, and after dinner we sat for a while, talking over our drinks. The waitress strolled over and said, ''Last call!''

''Let's have one for the road,'' I suggested, and we ordered fresh drinks. The waitress brought them, and we each took a sip, smoking and talking. After a moment, another woman, probably the owner, walked over. ''We're closing," she announced. "It's time to leave."

"Okay, okay, just let me finish my drink," I said, and we stayed where we were.

"No," she said "We're closing now. You'll have to leave."

I'd just gotten the drink! I assumed when the waitress said "last call," that meant we'd have time to drink what we'd ordered. I didn't pay for something to leave it on the table as I walked out.

"Fine. You've said you're closing. Just let me finish my drink," I said.

"I want you to leave now or I'll call the cops," she said.

"Go ahead. Call them. I'm going to finish my drink." I sat there, stubbornly exercising my rights as a patron in a restaurant that advertises itself as open to the public.

Not one but two policemen arrived on the scene and ordered us to stand up. Hands were put behind our backs, handcuffs were slapped on our wrists, and we were marched out the door. The policemen had arrived in separate cars. I was put in one and my friend in the other, and we were driven to the station house. The cuffs were tight, so tight they cut into the flesh of my wrists. I asked the policeman if he would take them off—I wasn't going anywhere. He did.

When we got to the police station and were standing at the desk waiting to be charged, I noticed my friend was still manacled. The handcuffs had cut into his wrists and blood was all over the cuff of his shirt. He'd been forced to sit with his hands wrapped by those steel manacles all the way to the station.

We were charged with "criminal trespass." Fortunately, the case was eventually "filed."

As one gets older, one's personal health becomes

more preoccupying. Now that I'm in my seventies, I make some concessions to a healthier life. One concession I have made for a long time is a yearly checkup. They started years ago with Vincent Carroll, Bette's doctor in Laguna Beach.

"I suppose you'll tell me to cut out the booze," I asked him at one point, steeling myself against the answer.

"Oh no," says he, "it's either booze or animal fats."

The animal fats left. I have been on a low-fat diet ever since, concentrating on chicken, fish, and vegetables. I'd always eaten well—just because I happened to like the things that are good for me. Vincent improved this diet.

I can't recall how I found Dr. Bethea in Beverly Hills, but he was another great one. Every year, the same questions:

"Is your booze consumption about average?"

"What's average, Doc?"

He thought for a while and came up with a figure.

"Oh, hell, way above average," said I.

He finally got back at me on one of his written reports: "Heart—so and so. Lungs—so and so. Genitalia—*below average.*"

When I was a relatively young man and was playing in *Born Yesterday* in New York, I had a case of hemorrhoids. I didn't know what it was. I hadn't been to a doctor since I was a kid, but it hurt so badly that Paul Douglas and Judy Holliday would change tempo, slowing down, because I had to sit so carefully. I saw Dr. Max Jacobsen, he injected a few things, and a few days later all was well. I called him "Magic Max," but others called him "Mad Max." He and I became good friends.

His waiting room was always full of people, some with little money, others with lots of it. When occasionally I got laryngitis, one shot of his magic formula would take care of it. Some of his patients were opera stars, who, if they strained or lost their voice before a performance, visited the office and then would be able to go on. Many famous people were his patients, including Jack Kennedy.

Years later, he was drummed out of the profession, accused of using illegal or harmful drugs in his "cocktails." I was out of the country at the time and wasn't able to help him. Although patients used him as a crutch, flocked to him for help, they were quick to turn against him.

When I first went to his office in the late forties, he had a sign, in *ten* languages, in the waiting room: NO SMOK-ING. He was that far ahead of his time. When we stood talking, which we were wont to do, he'd reprimand me, "Stand on both feet." He had a place on Long Island and every weekend, all year 'round, he swam in the ocean. He believed it to be a healthful practice. But he didn't recommend it to everyone. I said I'd try it. "Don't dive in, go in slowly," he advised. So home I went to Cape Elizabeth, and, with the children watching, I gave it a try. It was in the middle of winter and very cold. Over my trunks I wore a raccoon coat. I put on my boots and clumped down to the cove. I put one foot in, then the other, and very quickly turned around and ran back to the laughing household.

For years, I relied on a great general practitioner in Maine, Dr. Henry Finks, a terrific doctor who would come to the house if necessary, and had sometimes come at two or three in the morning. Often after the usual annual exam, he'd say, "I think you'd better cut out the cigarettes." Each year, we had the same cigarette talk. Finally, he retired. I asked him to recommend another doctor and, while he was thinking, he looked up and said, "Oh, about that smoking"—this was after twenty years of warnings—"I figure you're past the point of no return. You might as well keep going."

That's me, I'm past the point of no return. And I keep going.

12

MR. DO-NOTHING

How can a man's life keep its course
If he will not let it flow?
Those who flow as life flows know
They need no other force;
They feel no wear, they feel no tear,
They need no mending, no repair.

A sound man's heart is not shut within itself
But is open to other people's hearts:
I find good people good
And I find bad people good
If I am good enough . . .
I feel the heart-beats of others
Above my own
If I am enough of a father,
Enough of a son.

'Since true foundation cannot fail
But holds as good as new,
Many a worshipful son shall hail
A father who lived true.'
Realized in one man, fitness has its rise;

Realized in a family, fitness multiplies;
Realized in a village, fitness gathers weight;
Realized in a country, fitness becomes great;
Realized in the world, fitness fills the skies.
And thus the fitness of one man
You find in the family he began,
You find in the village that accrued,
You find in the country ensued,
You find in the world's whole multitude.
How do I know this integrity?
Because it could all begin in me.

> Lao Tzu
> *The Way of Life*
> by Witter Bynner

As Lao Tzu writes, I began with one man. Now, I have my family, I have my village—the village that is Maine—and I have my country and my world. My circle is complete. My commitment is now global. My role is now simply that of a world citizen. Which should not imply that my country and my world receive as much of my attention as my family and my village. Thank God for the state of Maine. It has sustained me through the years, and it is still my Gibraltar.

I woke this morning listening to the wail of foghorns across this bay that spills silver in my dooryard. I treasure the sounds and smells of this sea. I am one of the luckiest men alive to be able to live in this sheltered, solitary spot inhabited by sea ducks and the small creatures that I see only now and then as they scamper through the grass or the snow at dawn.

Looking back at my life has always been like looking across the bay to islands that disappear and reappear through the drifting fog. As this book has taken form, memory by memory, the fog has lifted, and I've been able to see more clearly the shape of past and present.

When Bette and I first started going to the Portland Country Club for dinners back in the fifties, we were greeted by our favorite waitress, Ellen Jordan, a Maine woman, attractive and always friendly. During the give-and-take of our bantering, she dubbed me "Mr. Do-Nothing." In response, I christened her "Tiger Lily." (Bette was "Dragon Lady.")

After all these years, Ellen is still at the club, and her table is the one I always ask for. She still calls me Mr. Do-Nothing, and I am reminded by her greeting that her sobriquet has become my all-purpose response. Whenever people ask the favorite American question, "What do you do?" (as opposed to "How are you?" or "What do you think?") I say, "I do nothing."

If they are interesting, or interested enough to pursue our relationship, I explain that my life has been spent avoiding chores and occupations I have never liked doing. Becoming an actor, as luck would have it, has allowed me the freedom to indulge my philosophy. I have, over the years, been able to turn away from joyless work and the drudgery and boredom of routine.

Discovering a lovely play: Now that's joy, not work. Being part of the building process; working with other actors and actresses, and (in the best of times) a brilliant director; to test it in Philadelphia or New Haven and then bring it to New York, where, after all the discipline, it becomes a hit—that's being alive, that's having fun! It's definitely not work, not by my definition.

After a time, when each evening's performance becomes a routine, when I've nothing more to give, then joy becomes drudgery—and I leave.

I've been leaving hit shows for most of my professional life, often leaving to go home to Maine. At the start of my career, radio seemed the perfect way for me to earn a living because the shows never lasted long enough to build any barriers of boredom. Radio was a pushover. In the studio, shaven or unshaven, dressed or nearly undressed, I would pick up the script, read my lines into the mike when the director's finger pointed my way, and then, wham, off to the golf course or the nearest watering hole.

At present I'm back to doing the same thing. I've come full circle: radio, the stage, Hollywood, television, and now, with TV voice-overs, back to "radio." Only it's not quite the same. The microphone is still there, I can show up with stubble on my face, or in my Maine golfing clothes, and a director still gives the signal, but now I'm pitching Volvos, or IBM computers, or United Parcel. I always talk for less than a minute.

The voice-overs I do for so many of the country's largest corporations are just the background music for television commercials, but the pay is a great deal better than the few dollars we got those long years ago for reading into the mikes that beamed soap operas into so many kitchens.

The rest of my life is spent soaking in the warm tub of *free time* my blessed occupation has allowed me to have. But I am not asleep. I try to exercise my mind, to find new ideas. Reading is my nourishment. I digest periodicals the way a squirrel chews acorns—a few each day. My reading room/living room looks like a library after a tornado. Copies of *The New York Times*, *The Washington Post*, *The Nation*, *Mother Jones*, *The Progressive*, *Commentary*, *Gay Community News*, *Public Citizen*, *Bulletin of the Atomic Scientists*, *In These Times*, *The Washington Spectator*, *Greenpeace*, *Nuclear Times*, *The Mobilizer*, *MagaZine* and dozens more gather in piles, like so many fallen leaves.

This list reveals my political interests and sympathies. The truths these publications tell energize my capacity for outrage, an emotion, I'm delighted to say, that does not diminish with age. I write letters, long ones, on yellow legal pads. There is no end to my outrage when I am reminded of how far this nation has drifted from the ideals that were mine as a boy growing up in Connecticut and Maine. We have become such a greedy, hypocritical society, making self-interest our new golden rule: Do it to the other guy before he does it to you.

So I use my free time battling the creed of self. I belong to Veterans for Peace, I work for and give to cultural institutions, I read poetry to schoolchildren (still my favorite "adults"), and I give my energies and wherewithal to efforts designed to encourage peace and reverse the destruction of this earth's fragile environment. It's an agenda to sustain perpetual outrage. What else can I fight for but life? What better calling than my commitment to peace and environmental sanity? It is a battle for being, a gratitude for my seven decades as Mr. Do-Nothing. I *owe*.

When I'm not reading, writing, and fighting, I spend time with friends, some of them—more, as the years pass—in hospitals or in wheelchairs. Over the past year, I sat at the bedside of a dying friend, watched her grit her teeth and never complain about the chemotherapy and drugs that drained her vitality—the way a torn doll spills sawdust.

I wonder, in the presence of such courage, if I will be as courageous. Having lived my three score and ten, I've had to acknowledge the inevitable last exit. My parents died in their early seventies. Now I try to prepare my grand-children, so my absence will not be unexpected.

Contemplating my own deterioration is not an occu-pation encouraged by my actor's vanity, so I say "To hell with it!" and revel in the luxury of outrage, draft one more letter, plan one more political campaign, organize one more protest. The cause has yet to be won.

GARY MERRILL'S FILMS

In order of release

This Is the Army, 1943
Winged Victory, 1944
The Quiet One,
    (narrator only) 1949
Slattery's Hurricane, 1949
Twelve O'Clock High, 1950
Mother Didn't Tell Me, 1950
Where the Sidewalk Ends,
    1950
All About Eve, 1950
The Frogmen, 1951
Decision Before Dawn, 1951
Another Man's Poison, 1951
The Girl in White, 1952
Night Without Sleep, 1952
Phone Call from a Stranger,
    1952
A Blueprint for Murder, 1953
Witness to Murder, 1954
The Black Dakotas, 1954
The Human Jungle, 1954
Navy Wife, 1956
Bermuda Affair, 1956
Crash Landing, 1958
The Missouri Traveler, 1958
The Wonderful Country, 1959
The Savage Eye, 1960
The Great Impostor, 1961
Mysterious Island, (US/UK)
    1961
The Pleasure of His Company,
    1961
A Girl Named Tamiko, 1962

Hong Kong, unaddio/
    Hong Kong Farewell,
    (Italian) 1962
Catacombs/The Woman Who
    Wouldn't Die,
    (UK/US) 1965
Run, Psycho, Run, (Italian)
    1966
Around the World Under the
    Sea, 1966
Ride Beyond Vengeance, 1966
Cast a Giant Shadow, 1966
Destination Inner Space, 1966
The Last Challenge, 1967
Clambake, 1967
The Incident, 1967
The Power, 1968
Amarsi male/Loving Badly,
    (Italian) 1969
The Secret of the Sacred Forest,
    1970
Huckleberry Finn, 1974
Thieves, 1977

PICTURE CREDITS